THE CRUSADES 1095-1204

The Crusades 1095-1204: A Study Guide for AS/A Level

Table of contents

Introductory Notes	2
Part One:	8
Part Two:	40
Part Three:	90
Part Four	135
Part Five:	194
Part Six:	263

Introductory Notes

The Crusades 1095-1204: A Study guide for AS/A Level

This study guide will assist you in your AS/A Level studies of Medieval History; the Crusades, a period of study that focuses on the years 1095-1204.

The aims and objectives of Advanced Level GCE in History include;

- Develop an interest in and enthusiasm for history and an understanding of its intrinsic value and significance.

- Acquire an understanding of different identities within society and an appreciation of aspects such as social, cultural, religious and ethnic diversity, as appropriate.

- Build on your understanding of the past through experiencing a broad and balanced course of study.

- Improve as an effective and independent learner.

- Develop the ability to ask relevant and significant questions about the past and to research these questions.

- Acquire an understanding of the nature of historical study.

- Develop your use and understanding of historical terms, concepts and skills.

- Make links and draw comparisons within and/or across different periods and aspects of the past.

- Organise and communicate your historical knowledge and understanding in different ways, arguing a case and reaching substantiated judgements.

Studying GCE History

This study guide has been written to provide a rewarding experience for those who are, or are interested in studying Medieval History. In particular, this study guide will assist you in understanding and examining the subject matter of the Crusades.

Who is this study guide for?

This study guide is intended to offer a satisfying experience for those learners who undertake an AS or A level qualification in History. This qualification pathway is offered by Edexcel, AQA or OCR examination boards and this resource is primarily designed to assist those who are studying this topic for an History qualification.

This study guide will help to lay a sound foundation for those who go on to study the Medieval World at a higher (degree) level as well as appeal to those who are interested in learning more about the medieval world generally and in particular, the establishment and demise of the Latin Crusader States of Outremer.

Please note that this study guide is not endorsed either by AQA or OCR and as such is not an officially recognised product by either Edexcel AQA, OCR or CIE examination boards.

This product is designed to be used as a study aide in order for learners to attain a qualification in the following examination units;

Edexcel Examination Board

- Pearson Edexcel Level 3 Advanced GCE in History (9HIO): Route A
- Pearson Edexcel Level 3 Advanced Subsidiary GCE in History (8HIO): Route A

AQA Examination Board

- AQA Advanced Level GCE in History (7042): Component 1A
- AQA Advanced Subsidiary Level GCE in History (7041): Component 1A

OCR Examination Board

- OCR Advanced GCE in History H505: Unit 2 Y203
- OCR Advanced Subsidiary GCE in History H105: Unit 2 Y233

About Athena Education Online

Athena Education Online are a specialist team of professional course writers based in Lincolnshire, UK. All course writers are specialists in their area and are all are experienced teachers and lecturers as well as experienced examination assessors for the main examination boards, including AQA, OCR, Edexcel and CIE.

About the Author

P Kenney is an experienced, course writer, college lecturer and tutor and examiner for several examination boards. A graduate of the University of Wales and Nottingham University in Classics and Archaeology, he has been examining, tutoring and writing courses and course materials since 2005.

Terms and Conditions of Use

Thank you for purchasing this product.

By purchasing this product you acknowledge that we the producers of these materials are not affiliated with any educational institution, that this product is authorised by, sponsored by, or affiliated with any educational institution.

Use of this product does not ensure any expected exam grade of anyone owning or using this product. Neither do Athena Online Education guarantee that this product is affiliated with, or suitable for, any particular examination board or examination unit, however Athena Online Education will strive to ensure that all of its products match as closely as possible the qualification for which it is intended to support.

Copyright Information

The materials contained within this product may not be incorporated into another body of work without prior reference to, and acknowledgement from Athena Online Education.

Whilst every effort has been made to ensure that the information provided in this product is up to date and accurate, no legal responsibility is accepted for any errors, omissions or statements which may otherwise mislead. It is the policy of Athena Online Education to attempt to obtain permission for any copyright material contained within their publications.

All images included in this product were sourced from wiki commons and other public domain material. Where an error has occurred Athena Online Education will happily rectify or remove images not in the public domain if contacted.

Disclaimers

This product is designed to be a supplement to learning only.

Although it may incorporate practice questions and material designed to follow the content of an examination specification. These learning materials are in no way an attempt to predict future examination materials and should not be treated as such. Athena Online Education does not make warranty as to future results users may obtain in examinations from the use of this product. Likewise, Athena Online Education does not make warranty as to the accuracy, content or reliability of the product. It is intended that this product be used appropriately and at the users own discretion. It is the user's responsibility to assess the suitability of this product to their own circumstances.

Athena Online Education is not affiliated with any examination board in any way nor is this product authorised, associated with, sponsored by or endorsed by, these institutions unless explicitly stated on the front page of the product.

Links to, and references to, other websites and resources are provided where appropriate. Athena Online Education is not responsible for the information of these sites and links and cannot guarantee, represent or warrant that the content contained on any website or resource are legal, accurate or inoffensive. Links to, and references to, websites and resources should not be taken to mean that Athena Online Education endorses these websites and resources in any way.

PART ONE: Introduction

PART ONE: Introduction

1.1 - The Geography of Europe and the Near East 1050-1100

1.2 - The Catholic Church 1050-1095

1.3 - Overview: The Byzantine Empire 1071-1095

1.4 - Overview: Islam 600-1095

1.5 - Overview: Christian Europe 1050-1095

1.1: The Geography of Europe and the Near East 1050-1100

In this topic we will;

- *Understand the Geography of Europe and the Mediterranean in the 11th century.*
- *Consider the divide of this physical area into spheres of Islamic and Christian control.*
- *Begin to consider the social and political considerations that led to the Crusades.*

Europe and the Mediterranean

The region depicted in the map was dominated by two faiths, Christianity and Islam.

The Old Roman Empire had been transformed, and not destroyed in 410AD with the sack of Rome. No longer centred in Rome, the Roman Empire had survived and even flourished in the East; a substantial part of the region depicted in this map was ruled by the Greek speaking successor to Rome; known commonly as, if somewhat misleadingly, as the Byzantine Empire. The Byzantine Empire was situated between the Danube River in the North and the Taurus Mountains in the East; with its capital in a central position called Constantinople; modern Istanbul.

Further North and West lay the 'Holy Roman Empire'. Rather than a unified Empire of Romans united in holiness, the Holy Roman Empire was a series of semi-independent dukedoms and counties located in central Europe; much of which is in Germany today. The ruler of the Holy Roman Empire claimed to be the direct inheritor of the Roman Empire in the West; a claim substantiated by, or challenged by, the Pope on many occasions. Further West was France, whose king likewise struggled to maintain control of many great lords.

In Northern Italy city states were emerging as powerful polities in their own right, some ruled by dynastic families, others as republics. These city states were dependent or independent of their larger neighbours as the scales of balance of politics shifted. In Sicily and Southern Italy Norman adventurers were in the process of carving out their own kingdom at the expense of both the Byzantine Empire whose hold on Southern Italy was being eroded as well as Muslim rulers of cities in Sicily.

Cities in 1100AD

Approximate population of cities

- *Baghdad – 500,000*
- *Cairo – 450,000*
- *Cologne – 20,000*
- *Constantinople - 600,000*
- *Cordoba – 100,000*
- *Florence – 40,000*
- *London – 20,000*
- *Milan – 30,000*
- *Paris – 20,000*
- *Rome – 35,000*
- *Venice – 40,000*

The British Isles were dominated by the Anglo Saxon kingdom of England which was to be overthrown by the Normans in 1066 at the battle of Hastings. In Ireland, Scotland and Wales the land was ruled by many clan chiefs and tribal kings.

In the Iberian peninsular the relatively new Christian statelets of Castile, Leon, Aragon, Navarre and Portugal were expanding their territory at the expense of each other as well as the independent Muslim *Taifa* kingdoms that remained after the Umayyad Caliphate crumbled in the early part of the 11th century.

To the East the Abbasid Caliphate commanded the actual or nominal allegiance of much of Syria, Iraq and Iran from their capital at Baghdad, but their rule was faltering as local Emirs refused to send their regular tribute to their distant overlord. The Sunni Arab Caliph was increasingly dependent upon Turkish Sultan who held the real power. To the South the rival Shi'ite Caliphate of the Fatamids was based in Egypt and commanded much of Palestine and Southern Syria.

In Central and Eastern parts of Europe lived peoples newly converted to Christianity, such as Slavic peoples in the Balkans, Poland and parts of southern Russia and Ukraine. In Hungary the Magyars had settled in the old Roman province of Pannonia after centuries of migration and established a new and energetic kingdom both courted and contested by their neighbours in the Byzantine and Holy Roman Empires.

Groups of people continued to migrate throughout this period. Normans and Scandinavians sought land in several regions and the men of these peoples often served as mercenaries in the Byzantine Empire or for a minor lord. In a general migration from Central Asia, Turkish tribes, such as the Pechenegs headed west, some passing north of the Black Sea and putting pressure on the Danube frontier of the Byzantine Empire, or the eastern regions of the Holy Roman Empire. Other Turkish groups moved into lands ruled by the Abbasid caliphate, here they were converted to Sunni Islam and would become key players in the crusades.

In 1000 AD most Christian countries the majority of the inhabitants were Christian, there were a few Jewish communities settled in towns along the trade routes which connected the West to the East. In contrast, the territories controlled by Muslim rulers had much greater diversity of religion amongst their populations. Christian communities of many sects existed alongside Jewish communities under Muslim rule and whilst some persecution occurred at times, these communities often thrived.

In general, at the time of the 1st Crusade, the cities of the East were much larger in size and splendour than the cities in the West. Some old cities like Rome had gone into decline in the West, however the city of Cordoba in what is now southern Spain had by far the largest population amongst the cities in the West.

In the 1050s the Seljuk Turks became the effective rulers of the Abbasid Caliphate. Taking the title of *Sultan* ('Power' in Arabic), the Seljuks would rule in all but name in Iraq and Syria and decisively defeat the Byzantine Empire at the battle of Manzikert in 1071 that would enable Turkish groups to migrate into Anatolia. One of the indirect consequences of this battle would be the 1st Crusade.

As an indirect result of the 4th Crusade in 1204, another Turkish dynasty; the Ottoman Turks would in 1453 replace the Christian Byzantine Empire with a Muslim Empire. In doing so they would kill the last Byzantine Emperor in battle and capture the city of Constantinople.

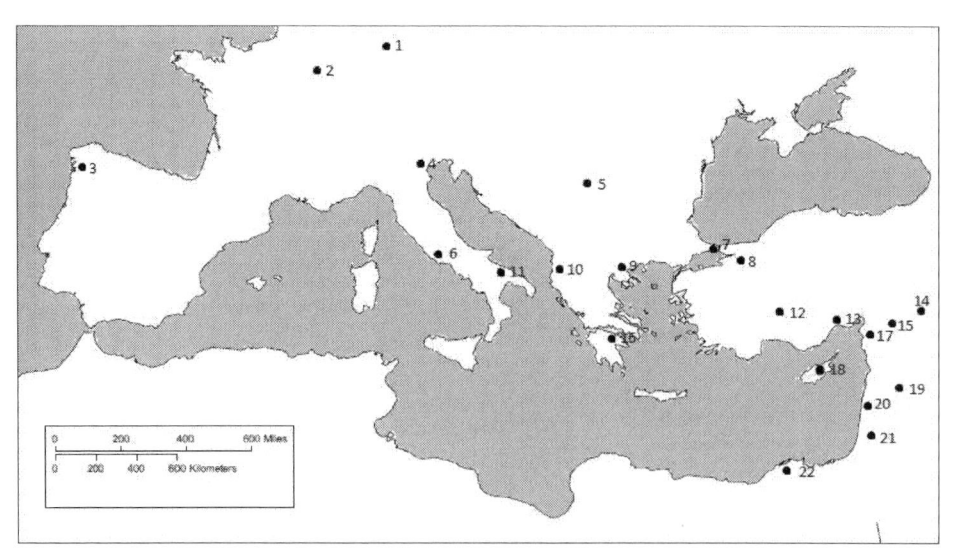

THE CRUSADES 1095-1204

> **Task: Cities Identification task**
>
> Look at the map and the list of cities below. Try to identify each city from the list provided below.

Thessaloniki	Antioch	Belgrade	Iconium
Jerusalem	Santiago De Commpostela	Acre	Venice
Nicaea	Tarsus	Rome	Mosul
Corinth	Constantinople	Edessa	Cologne
Durazzo	Damascus	Paris	Alexandria
Nicosia	Bari		

ATHENA CRITICAL GUIDES

1.2 Christianity

In this topic we will;

- Consider the legacy of the Roman Empire to Christianity.
- Understand the development of Christianity from the 4th-11th centuries.
- Understand the role and function of the Patriarchal seats.
- Begin to consider the importance of Christian belief in launching the Crusades.

The beginning of a World Religion

The Patriarchal Seats

In order of seniority

- Rome
- Constantinople
- Alexandria
- Antioch
- Jerusalem

As a religion, Christianity has its roots in Judaism. Despite occasional bouts of persecution in its early centuries, the religion took hold and spread throughout the Roman Empire. Christianity received a major boost as a religion when it was adopted by the Emperor Constantine I and subsequently became the state religion of the Empire in the early 4th century AD.

Christianity expanded in these early centuries through small groups of faithful often focused around a small group leader who may or may not have been responsible for converting the group. These communal leaders were spokespeople (in Greek *episkopos*) who often represented the group in the wider community. In time, and increasingly in the 3rd and 4th centuries these communities and their appointed spokespeople would congregate in ever larger and more magnificent meeting places, basilica in towns that would evolve into churches, the spokesperson would evolve into a priest or a bishop. Even before the reign of Constantine buildings were being purpose built as churches across the Roman Empire.

The Council of Nicaea and its successors

In 325AD the most prominent Christian leaders were invited to attend a great meeting of the faith in the city of Nicaea by the Emperor Constantine I. At this council, over which the Emperor presided, the church delegates established a commonality of worship; modern Christianity. The dates of Easter and Church law were established and a common unity imposed to have the same doctrine in the Trinity of the Father, The Son and the Holy Spirit.

Other Roman Emperors would also summon meetings of Bishops to resolve some issue or condemn some heresy, with the last

'Oecumenical' meeting of the church being held in 879/880AD. These meetings were summoned by the Emperor – who often participated. The Emperor at Constantinople then had a great influence in the development of the Christian faith into a World religion.

In 381AD the last Emperor of the united Roman Empire, Theodosius I (379-395AD) ordered an oecumenical meeting. This council saw the establishment of the Patriarchal Seats, bishops that were of the most senior rank in cities were Christian worship was established either by apostles or that had special significance. Rome, Antioch and Alexandria were established by the apostles, Jerusalem was made a Patriarchal seat because of its unique significance to Christians. That left Constantinople, this city as the New Rome was the capital of the Empire and seat of the Emperor, it was only right therefore that a patriarch be appointed to maintain the close link between the Church and the Emperor.

However, the question of pre-eminence among the Patriarchs remained unanswered. Another Church council was required and in 451 the Council of Chalcedon established a hierarchy amongst the Patriarchal Seats.

The Patriarchal Seats of Christendom

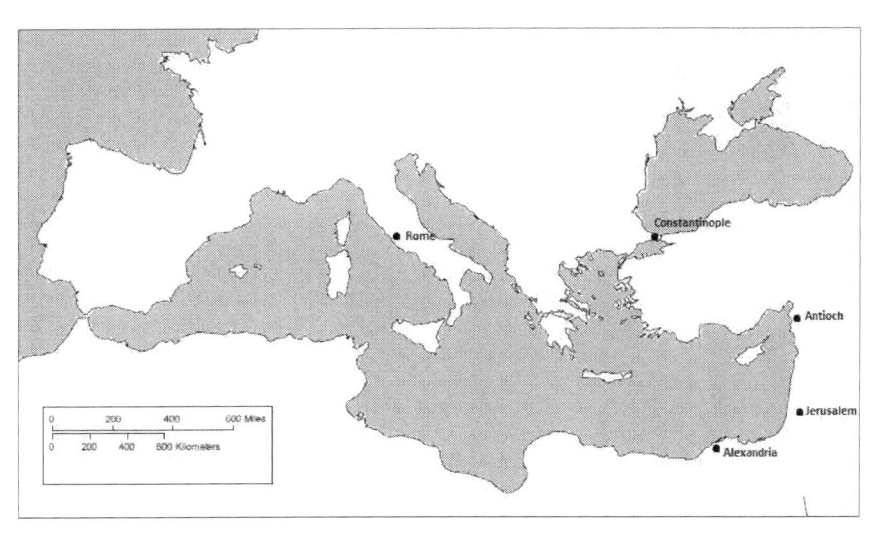

The Papacy and Patriarchs in the 11th Century

The Patriarchs were responsible for maintaining a united and correct belief in Christianity and church organisation. However despite attempts to maintain a united doctrine of faith, the differences in belief in the various parts of the Roman Empire ensured that various churches and peoples worshipped Christianity in slightly different ways. Debates over the role of Mary Mother of Jesus, the nature of Christ and the wording of prayers led to differences; many of which are still maintained today. Copts in Egypt, Greek Orthodox and Latin Catholicism formed in the centuries following the adoption of Christianity as the state Religion of the Roman Empire.

After the rise of Islam in the 7th century the Patriarchal seats of Antioch, Alexandria and Jerusalem remained, but they were under the secular control of Islam. As a result of being no longer in the Roman Empire; their influence and prestige with Christians still within the Empire and in Western Europe was much diminished. Sometimes these Patriarchs were persecuted by local Muslim leaders, sometimes they prospered. At the time of the First Crusade the Patriarch of Antioch was in exile in Cyprus, likewise the Patriarch of Jerusalem had also been ejected from the city by the Turks.

Pope Gregory VII's call for a Crusade, 1074

...a pagan race had overcome the Christians and with horrible cruelty had devastated everything almost to the walls of Constantinople, and were now governing the conquered lands with tyranny, and that they had slain many thousands of Christians as if they were but sheep. If we love God and wish to be recognized as Christians, we should be filled with grief at the misfortune of this great empire and the murder of so many Christians...

...Know, therefore, that we are trusting in the mercy of God and in the power of his might and that we are striving in all possible ways and making preparations to render aid to the Christian empire as quickly as possible. Therefore we beseech you by the faith in which you are united through Christ in the adoption of the sons of God, and by the authority of St. Peter, prince of apostles, we admonish you that you be moved to proper compassion by the wounds and blood of your brethren and the danger of the aforesaid empire and that, for the sake of Christ, you undertake the difficult task of bearing aid to your brethren."

The rivalry of the Pope and the Patriarch

The Pope of Rome and the Patriarch of Constantinople often saw each other as rivals. The Pope was the ranking Patriarch, however the prestige of his city was much less than that of Constantinople which was called the 'Queen of Cities'. The Patriarch of Constantinople had the ear of the Emperor, but since he was often appointed by the Emperor he was often perceived as a political appointee. As the Empire diminished and Rome became increasingly removed from the authority of the Emperor in Constantinople the pope at Rome could become a much more independent and authoritative figure. Legal forgeries such as the 'Donation of Constantine' gave the Pope theoretical control of the former provinces of the empire in the West. However, the Pope's position was also increasingly a political one and all too often the Pope was selected by the local Roman aristocracy. Religion had little to do with the choice.

In 1054 doctrinal differences combined with pig headedness led to the great Schism, which still remains an issue today. Both the Pope and the Patriarch excommunicated each other and neither accepted the authority of the other.

A new Emperor

By 800 the Pope of Rome was in need of powerful external support. The Byzantine Emperors of the previous century had often been influenced by Iconoclasm; a form of Christianity that abhorred the use of imagery in religious services. The Pope faced with opposition at home needed the support of a powerful ruler to help safeguard the Papal position. In 800AD the most powerful ruler of Western Europe and King of the Franks, Charlemagne was crowned Emperor of the Roman Empire in the West. Thereafter the title of Emperor was bestowed upon many rulers of what became known as the Holy Roman Empire. This Western Emperor was seen as counterbalance to the Byzantine Emperor, but the policy was not well received in Constantinople, despite talk at the time of a marriage between Charlemagne and the then Empress Irene.

The policy of creating a Western Emperor was not always a happy one for the Pope though. The Holy Roman Empire often tried to manipulate the appointment of new popes and bishops, whilst the local Roman aristocracy still fought amongst themselves in order to have their own chosen pope appointed. The Papal throne increasingly became a prize over which rival parties fought. This struggle increased with the establishment of a Norman kingdom in southern Italy and Sicily. By the 11th century papal rivalries sometimes resulted in multiple popes (called anti popes) and often the Pope was unable to actually live in Rome, so fierce was the competition.

Alexius and the Papacy

The Byzantine Emperor Alexius I sought to heal the breach between Constantinople and Rome. That had been an open wound since the mid-11th century. Alexius had a genuine piety but his aim was primarily political. Seeking assistance wherever he could against Robert Guiscard of Southern Italy with who he was at war, Alexius sought to restore good relationships with the Papacy. Good relationships with the Pope might deter Guiscard and help to repair relationships with the kingdom of Hungary who had also attacked the Empire. It might help encourage western soldiers to come to defend the Byzantine Empire.

The Pope Urban II was also in need of some assistance, he had been driven out of Rome but his authority was not fully established there. Urban II also welcomed the opportunity to be seen as the foremost Christian leader and to reassert his authority over the Patriarch at Constantinople.

Communications were slow and hampered by a succession of new Popes but by 1095 Alexius had built reasonably good relations with the then pope Urban II. In his letters of that year Alexius passed along the hopes that soldiers would be willing to come to the empire to serve as mercenaries. He also mentioned that the established pilgrim routes across Asia Minor were severely disrupted by these incursions. Alexius also passed along the news of the wars between the Fatamids of Egypt and the Seljuk Turks as well as the expansion of the Turks into Asia Minor. He asked Urban II to support his appeals for soldiers who were about to tour Western Europe in an attempt to consolidate his own authority over the secular leaders of the West. Alexius expected and hoped that his appeals would encourage mercenaries to come and join his army.

What he got was the First Crusade.

Task: The importance of the Pope

Write a response of *no more than 750 words* on the following topic;

"To what extent was the Pope the single most important figure in the Christian World?"

Consider the relationships between the Pope and;
- The Byzantine Emperor
- The Patriarch of Constantinople
- The Rulers of Germany and France

1.3 - Overview: The Byzantine Empire 1071-1095

In this topic we will;

- *Identify what is meant by the Byzantine Empire*
- *Understand the geography and political situation of the Byzantine Empire in the 11th century.*
- *Consider the relationships the Byzantine Empire had with its neighbours.*
- *Understand the importance of the battle of Manzikert.*
- *Begin to consider the role of the Empire in the Crusades.*

The Byzantine Empire

For much of the 11th century the Byzantine Empire stretched from Southern Italy to Armenia, from the Crimea and the Danube River in the north to Cyprus and Antioch in the South and East. Despite having shrunk in territory since the rise of Islam, in many ways at the time of the death of the Emperor Basil II (The Bulgar Slayer) who had reigned from 976-1025AD the Empire was at the height of its power. It was well led, its administration well organised, its armies were strong and well equipped and Constantinople dominated trade between the East and West.

The Byzantine Empire c1025

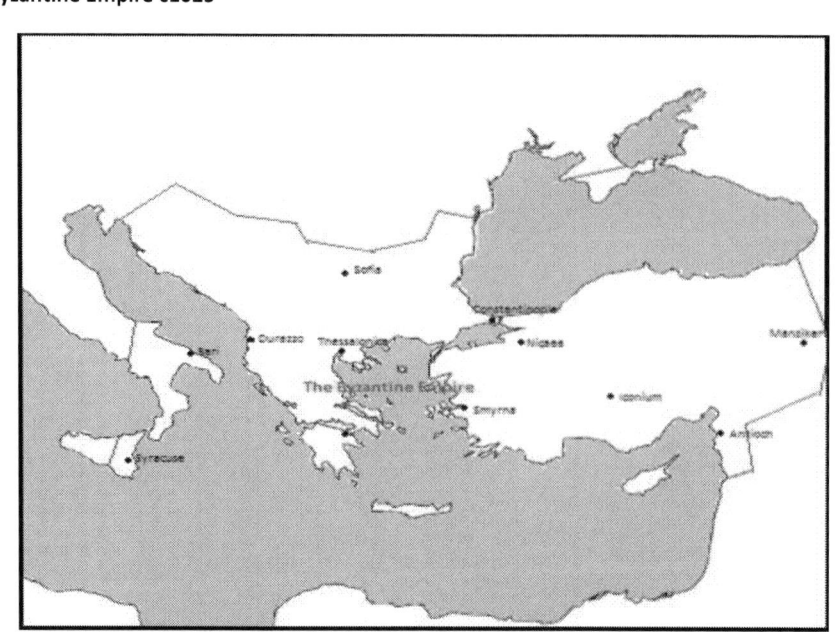

> **Byzantine Losses 1071-1095**
>
> - *1071 Manzikert*
> - *1071 Bari*
> - *1081 Nicaea*
> - *1084 Iconium*
> - *1084/5 Antioch*

However, after the death of Basil II in 1025 a series of less effective rulers mis-administered the state and the political landscape increasingly became a battleground between the bureaucracy based in Constantinople and the increasingly powerful dynastic families that owned vast tracts of Anatolia the East upon whom the Byzantine increasingly depended upon for military support along the Eastern frontier. The Emperor maintained an imperial army, but increasingly it was used to safeguard the Emperor's position in the Capital. The old system of an army raised from among the Byzantine peasantry and small landowners went into terminal decline as a result of the landed aristocracy of the East buying up all the land. As the tax revenue declined so also did the armed forces that were maintained by the Emperor to maintain the frontier. Emperors consistently reduced the funding available for the maintenance of these border forces in order to fund an ever larger bureaucracy and other funds were lost through widespread corruption.

The new state of affairs in the provinces of Asia Minor (also known as Anatolia; or the area of modern day Turkey) meant that the empire was less able to defend the eastern frontiers should a new threat appear. This new threat was not long in arrival; in fact it had arrived before the death of Basil II. In 1016-17 the first Turkish raids are recorded in the sources. Seeking new pasture lands for their nomadic lifestyle the Turks began pressing against the Eastern frontier of the Empire in the same way that the Northern Danube frontier had long been threatened by migrating tribes. By the 1040s the Turks along the frontier had increased in both numbers and the threat that they posed. In spite of this increasingly apparent threat to the security of the Byzantine Empire, the process of reducing the Empire's armies continued. Experienced regiments were seen to be too expensive to maintain and were disbanded and replaced with mercenary companies who were often less effective and almost as expensive to maintain. Despite this, the Empire continued to prosper at its centre whilst the frontiers deteriorated.

> **Byzantine Emperors 1071-1081**
>
> *1068 Romanus IV Diogenes*
> *1071 Michael VII Ducas*
> *1078 Nicephoros Botaneiates*
> *1081 Alexius I Comnenus*

The Importance of the year 1071

The year 1071 was one of the most important years in recorded history. It was a year in which the terminal decline of the Byzantine Empire is first identifiable, a series of events occurred which wounded the Empire and ensured that future wounds would spell the death of the Empire. The year 1071 also produced other legacies; it would be a year which would see the beginnings of Turkish domination of Asia Minor and a year after which Western Europeans would see increasing opportunities in the East. As a result of the events of 1071, the Byzantine Empire lost its prestige in the East as well as the West as well as territory. One of the legacies a legacy of 1071 was also the Crusading Movements of 1095-1204 which is the focus of this work.

In 1071 the Byzantine Emperor Romanus IV Diogenes was determined to restore the prestige of the Empire. In the West the Normans of Southern Italy led by Robert the Guiscard was intent on driving the last Byzantine outposts out of Italy. He laid siege to Bari, the final Byzantine held fortress in Italy. In the East Seljuk Turks led by the Sultan Alp Arslan had captured a number of fortresses along the frontier including Manzikert. Romanus IV determined to deal with Alp Arslan. He gathered an army and led it East, It would have been better for him and the Empire if he had remained in Constantinople.

At the battle of Manzikert Romanus IV was defeated and captured by Alp Arlsan. Although freed soon after, Romanus was discredited and soon deposed and killed. In the same year Bari was captured by the Normans of Southern Italy who began to see opportunities for further expansion in Greece and the Balkans.

A succession of Emperors was unable or unwilling to retrieve the military situation in the East. Turkish bands migrated into Anatolia and ousted much of the local population from the countryside. The cities of the East and Constantinople were flooded with refugees from the countryside and the cities of Anatolia gradually surrendered to Turkish rulers. By 1081, the Seljuk Turks had established a new capital at the city of Nicaea, some 200 miles from Constantinople.

The accession of Alexius I Comnenus

Alexius Comnenus was one of the youngest and most skilful of the Byzantine Empire's generals after Manzikert. Well connected, Alexius was the nephew of a former Emperor and related to many of the most powerful families of the Empire. In 1081 the elderly Emperor Nicephoros Botaneiates who had reigned since 1078 abdicated in favour of Alexius.

Upon coming Emperor Alexius faced many grave challenges; other people hungered for the throne of the Empire. Enemies were crossing the Danube frontier as well as the Turkish groups that were penetrating further into Asia Minor. The treasury was empty; Alexius' armies were small and scattered and mostly composed of mercenaries; likely as not to desert as to fight.

Alexius however had a few assets at his disposal. The Empire may be poor, but his relatives and the church were wealthy. They were called upon to provide funds. Alexius was a skilled general and respected by the remaining loyal military commanders. He was also well connected and had the support of his own family the Comneni as well as the Ducas and Dalassena families.

Alexius chose to focus his efforts against the nearer and greater of the immediate threats; In Europe the Pecheneg tribes had crossed the Danube, the Normans of Sicily were about to launch an attack on the Empire and the Hungarian kingdom was also seeking to take advantage of its vulnerability. The Normans of Italy, led by Robert Guiscard made much early progress capturing the port city of Durazzo (in Modern Albania) in 1082 and defeating Alexius in battle a year later. However, Alexius used diplomacy to incite rebellion in Southern Italy and also made alliance with Venice who was also concerned about the sudden rise of Guiscard. Robert the Guiscard was forced to return to southern Italy by these distractions leaving his son Bohemund to continue the attack. Guiscard returned years later but the impetus had gone and he died as a result of a plague that devastated his army in 1085. Durazzo was reclaimed for the Empire and the Normans ejected. Alexius also campaigned against the Hungarians and the Pechenegs, achieving a great victory over the latter in 1091 at the battle of Levounion. The surviving Pechenegs were compelled by Alexius to serve in his armies in return for land to settle on.

By 1095 The Emperor Alexius then had recovered much of the Empire's former position in Europe, but it had been at the cost of neglecting the Turkish advance in Asia Minor. As the situation improved in the West, Alexius began to look at how he could turn the tide in the East and restore the Empire there. Alexius had rebuilt the economy and stabilised the Western provinces. But his armies were still small and reliant upon mercenaries. He needed manpower from the West and he respected the battle prowess of western knights.

Western soldiers had been serving in the armies of the Byzantine Empire for some time; Norman adventurers, Russians, Anglo Saxons and French knights all had come to the Empire to serve in the armies of the Emperor. In 1088 some 500 knights from Flanders had served the Emperor well and Alexius no doubt considered that European Christian soldiers who would hopefully be more reliable in battle against the Muslim Turks and many French and German knights fought annual campaigns against Muslims in Spain in the past few decades.

It was with this aim of acquiring Christian mercenaries that he contacted the Pope of Rome, Urban II. Alexius hoped for soldiers and knights who would serve in his armies. He did not get quite what he expected.

Task: Threats to the Empire 1081-1095

Part a) Using the information you have learned so far make a list of threats, real and potential, to the Byzantine Empire in the years 1081-1095 (The early years of Alexius' rule). *Spend no more than 10 minutes on this part of the task.*

Part b) Once you have written your list try to identify threats which are minor and major. Minor being threats that could damage the Empire but not destroy it. Major threats being those that could topple Alexius from his position or even destroy Greek rule of the Empire. *Spend no more than 10 minutes on this part of the task.*

Part c) Try to decide which of these threats is the most threatening to the Byzantine Empire in the short term and long term. *Spend no more than 10 minutes on this part of the task.*

1.4 - Overview: Islam 600-1095

In this topic we will;

- Understand the reasons why Islam became a World religion so quickly.
- Consider the geographical and political landscape of the Islamic World by the 11th century.
- Understand some of the terminology used in Islam.
- Begin to explore the World of Dar al-Islam.
- Begin to consider the social and political factors in the Islamic World that that led to the Crusades.
- Consider the importance of the Turks in the 11th century.
- Understand the relationship between the Byzantine Empire and the Islamic World and why this relationship was unbalanced by the Turks.
- Continue to consider the social and political factors in the Islamic World that that led to the Crusades.

Islam

The death of Muhammad at Mecca in 632 signalled the beginning of the expansion of Islam out of the Arabian Peninsula across the Near East, North Africa and into Europe.

Armies led by Arab converts to the new religion invaded the neighbouring territories and their successes transformed the political and religious landscape. The two major powers in the Near East – the Christian Byzantine Empire and the Sassanid Persian Empire had fought for centuries for control of Palestine. The latest war, lasting from 602-628 had been particularly exhausting to both sides and neither the Persian nor the Byzantine Empires were prepared to tackle the new force emerging from Arabia.

The conquest of the Near East was both rapid and impressive. Several Byzantine armies were soundly defeated in battle and by 641 Syria and Palestine were controlled by Islamic forces. The Byzantine capital Constantinople was besieged from 647 but the armies of Islam were unable to capture the city.

Egypt and Persia soon followed and North Africa was under Muslim rule by the end of the 7th century. At the beginning of the 8th century the Arab led armies were invited into Spain and soon put an end to the Visigothic kingdom there. In 732 Muslim raiders were in central France until they were pushed back into Spain after a battle at Poitiers.

The conquests of Islam

Syria and Palestine – 635-641

The Persian Empire overthrown – 637-648

Antioch captured - 637

Jerusalem captured - 638

Egypt captured – 640-642

Afghanistan invaded - 664

North Africa subdued– 698

Bukhara, Tashkent and Samarkand Invaded -711

Spain Invaded– 711-713

Southern France (until defeated at Poitiers) - 732

Sicily - 830

Islam and Jerusalem

The Patriarch of Jerusalem, Sophronius surrendered the city to the Caliph Umar in February 638 after a long siege. The occupation was a peaceful and orderly one, one which contrasted sharply with the capture of that same city by the forces of the First Crusade in 1099 and more recently the sack and massacres that had taken place during the war between Byzantium and the Sassanid Persians.

Entering the city on a camel and wearing tattered clothes the Caliph Umar established new mosque which survives to this day; the Al-Asqa, whilst leaving the Christian and Jewish places of worship untouched. The capture of this city was a humiliation to the prestige of Christianity on the one hand, but on the other hand it confirmed to the followers of Islam what the caliph and the prophet had been saying all along; as Christianity had replaced the old religions of Judaism and the pagan faiths of the Roman Empire, so to Islam was replacing Christianity as the final revelation from God.

> **The significance of Jerusalem to Islam**
>
> According to Islamic belief, the city of Jerusalem is the place where the Prophet Muhammad ascended to Heaven. After Mecca and Medina it is considered to be the most holy place in Islamic faith.

Islam

In a little more than a decade the Byzantine Empire lost over half of its territory to Islam. The successful tactics of the Arab led armies of Islam combined rapid movement by soldiers mounted on camels as well as horses, fierce raids and a sophisticated understanding of siege warfare. In 636 a huge Byzantine army was destroyed on the banks of the river Yarmuk. Establishing themselves at Damascus, the Muslim armies made annual invasions into Byzantine territory. In 661 so severe a threat were these armies to the Byzantine Empire, that the then Emperor considered removing his capital to Sicily.

The newly conquered lands were known as *Dar al-Islam* (The house of Islam). In the Qur'an, Religious tolerance was accorded to the peoples of the book; Christians and Jews.

Christians and Jews had to pay for Islamic rule and protection however through a tax known as the *jizya*. Non-Muslims were also banned from bearing arms and riding on horses. However, for many of the inhabitants of Syria and Palestine these inconveniences were still much less resented than the long years of warfare, high taxes and religious infighting that had been the case when the areas were governed by the Byzantine Empire and the Sassanid Persians. In many areas the Islamic conquest was welcomed.

> **Task: Excerpt analysis**
>
> Read the following passage translated from the Qur'an;
>
> *"Unbelievers, I do not serve what you worship, nor do you serve what I worship. I shall never serve what you worship, nor will you ever serve what I worship. You have your own religion, and I have mine."*
>
> Sura 109
>
> What does this passage tell you about how people of different religions should be treated in *Dar al-Islam*?

Byzantium and Islam

When the Islamic Caliphate was transferred to Damascus, the Byzantine Empire was faced with a powerful rival that could utilise the resources of Syria, Egypt and Iraq to make further inroads into the territory of the Empire. Proximity to the Mediterranean enabled the Caliphate to launch naval expeditions against the Empire as well as overland.

However by the 8th century the Umayyad Caliphate were overthrown by the Abbasids and this new dynasty moved the centre of power Eastward to Baghdad. The Abbasid interests lay primarily to the East and in 798 the Caliph Harun al-Rashid made alliance with the Chinese Tang dynasty against the threat of the Tibetan kingdom, at the same time new wealth came into Abbasid Caliphate through trade routes with India.

The reorientation of Abbasid policies to the East allowed the Byzantine Empire some breathing space along their Eastern frontiers. Throughout the 9th and 10th centuries energetic Emperors reformed the army and led it to many victories in Armenia, the Taurus Mountains and south of Edessa and Antioch. Another consequence of the reorientation of Abbasid focus to the East meant that Egypt, which had once been part of the heartland of Umayyad power, was now on the edge of the Abbasid Caliphate. It was therefore possible for new Islamic leaders to create a state independent of Baghdad. In the 8th and 9th centuries the extension of Muslim power into the Mediterranean against Crete, Sicily and Southern Italy came from North African Emirs. Arab and Berber led armies entered Spain in 711 from North Africa and raids were also launched against the islands of Sardinia and Corsica as well as Rome. Byzantine resources were insufficient to advance in the East as well as adequately protect their possessions in the Mediterranean.

The Seljuks and the Abbasid Caliphate

The Turks originated in Central Asia and were a people of many tribes who migrated gradually Westwards over the centuries. The Cumans and Pechenegs were Turkish peoples for example who were encountered in the Western sources long before the Seljuk Turks arrived in the region. Groups known specifically as Turks however are first recorded along the Byzantine frontier in 1016 AD.

The Seljuk Turks first appear in the sources around 950 AD in Transoxania near the Aral Sea. It was here that they were converted to Islam and as devoutly Sunni they were often opposed to the Shia Muslims whom they saw as heretics.

Often employed as mercenaries, the Seljuk Turks migrated westwards gradually over the following decades where they took service with the Abbasid Caliphate. The Caliphate was in decline, a victim of its own success, the Abbasid Caliphate was unable to maintain adequate control of outlying territories. Replacing the traditional land tax the *Kharaj*, the Caliphate instead instituted the *iqtas*, local taxes would thenceforward by kept locally, the regional rulers instead obliged to send armies as required. Gradually starved of wealth as well as soldiers as regional rulers neglected to pay their taxes and send their men, by the end of the 10th century the Abbasid Caliphate was bankrupt. It was therefore the Turks who became the power in the land.

By 1045 the Seljuks under their leader Tughrul Bey were in Persia, by 1055 Tughrul Bey was settled in Baghdad with the title of *'Sultan and King of East and West'*, the real power in the Abbasid Caliphate. Whilst the Sultan resided in Baghdad ruling in the name of the Caliph, who was kept as a virtual prisoner in his own palace, the other Seljuk princes established themselves as the military representatives of the Sultan in Mosul, Aleppo and Damascus amongst other cities.

The Seljuks, the Fatamids and the Byzantine Empire

Contrary to the belief of many Western orientated sources, the main enemy of the Seljuk Turks was not the Christian Byzantine Empire; it was the Fatamid Caliphate of Egypt who were Shi'ite Muslims as opposed to the Seljuk Turks who were Sunni Muslims. In the 1050s the Fatamids controlled much of Palestine and Syria including Aleppo. The Seljuks were determined to drive the Fatamids back from encroaching on territory that was perceived to belong to the Abbasid Caliphate. Any army advancing against the Fatamids would need to ensure that their lines of communication with Baghdad and Mosul were secure. In order to secure these lines, the Seljuk Turks needed to ensure that the Byzantine Empire would not launch an attack through Armenia and down the Euphrates towards Baghdad. This may have appeared likely to the Seljuks, as the Byzantine Empire and the Fatamid Caliphate had reasonable relations with each other.

From 1046 AD the Seljuks sought control of Armenia; taking advantage of the Byzantine Empire reducing its frontier armies in this area and the following decades in order to save money. In 1054 Tughrul Bey raided Armenia and thereafter raiding parties were sent annually. Tughrul Bey died in 1063 and was succeeded by his nephew Alp Arslan. In 1064 Alp Arslan renewed the assault on Armenia by destroying the city of Ani; the Armenian capital. By 1067 Alp Arslan had penetrated as far as Caesarea in Cappadocia. As a result of these incursions the Byzantine Emperor Romanus IV Diogenes determined to put an end to this threat. He led expeditions in 1068 and the year after. In 1071 he led his army to defeat against Alp Arslan at the battle of Manzikert.

After Manzikert Turkish groups, not just Seljuks but other groups such as the Danishmends and the Ortoqids sought new pastures and land in which to live on and raise their horses at the expense of the Byzantines. These groups, far from the central control of the Sultan at Baghdad established new semi- independent territories. The Sultan at Baghdad was unable to exert control and authority of these areas and members of the Seljuk dynasty began to establish themselves in their own right. In the 10 years after Manzikert, Alp Arslan's successor, Malik Shah had established a new Sultanate in Asia Minor called 'Rum'. Its capital by 1081 was at Nicaea. Other Turkish groups established themselves further East; the Danishmend

Turks in the North East of Asia Minor and the Ortoqids further East still in Armenia and Syria.

The Seljuks did not just advance against the Byzantine Empire. Most of Syria and Palestine were under Seljuk control by 1079 AD. These territories were controlled by a patchwork of Emirs; some Turkish, some Arab. Some were controlled by military governors called Atabegs who quickly became the de facto ruler in these lands through their military reputation and retinues. To this end the Atabegs maintained retinues of Mameluks – both warriors and slaves who were loyal to their leaders and fierce in battle.

Throughout this period the Turks largely retained a nomadic lifestyle, moving in small clans and extended family groups with their horse herds seeking pasture. This lifestyle in part was represented in their military prowess. Fighting as mounted archers, the Turks could out manoeuvre and decimate infantry armies by shooting their arrows from a distance and avoiding hand to hand fighting.

The Seljuks and the Holy Land

The Turks ruled a wide variety of people in Syria and Palestine. There were Orthodox Christians, Jacobite Christians, Jews, Armenians, Arabs and Shia converts from amongst the Syrian and Palestinian peoples. Likewise, the Fatamids also ruled over Christian Copts in Egypt as well as those mentioned above. The Near East in the century before the Crusades was a melting pot of different ethnic and religious groups.

The migrations of the Turks into the Near East did more than change the political landscape. Trade routes were disrupted and roads long used by merchants and pilgrims from the West to the Holy land were made almost impassable by the disruption.

In 1087, the Seljuk Turks captured Jerusalem from the Fatamids. News that the Holy city had been lost to the Turks and that pilgrims could not now reach there without greater danger and hardship spread quickly Eastward.

1.5: The Geography of Europe and the Near East 1050-1100

Introduction

In this section we will;

- Understand the lands and nations of Medieval Europe and the Middle east
- Consider the key differences and similarities of these lands and nations
- Explore the characteristics of Nobles and Knights in Europe
- Investigate the traits of Nobility

Nobles and Knights in Europe

The development of kingdoms in Europe such as the kingdoms of France and Germany depended to a great extent on the complex relationships between Rulers and Nobles, the relationships between Nobles and Nobles and the relationships between Nobles and non-nobles.

A King or Noble (or someone who aspired to be either) needed certain requirements in order to maintain or improve their standing including;

- The trait of nobility
- A family name
- Primogeniture and Inheritance
- Land acquisition
- Military skill and reputation
- A fortified home; a Castle
- Knights

The trait of nobility?

Straightaway here we run into a potential problem; Nobility is a term that in practice is not easily defined or applied. Some people might be described as noble due to their birth into a family of nobles; others might equally be defined as noble through their virtues and moral behaviour. In the loosest terms of definition we could perhaps equate the trait of nobility with links to families of power and status within a given area.

Nobles could be described as those who managed to acquire control or ownership of a castle or town or could even be used to describe anyone who was born as a 'Freeman'. This could therefore even include very poor peasants that lived in areas not under the control of any 'Overlord'. The definition then is loose, subject to change and prone to misconceptions.

One common misconception of nobility then was that with nobility came wealth. This misconception is false. Baldwin I (king of Jerusalem) was relatively poor before he joined the First Crusade. Another misconception that commonly occurs is that a knight by definition must be noble. This was never the case. The status of fighting men was often equated with being a knight; yet there were many kinds of fighting men who came from many different backgrounds. Soldiers of the Byzantine Empire for example might come from peasant families who were obligated to provide their own horse and weapons, but were not described as knights.

A family name

A Noble ideally possessed a family name; they could link themselves through their family tree and ancestry to men and families of wealth and status. In an ideal world a noble would be able to point to their family tree and identify a link of either blood or marriage ties to the idealised Christian king that united much of Europe in the late 8th and early 9th centuries under his rule; Charlemagne.

Another way to acquire the trait of nobility was to marry into a family that already possessed this trait. Many nobles had daughters that required marrying off and, whilst many of these daughters married other noble families, occasions did occur when a noble lord would permit his daughter to marry someone from a much less illustrious background. Sometimes these were the youngest sons of lords who had little to recommend them except their family name, but sometimes a lord may allow his daughter to marry non-nobles of wealth and means, such as merchants or even peasants that had acquired wealth and success. This strategy of marrying noble to money had its dangers however, having ancestors of poor or servile origins in your family tree could jeopardise your own nobility. In the early 11th century for example, the Count of Flanders, desperate for additional funds threatened to strip the land and assets of noble families within his county that had any suggestion of non-noble origins.

The case of Bohemund.

Bohemund was the eldest son of Robert the Guiscard, a Norman adventurer who through cunning, luck and outright violence dominated the peninsular of Italy in the latter 11th century and came close to toppling the Byzantine Empire in 1081-1085. Whilst Bohemund was the eldest son, when his mother died, Guiscard married again (to a rather war-like princess) and it was to his eldest son of his second wife, Roger Borsa; that the bulk of Guiscard's inheritance went. Despite his fearsome record on the battlefield, Bohemund was in possession of much less land and wealth than his younger brother (who became king of Naples and Sicily) and it was this relative poverty that encouraged Bohemund to seek richer lands along the eastern fringes of the Byzantine Empire.

In this he was successful in the short term - becoming Prince of Antioch for a time, but being defeated in his designs on the Byzantine Empire in 1108, Bohemund was required to acknowledge the over lordship of the Byzantine Empire of the city of Antioch. In despair at being forced into this acknowledgement, Bohemund returned to live out his days in relative obscurity on his original estates in Italy.

Primogeniture and Inheritance

Anyone born into a noble family could easily describe themselves as 'noble', however, all too often these 'nobles' lacked the other necessities required to truly merit the accolade of being a noble. Much of what was missing was wealth and land.

When a noble lord died, it was often the case that all of the deceased wealth and lands and titles went solely to the eldest male child. Other children, male and female, would not inherit anything. This rule of inheritance is known as ***Primogeniture***.

Whilst female children were typically married off to remove them from the household (and to create links with other families), younger male children were either left with the choice of joining the Church as priest (hoping in turn to gain the wealth and status that came from high churchly rank), staying at the side of their brother as a sometimes reluctant and unwanted house guest, or leaving home to seek land and wealth elsewhere.

More often, a noble would inherit something from their father's lands and wealth; it might be a manor house or a small castle on the edges of the family land. In any event, in order to be granted this land or possession, the second or third son would be required to perform an act of homage to their sibling, who became their liege lord. Sometimes this grant of land and home would be too small to satisfy the ambitions and hope of the younger or ousted child.

Land acquisition

In Medieval Europe, much of what we understand as wealth could actually be translated as 'land'. Land was the basis of almost all economies in Western Europe. Land was used to grow crops and rear livestock on, which all who lived in the area depended upon for sustenance and the slight hope of improving their wealth. Without land, a noble had no real means to generate income and therefore maintain their standing in society. Land could be used by nobles to generate wealth as well as to meet the obligations imposed upon them by their overlords. Land could be used to reward followers with and could be increased.

Policies and tactics which nobles could use to increase their ownership of land included;

- De-forestation, land drainage and reclamation works - (much land in Europe in the late 11th century was uncultivated and needed only to be cleared and settled in order to be acquired). This method would be time consuming and expensive.

- Serve a lord in return for them granting you land – this technique would usually result in the land being granted conditionally and may not be permanent. As a poorer noble, you might already own land elsewhere which would also have conditions attached to it. What if your overlords disagree?, you might have to serve one against the other.

- Emigration - Nobles needed to be able to provide for themselves and their followers, and this provision often came from the acquisition of land. If a noble could not inherit land, they could emigrate to other parts of the world and gain land through service elsewhere where they were encouraged to journey to. Many French nobles moved to England for example after 1066, whilst others took up service in the kingdom of Sicily or in the Byzantine Empire.

- Seizing land from non-Christians – one option for a landless noble was to try and take land from others by force. The Eastern areas of Europe where pagan peoples still lived was one area exploited by German nobles in particular. French (particularly from the southern parts of France) were encouraged to participate in the wars in Spain between Christian and Muslim rulers in the hope of gaining land.

- Seizing land from your neighbours – a final option for the landless noble of Western Europe was to raid neighbouring lordships in the hope of acquiring some wealth through plunder or event to forcibly seize parts of their territory.

Many of these methods of land acquisition required the aspiring noble to be able to fight.

Military skill and reputation

Kings and great lords were required to be military leaders in practice. Their claims to large areas of lands and wealth would be jeopardised by a reluctance to, or inability to fight. If a noble had a great reputation as a warrior it could deter others from seeking to exploit them. However, a poor military reputation and numerous defeats could be an invitation for others to try and take advantage.

In order for a king or lord to fight then, it follows that they required the means to be able to fight. A retinue of armed warriors was an essential must have for a lord or noble. This armed retinue likewise had to be skilled in battle and or of sufficient size so that when conflict occurred, the lord could lead his men to victory. This armed retinue could either be paid in cash, paid in booty and plunder acquired by force, or paid for in land. The armed forces of a lord might be recruited as mercenaries from other areas, be men obligated to serve from the lord's territories or may be landless nobles hoping to acquire land through service to another.

Knights and Castles

In Medieval Europe, war was typically fought in order to achieve one of the following aims;

- Plunder

- Conquest

THE CRUSADES 1095-1204

In order for the war mongering noble to succeed in the attack the noble needed a core of professional force of armed fighting men – what we might call knights. For a noble to be able to protect his possessions, a noble would need not only a force of professional force of armed fighting men, but also means of defence to protect his valuables. A common means of defence was to safeguard wealth in fortified locations – castles.

When we think of knights we must not think of King Arthur and his Knights of the Round table. Brave in battle, courteous to women and the poor and galloping around on white horses in shiny silvered armour. Whilst this was the image that many knights would like to portray it is far from accurate.

Knights were trained mounted soldiers, but they were almost certainly less than courteous to the poor and the vulnerable. Indeed, their favourite targets in war were often precisely the poor and defenceless. These were rough men, used to fighting in all conditions against other rough men. They were armoured (usually with types of chainmail armour) and equipped with lances, spears, swords and a variety of blunt objects such as hammers and maces which they used to knock each other from their horses (which too had been trained to fight in battle and were also sometimes armoured). Knights were recruited from a variety of backgrounds, from the local nobility for certain, but also illegitimate sons of nobles, as well as men from the fields that their neighbours and lords knew had an aptitude for violent work. Landless nobles from other areas too would flock to regions beset by violence in the hope of gaining employment, bringing with them little but the possessions that their animals and few retainers could carry and there training in the ways of medieval warfare. Despite being in the minority on any given battlefield, the knights could fight off many times their numbers of badly equipped and nonskilled foot soldiers.

Castles were fortified places, areas from which the noble could stay relatively safe whilst under attack, house his property and keep supplies of food. They also provided a focal point for the noble's lands and a place where the affairs of his land (law courts and business) might also take place.

Castles could be built of earth, timber or stone and could be small or large in size. Some castles were very simple, a wooden fence atop a hill of earth, others were extremely elaborate, capable of housing hundreds of people in times of danger and having their own community in their own right. A Noble might require a stone castle – from either the grounds of prestige or necessity, but a stone castle could take years to construct and was extremely expensive. A noble might pay for a castle by increasing the taxation on his subjects, borrowing money or acquiring the wealth through attacks on their neighbours.

An individual with luck, skill or determination then could be created through the acquisition of land, a castle and a retinue of knights. He might construct a crude castle close to a road, people it with a group of local toughs and prey on the inhabitants and trade passing through a local area. The locals might pay off the bully in the castle in return for peace, whilst at the same time the king or overlord may overlook the behaviour of the bully in the castle in return of some service, money or acknowledgment of over lordship, with such acknowledgment comes nobility, and within a relatively short amount of time, an area might have a new noble lord.

The aspirations of the landless noble and the needs and requirements of the lords of the land therefore intertwined. Lords had land, men and castles, without these a lord, no matter how noble, was not a lord. Landless nobles neither land, men nor castles, but were usually better placed than those without nobility to acquire these from those that did.

Task: Ranking exercise: Traits of nobility?

Look again at the characteristics discussed earlier;

- *A family name*
- *Primogeniture and Inheritance*
- *Land acquisition*
- *Military skill and reputation*
- *A fortified home; a Castle*
- *A retinue of Knights*

Which of these characteristics do you think is the most important requirement for someone to be considered as Noble in the period of the Crusades?

PART TWO: The First Crusade 1095-1100

PART TWO: The First Crusade 1095-1100

2.1 Pilgrimage and the Origins of Holy War

2.2 Summoning the First Crusade

2.3 Launching the First Crusade

2.4 The motives of the Crusaders in the First Crusade

2.5 The First Crusade 1095-1100: From Nicaea to Jerusalem 1097-1100

2.1 Pilgrimage and Holy War

In this topic we will;

- Understand what is meant by the term Pilgrimage.
- Consider the reasons why pilgrimage flourished in the 8th, 9th and 10th centuries
- Understand the importance of the Church in encouraging Pilgrimage.
- Explore the factors that were required in order for mass pilgrimage to the Holy Land.
- Consider the concept of Holy War.
- Understand why the concept of Holy War developed.
- Begin to consider the relationship between Holy War, pilgrimage and the Crusades.

Pilgrimage and Jerusalem

Unlike the *Hadj* of Islam, pilgrimage is not considered to be a necessary act of faith in the Christian religion. Early Christians of the 1st through 4th centuries did not tend to go on pilgrimage. Indeed, there would have been little for them to see and limited infrastructure to accommodate them if they had gone. Jerusalem had been ruined by the Romans in the 70s AD by the future Emperor Titus after a Jewish revolt. The city remained ruined for some fifty years until rebuilt and renamed *Aelia* by the Emperor Hadrian.

It was not until the 4th century that Jerusalem became a destination for pilgrims. The mother of the Emperor Constantine I and first great pilgrim and archaeologist of the Late Classical World; the Empress Helena journeyed to Palestine and through a combination of her Christian faith, fame and family wealth many of the sites mentioned in the Bible were identified and lavished with churches. It was through Helena that the most holy church in Christendom was built; the Church of the Holy Sepulchre at Jerusalem.

Thereafter, pilgrims began to journey to the Holy land from across the Roman Empire. Despite this Imperial patronage, opinion amongst early church authorities disputed whether the act of pilgrimage was a worthwhile one or not. As pilgrims journeyed to the Holy Land they sought mementos of their visit. Poor pilgrims were satisfied with Palm leaves from the banks of the river Jordan. Wealthy pilgrims and pilgrims of authority in the early church sought historical mementoes. The relics of the past; often the physical remains of saints that they could bring home and place as a centrepiece in their local place of worship.

Relics were first taken to Constantinople to be housed in the great churches there. Later, other pilgrims took relics to churches further west. These relics, the fragments of martyrs and saints began to be honoured in their own right for the miracles they were reputed to give. Churches were built to house them and were often named after the individual saint whose relics they housed.

The rise of Islam disrupted the pilgrim routes to the Holy lands and caused a realignment of trade routes, however, although the pilgrims were disrupted and inconvenienced, this did not stop them from attempting the journey. Throughout the 7th and 8th centuries individuals are known to have journeyed from Western Europe to Palestine.

The Major Pilgrim routes

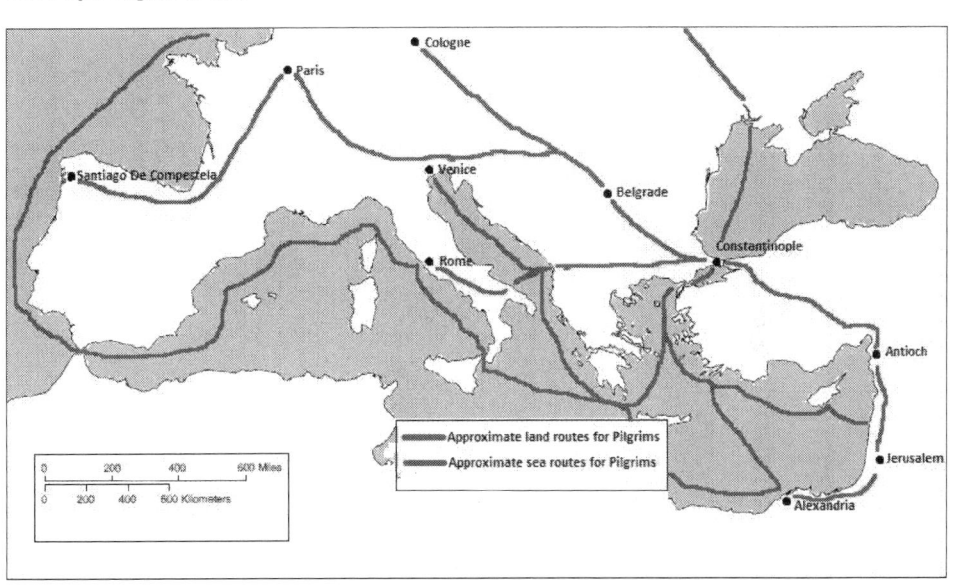

In the 8th and 9th centuries the numbers of pilgrims increased. The Frankish Emperor Charlemagne established good relationships with the Caliph at Baghdad and was able to sponsor the construction of hostels throughout the Holy land to accommodate the increasing traffic of pilgrims. These hostels were run by nuns from the West who gave pilgrims places of rest and food whilst on their travels.

By the end of the 10th century the Hungarian kingdom that lay between the Holy Roman Empire and the Byzantine Empire was converted to Christianity. It was now possible to travel overland through central Europe and to Constantinople, then across Asia Minor and into the Holy lands. The Byzantine Empire also mad safe the sea routes of the central and eastern Mediterranean, permitting those who had the money to travel by ship to do so in relative safety from pirates that had been a problem in the previous centuries. Pilgrims could travel from one of the Italian merchant city states to either Palestine or Egypt and then journey to Jerusalem from there. Both men and women travelled as individuals or in large groups. Land travel was slow but it was cheap and it allowed large groups of pilgrims to travel together.

The Muslim lords of Palestine and Egypt welcomed pilgrims in the main. The pilgrims travelled established trade routes and also brought wealth that they would spend. Other pilgrims travelled to Constantinople to see the large collection of relics housed there and then either went home or continued on to Palestine. However in the middle of the 11th century access to Palestine was at times restricted. Some pilgrims were denied entry to Palestine and in 1056 Christians were ejected from Jerusalem for a time. The Byzantine Empire too attempted to profit from pilgrims. Taxes were placed on pilgrims and their horses from 1020s-1050s. These actions, did not however dissuade pilgrims from attempting the journey.

Scandinavian pilgrims could sail from their homelands and enter into the Mediterranean via Gibraltar, then journey to Palestine and return home via Constantinople and the Black Sea, crossing Russia overland. Some of these Scandinavians took employment in the Varangian Guard of the Byzantine Empire for a few years as well as become pilgrims. Harold Hardrada did so in 1034.

Some Pilgrims made the journey more than once. St. John, Bishop of Parma went to Jerusalem as a pilgrim on six occasions. Fulk Nerra of Anjou was a pilgrim three times. Each time he went was to salve his soul for his constant acts of warfare and massacre. Not all pilgrims survived the journey however, Swein Godwinson died on his pilgrimage in 1051/2. He had travelled barefoot in penance for committing murder. He died of exposure in Asia Minor.

Nobles who travelled to the Holy land did so accompanied by many poorer pilgrims. As numbers increased the Christian authorities sought to create an infrastructure to assist and maintain control of the pilgrim experience. The Cluniac order of Monks approved of pilgrimage and established hostels throughout Europe to facilitate the travels of pilgrims and profit from providing this service; not just to Palestine, but also in Spain to help pilgrims travel to the Church of Santiago de Compostela. Whilst poor pilgrims may donate to the upkeep of these hostels, the great lords provided land and donations of money to the Cluniacs.

According to Sir Steven Runciman, the success of large scale pilgrimage rested on two factors;

- Palestine needed to be settled and orderly.
- The journey to Palestine needed to be safe and cheap to do.

The influx of Turkish rule into Palestine and conflict between the Turks and the Fatamids from the 1050s onwards disrupted the first factor; the second factor was disrupted by the Byzantine defeat at the battle of Manzikert.

Christianity is usually claimed by those that adhere to this faith to be a religion of love, morality and duty. How then could tens of thousands of men and women who went on crusade justify their claims of piety and devotion through acts of murder, warfare and wholesale massacre of people of other faiths, let alone people who also professed the same Christian faith as their killers?

According to the Historian Sir Steven Runciman;

> '*The Holy War itself was nothing more than a long act of intolerance in the name of God, which is the sin against the Holy Ghost*'
>
> Runciman (1954, iii, 480)

A closer reading of the works of both the Old and New Testament can reveal justification for such acts should people choose to interpret them so.

Throughout the Old Testament there are many references to acts of murder and warfare that are not only condoned, but are stated as being pleasing to God. In Exodus XXXII:26-8 Moses is told to slaughter unbelievers, whilst in the books of Maccabees, which are dated to the 3rd century BC, the Jews are praised in their battles against the Seleucid Empire as they kill their enemies in the name of God. The New Testament also is liberally scattered with references to fighting and dying in the name of God. In the final book of the

New Testament, the apocalyptic vision of the end of days outlined in the book of Revelations depicts scenes of battle and slaughter and conflict. There are then many examples of acts of violence in the major Christian texts.

Christianity and the defence of the Roman Empire

When Christianity was adopted by the Roman Empire as the state religion, Christianity also took on the obligations of the old Pagan deities that were responsible for maintaining the security of the Empire. Christian leaders, including the Emperor were then required to justify acts of warfare and violence in the name of the defence not just of the Empire, but of the Christian religion of its citizens.

Whilst this was easier when the Empire was at war with its rival non-Christian Sassanid Persian Empire, the fact that many of the Barbarian invasions that plagued the later Roman Empire were comprised of peoples who were also Christians. However, this difficulty was overcome on the grounds that many of these Christian Barbarian invaders (Goths, Vandals and Franks) were of Arian and other heretical beliefs. In short they belonged to the 'wrong' kind of Christianity.

Since the Roman Empire was now a Christian one after the 4th century. It was argued by leading Christian authorities such as Ambrose, Bishop of Milan (died 397) that any wars it fought, defensive or aggressive, were Christian wars.

Later in the Byzantine East wars would be fought in the defence of Christianity. The Emperor Heraclius was known as the 'First Crusader' due to his long wars against both the Sassanid Persians and also the Arab led armies that surged out of Arabia in the 7th century. These wars included long struggles over Jerusalem and the Holy Land which added to tradition that the wars he fought were in fact in the defence of the Holy land. Despite his efforts Heraclius was unable to save the three Patriarchal seats of Jerusalem, Alexandria and Antioch for the Empire and the losses broke him.

Charlemagne and the Western tradition of militarised Christianity

In the West, the Roman Empire was replaced by Germanic peoples who founded new states in Britain, Germany, France, Italy and Spain. Some of these new states were pagan initially, others were Christian but after a few hundred years most of Western Europe was Christianized. Initially, the new lords; Pagan or Christian, imposed themselves upon the existing Roman administration who maintained their position through the retention of armed military retinues, who usually served in return for the reward of land. The feudal system had arrived in Western Europe.

However, although they had adopted Christianity, these local aristocrats did not relinquish their military authority and continued to justify their violent habits in the name of their religion. Many lords and knights continued to war on their neighbours in the name of God and at times it was irrelevant whether their opponents were Pagan or Christian. Oswald, King of Northumbria was martyred fighting pagans in the 7th century. In 1066 King Harold of England was killed by Duke William of Normandy at Hastings, both were Christians and William had Papal approval of his conquest of England. The fighting was not restricted to aristocrats however; Church leaders such as bishops emulated the secular leaders of the lands and also kept armed retainers who fought in battle alongside their Bishops.

In 885/6 a Viking attack on Paris was repelled in part by an Abbott who was very skilled in the use of medieval artillery;

"He was capable of piercing seven men with a single arrow;

In jest he commanded some of them to be taken to the kitchen".

De bello Parisiaco; Abbot of St. Germain

In 800AD The King of the Franks, Charlemagne was crowned as Emperor of the West by the Pope. Charlemagne had already united much of Western Europe through a combination of the power he inherited along with many victorious military campaigns. Crowned as Emperor, Charlemagne was keen to portray himself as the leader in the defence of Christian faith. Later Christian knights would hold Charlemagne as the ideal Christian warrior. To the knights of the Crusades, the act of being a good Christian coincided with the act of being a good warrior.

Charlemagne's armies indulged in prayers and mass confession before fighting Pagan enemies and the promotion of relics to help inspire his soldiers to greater efforts. Charlemagne's victories were accompanied by miraculous acts in the historical sources. Charlemagne's wars of conquest against the Pagan Saxons of Northern Germany were amongst the most brutal fought in Early Europe. Victory in battle was followed by a determined policy of massacre and terror; forced conversions and the deliberate destruction of Saxon holy sites resulted in the conversion of the Saxons, who according to Charlemagne were a threat to the safeguarding of Christian peoples elsewhere. Charlemagne's victories in the name of Christendom were inextricably linked with systematic acts of terror and violence.

Task: An early view of Holy War

Read the following quote by Pope Leo IV;

"We hope that none of you will be slain, but we wish you to know that the kingdom of heaven will be given as a reward to those who are killed in this war. For God knows that they lost their lives fighting for the truth of the faith, for the preservation of their country, for the defence of Christians. God will give then, the reward which we have named."

Pope Leo IV (847-855)

What does this passage tell you about how the idea of Holy War?

Spend no more than 10 minutes on this task

2.2 – Summoning the First Crusade

In this topic we will;

- *Consider the extent and purpose of Pope Urban II's tour 1095-1096*
- *Explore the extent of the response to the Papal tour*
- *Consider the reaction of Emperor Alexius and his preparations*
- *Examining the successes and failures of Urban's tour*

Pope Urban's Tour 1095-1096

In March 1095, envoys from the Emperor Alexius reached Pope Urban II in Italy. Amongst other business, including discussion aimed at improving the relationship between the Catholic and Orthodox churches was a request for assistance in seeking military aid from the West.

Urban II was a new Pope and faced difficulties. He was opposed by an *Anti-Pope*, appointed by the German Ruler Henry IV and this *Anti-Pope* held the city of Rome. Urban then needed to oust the Anti-Pope from Rome and assert control of the Church and the secular rulers who professed to obey the dictates of the Church.

Urban II determined to accomplish this by launching a Papal tour. This tour was to last fourteen months (between July 1095-August 1096) and was both wide-ranging and select in where Urban visited and where he did not. He would visit much of France, from Toulouse in the South to Le Mans in the North. However, Urban II did visit those areas of France that were no directly under the control of the French King Philip (whom the Pope was to be excommunicated in November 1095 due to his adultery), likewise Urban II would not visit Normandy, control of which was hotly disputed between King William II of England and his brother Robert, Duke of Normandy. Germany too was avoided due to the potential danger of falling into the hands of Henry IV; Urban's political enemy. Urban then was to tour areas where he felt he could gather political support.

Midway through his tour, Urban had arranged for a large meeting of bishops and other clerics at the town of Clermont between 18th-28th of November 1095. This meeting was to be one of the most important events in medieval history.

The Council of Clermont, November 1095

At Clermont Pope Urban II was met by some 300 Clerics, Bishops and Archbishops; this large meeting was a sign that the Pope had the confidence and support of much of the clergy of France and with some attendees also travelling from England and Germany, the Council was a clear attempt by Urban II to solidify his position as the most prominent leader of Christianity in Europe. Much of the ten day meeting was spent in Church business. Decrees were established designed to prevent secular rulers from appointing bishops without permission of the Pope. Priests were to be banned from marriage and anti-corruption decrees were passed, with one bishop being excommunicated for *Simony*.

Term

Simony – the buying and selling of spiritual privileges associated with matters of the Church and faith

As mentioned above, the French King, Philip was excommunicated for adultery. This decision was political as much as moral, the French King was in a relatively weak position, controlling only a tiny part of France, but he was still the acknowledged king. By excommunicating King Philip, Urban II was asserting his authority over the highest secular authority in the land. If he could force Philip to accept his authority, then others would also.

Finally, it was declared that on the 27th November a great announcement would be made.

Urban's Speech at Clermont

Urban II spoke to a large crowd at Clermont on Thursday 27th November 1095. The crowd was so large that the event occurred outdoors as the Cathedral at Clermont was too small to hold the crowd.

Elements of Urban's speech have survived in four contemporary chroniclers who all wrote their accounts some years after the actual event and these chroniclers may or may not have been present at Clermont.

These chroniclers were;

- Robert the Monk
- Baudri of Dol
- Fulcher of Chartres
- Guibert of Nogent

These accounts all differ in places but it is possible to identify some elements of Urban's speech. The Christians that lived in the East were appealing for assistance against the Turks who had invaded their lands, desecrated holy sites and mistreated the local Christians. Christian pilgrims to Jerusalem had been obstructed and harassed on many occasions in recent years and undergone many sufferings whilst on pilgrimage. Urban II stressed the holiness and importance of Jerusalem for all Christians and urged Christians in the West, rich and poor alike, to go and help their fellow Christians in the East. Those that go and die on the journey would receive absolution and the remission of their sins.

According to tradition, the speech was responded to with great enthusiasm by the audience with cries of *'Deus Le Volt'* ('God Wills It') and the very first person to volunteer to go was the Bishop of Le Puy and after him many others present too volunteered. In fact, the speech was probably less successful. No great lord attended the Council of Clermont and since the audience was almost entirely composed of priests, townsfolk and peasants the military capabilities of the crowd would be of limited use in an armed expedition to the East.

Planning and preliminaries

Urban II persevered with his crusade plan and subsequent declarations furthered shaped the form that the crusade would take place;

- Those that went on the expedition would have their possessions protected by the Church whilst they were away.

- Those that go would be identified by wearing a red cross.

- All who go should seek spiritual advice from their priest.

- Those that declared they would join the crusade but then failed to set out, or turned back before the crusade was complete would be excommunicated.

- Clerics could only go with permission of their superior in the Church.

- The Crusaders should be ready to leave by the 15th August 1096 and journey to Constantinople.

Early in December, only a few days after the speech at Clermont, Count Raymond of Toulouse declared that he wished to join the crusade. Raymond lived far away from Clermont and therefore must have had prior knowledge of what the Pope was about to announce. This indicates that Urban's plan to launch the campaign was both premeditated and that the groundwork was laid well in advance of Clermont. Likewise, the Bishop of Le Puy had been visited by Urban before Clermont (indeed they had travelled to Clermont together) and had knowledge of Jerusalem, having already visited the city in 1086 on pilgrimage. No doubt, Urban would have interviewed the Bishop of Le Puy and others like him, about Jerusalem and the potential difficulties faced in travelling there.

Once Pope Urban II had returned to Italy he had succeeded in attracting mass support for his crusade, the armies were in the process of being gathered and could confidentially expect these armies to start their marches to Constantinople on or after the feast of the assumption, 15th August 1096. Despite his instructions, the Pope heard rumour that many were so eager to take the cross; that they would not delay their march indeed; some thousands of pilgrims had already set out.

Alexius' Preparations 1096-1097

The Byzantine Emperor Alexius received news of the success of Pope Urban II's tour and began to make preparations for their reception. Despite the difficulties faced by the Empire, it was still comparatively speaking much better organised than the Western European kingdoms.

Alexius ordered stockpiles of food and other necessary equipment to be gathered at strategic points along the predicted routes, welcoming parties were likewise dispatched to border towns were the Crusaders were anticipated to enter the Empire and in order to ensure the good behaviour and rapid movement of the Crusading armies across his Empire, the Emperor ordered that strong detachments of the Imperial army be ready to escort the crusaders and be prepared to enforce punishment and discipline upon the Crusaders should they require it.

However, these preparations were not entirely successful. Alexius expected the Crusaders to reach him in the months following August 1096. However, the enthusiastic group commanded by Peter the Hermit as well as other less well documented groups set off earlier and so arrived earlier than expected. Also problematic was the unexpected arrival of large numbers of Crusaders arriving via the Hungarian border. Alexius had been getting most of his news from the Pope who sent messages from Italy, therefore many of the supply depots and Imperial garrisons were in the wrong locations.

Alexius expected most of the Crusaders to arrive from Italy and use the old and established Roman road called the Via Egnatia, which led from Durazzo on the coast opposite Italy and led due East to Constantinople. However, many pilgrims and crusaders preferred the cheaper, but longer land route through Hungary and down through the northern (and among the poorest) provinces of the Byzantine Empire.

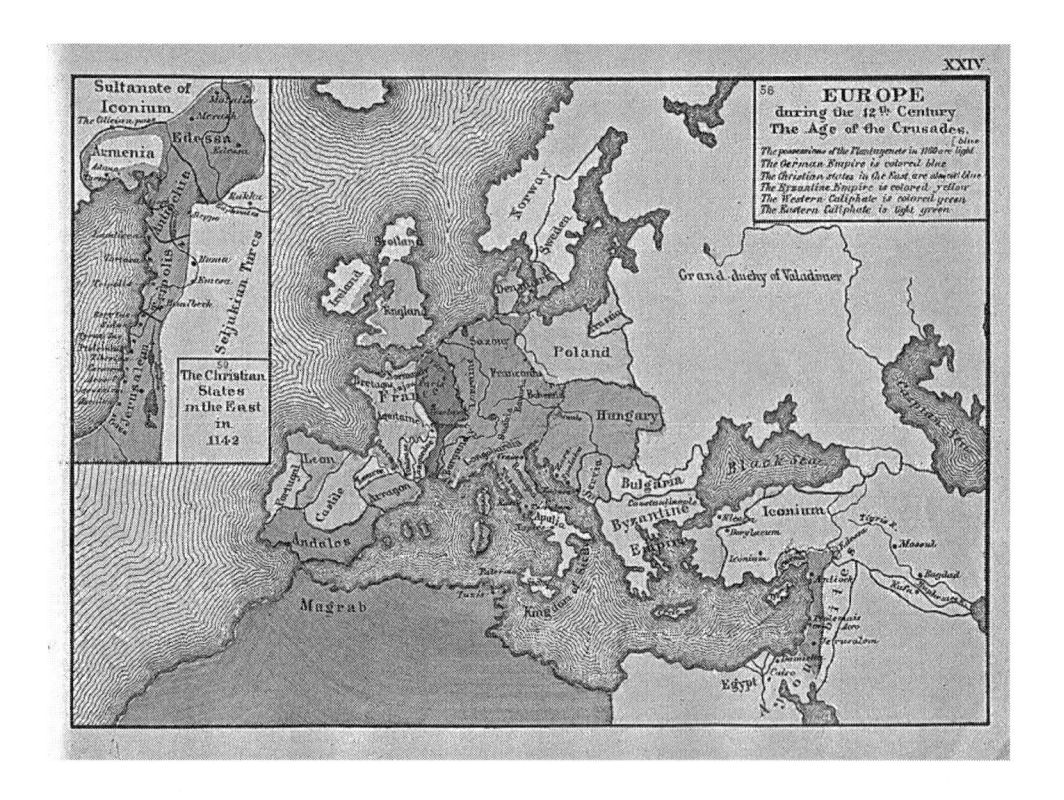

THE CRUSADES 1095-1204

2.2 – Launching the First Crusade

In this topic we will;

- *Understand the extent of the planning and preparations made by Crusaders*
- *Explore the differences between the 'Popular' and "Princes'" Crusades*
- *Understand who were the leaders of the First Crusade*
- *Consider why the Popular Crusades met with disaster*

The Leader of the First Crusade?

According to the sources that record events at Clermont in November 1095, the first person to pledge themselves to go on Crusade was a Churchman.

Bishop Adhemar de Monteil was Bishop of Le Puy. Bishop Adhemar was a Frenchman, middle aged and a member of the nobility. He was related to the Count of Valentinois and several members of his family accompanied him on the Crusade. It is probable that Pope Urban II was not surprised by Adhemar's decision to go on the Crusade. He had accompanied Urban on his tour of France and almost certainly discussed the project with the Pope. If Urban desired a Churchly leader for the Crusade, then Adhemar was a wise choice.

A member of the nobility, Adhemar was used to dealing with powerful lords. He was middle aged, so not too old for the rigours of the journey and not too young so that he was inexperienced in negotiations. Adhemar had another important qualification; he had been to Jerusalem before. Adhemar had been on pilgrimage to Jerusalem a few years previously, having travelled there in 1086. No doubt Pope Urban II had interrogated Adhemar extensively on the perils and tribulations of the pilgrim routes to the Holy land.

Successful negotiations would be essential for the enterprise to achieve its goals. Adhemar would need to be able to bring together the noble leaders of the crusade, who might be headstrong and quarrelsome. He would be able to deal with peasants and religious fanatics such as Peter the Hermit. As the official legate of the Pope, Adhemar would also need to be able to converse not only with the Byzantine emperor in order to ensure that the passage of the Crusade across the empire would be viable, but also seek to improve relations with the leaders of Eastern Christian faiths, including the patriarchs of the Eastern Church (Constantinople, Antioch and Jerusalem). Adhemar then had a large task and it is a measure of his success that the Crusade kept its unity of purpose until his death in August 1098 at Antioch.

Peter the Hermit and the 'Peoples' Crusade'

A number of evangelists had preached the Crusade in the wake of Clermont. One such individual was Peter the Hermit. Peter was a monk from Amiens in France. Peter was a short man with a long face that some thought that had a more than passing resemblance to the donkey that he rode. Dressed in filthy rags and walking barefoot, Peter's diet was limited to fish and wine.

It is possible that Peter had been recruiting for a pilgrimage of his own even before Pope Urban II had preached at Clermont; one source, Albert of Aix, credits Peter the Hermit as being the initial drive behind the Crusade. It is known that Peter had attempted to journey to Jerusalem a few years earlier, but had been turned back by the hostility of Turks that he had encountered.

A Popular Movement

Peter the Hermit toured parts of Northern and Eastern France as well as Western parts of Germany. His preaching tours do not seem to have overlapped with the Pope. People listened with such enthusiasm to Peter that by the time he reached the city of Cologne in Germany it is estimated that he had gathered at least 15,000 followers. These people were predominantly non-combatants with a scattering of knights and minor nobles. No great lords joined Peter and preferred to wait for the armies gathering under established military leaders.

By June and July 1096 many pilgrims began to journey towards the East.

> **Task: Peter versus Adhemar**
>
> Peter or Adhemar?
>
> Who do you think was better qualified to lead the Crusaders in their journey to Jerusalem?
>
> Who had the best qualifications, but who had attracted the most recruits to the Crusade?
>
> Try now to put yourself in the place of a Crusader – if you were a knight, which might you prefer as leader? What about if you were a peasant who had taken the cross? What if you are a landless noble that went on Crusade in order to find land and wealth in the East, who might you prefer to be in charge then? Who might you find more appealing if you were a German who was loyal to the German Emperor?
>
> These questions are important to consider as we continue in our exploration of the Crusades, although the majority of Crusaders were genuinely pious, others had different and at times conflicting motives, desires and obligations that might place them at odds with others in the Crusading movement.

The Expedition of Peter the Hermit

Peter the Hermit arrived at the German city of Cologne around the 12th April 1096. A group of his followers, perhaps some 2-3,000 men led by a knight called Waltar of Sans Avoir decided to leave soon after. Waltar's group reached the Hungarian frontier around the 8th May and despite some pillaging attacks on both Hungarians and Byzantines reached Constantinople around mid-July 1096.

Peter the Hermit followed more slowly, leaving Cologne on the 20th April and reaching the border with Hungary towards the end of May. Despite crossing Hungary without serious incident, the group began to lose their discipline and sacked towns on the border of Hungary and the Byzantine Empire; Semlin and Belgrade. The Semlin attack was severe with thousands of Hungarians reported killed and wounded. This event was to cause the Hungarian King, Coloman, to act with some hostility towards other subsequent Crusaders crossing his lands.

Peter's army continued with its poor discipline in the provinces of the Byzantine Empire. The army repeatedly raped and pillaged its way across the northern territories of the Empire. This might have been due to lack of supplies offered by the Byzantines (who had not expected the Crusaders to arrive so soon, from such an unexpected direction), however we can be sure that Peter had little real practical control over his followers when his own resources to help supply them ran short. Also, Peter's expedition was a hodge-potch affair of non-combatants, ill-equipped peasants and minor lords and knights. There was no clear military leader in his expedition.

Matters came to a head in early July, when the Byzantine Army and Peter's force came to blows over their lack of control. Peter's forces also soon demonstrated their lack of organisation and skill in battle. It is reported that the Imperial army killed or scattered as much of a quarter of Peter's expedition in the short battle that followed. Thereafter the chastened force marched (still on occasion causing problems for the local inhabitants) on, reaching Constantinople by the 1st August 1096. Their poor behaviour continued with thefts and other crimes resulting in the Byzantine Emperor rapidly arranging the transportation of Peter's force across the Bosporus around the 6th of August.

Indiscipline and Disaster

Peter the Hermit's expedition was in Asia Minor but its stay there would be short-lived and tragic. Whilst Peter spent increasing amounts of time at Constantinople organising supplies, the bulk of the army was based at Civetot; a military base prepared by Alexius to house mercenary forces. Almost at once, the indiscipline that had cost the expedition so heavily previously broke out again. Peter's force had been a collection of French and Germans. The army now divided along these lines and began to raid the area around Civetot and towards the Turkish held city of Nicaea. Most victims of these attacks were Greek and Christian subjects of the Emperor.

A French force raided close to Nicaea and acquired much plunder. Jealous, the Germans raided the lands beyond Nicaea and captured a small castle at a place called Xerigordon. By the end of September the Seljuk Turks had sent reinforcements to Nicaea and began to strike back. Xerigordon was recaptured early in October, the survivors being given a choice, slavery and conversion to Islam; or death.

The Turks approached the main body at Civetot. On the 21st of October 1096 Peter's force was ambushed and mostly annihilated. Some 3000 survivors managed to defend themselves at a small castle close by until rescued by Byzantine forces sent by sea from Constantinople. The survivors were taken aboard and housed at Constantinople along with Peter the Hermit until the arrival of the other Crusading armies.

Gottschalk

Little is known about this German preacher except that he was a follower of Peter the Hermit who remained behind in Germany to continue recruiting. It is thought that his followers numbered some thousands of followers when they began their march towards the East a few weeks. At Ratisbon, Gottschalk's followers massacred Jews and raided their property, but their discipline on the march ruined them. They were admitted access across Hungary, but having committed numerous acts of lawlessness, they were attacked and destroyed by the Hungarian army. Of Gottschalk we have no further knowledge.

Emich

Count Emich of Leisingen raised a crusading force and used this force primarily against the Jews of Germany. On the 3rd May 1096 Emich's forces killed dozens of Jews at the town of Speir, but this was just the beginning. Perhaps 500 Jews were killed at the town of Worms on the 20th May and more still at Mainz during a two day massacre, followed by another on the 1st June at Cologne. These Pogroms (Persecutions of the Jewish communities) included theft, rape and murder of Jews as well as forcible conversions and arson of Jewish property and synagogues. Not content with his work in Germany, Emich attempted to repeat his actions in Hungary, however at the town of Wiesselburg, the local townsfolk refused admittance to Emich and his men. Laying siege to the town Emich's crusade was destroyed by the Hungarian army when it arrived and the survivors, including Emich went home; their crusade was over.

THE CRUSADES 1095-1204

Volkmar

Another preacher about whom we know very little was a priest who raised an expedition of some thousands. Volkmar took his army to Prague and massacred the Jews resident in the area on the 30th June 1096. This action may have influenced the Hungarian decision to destroy Volkmar and his force once it entered Hungary. Probably, Volkmar's expedition, about which little is known had a distinct lack of discipline and had committed acts of violence in Hungary resulting in the Hungarian response.

Task: The Popular Crusades of 1096

Consider again the crusade expeditions of Peter the Hermit, Emich, Volkmar and Gottschalk.

What do you think were the main reasons for the failure of these expeditions?

You should consider the following factors;

- Lack of leadership
- Lack of organisation
- Lack of discipline
- Lack of direction by Pope Urban II
- The opposition of the Hungarians

Write a response of no more than 500 words

The "Princes'" Crusade

The term above is slightly misleading and inaccurate but serves the purpose of distinguishing between the popular crusading movements led by people such as Peter the Hermit with those led by the great nobles of Western Europe.

Unlike in the Second and Third Crusades, no king or secular ruler of a kingdom or Empire took part in the First Crusade. Instead just over half a dozen Great Lords organised and led their own armed expeditions on the First Crusade.

The following lords commanded the several contingents;

- Hugh, Count of Vermandois
- Godfrey of Bouillon, Duke of Lower Lorraine
- Bohemund, Prince of Taranto
- Raymond of St.Gilles, Count of Toulouse
- Robert, Duke of Normandy
- Stephen, Count of Blois
- Robert, Count of Flanders

The routes taken by participants in the First Crusade from West to East 1095-1100

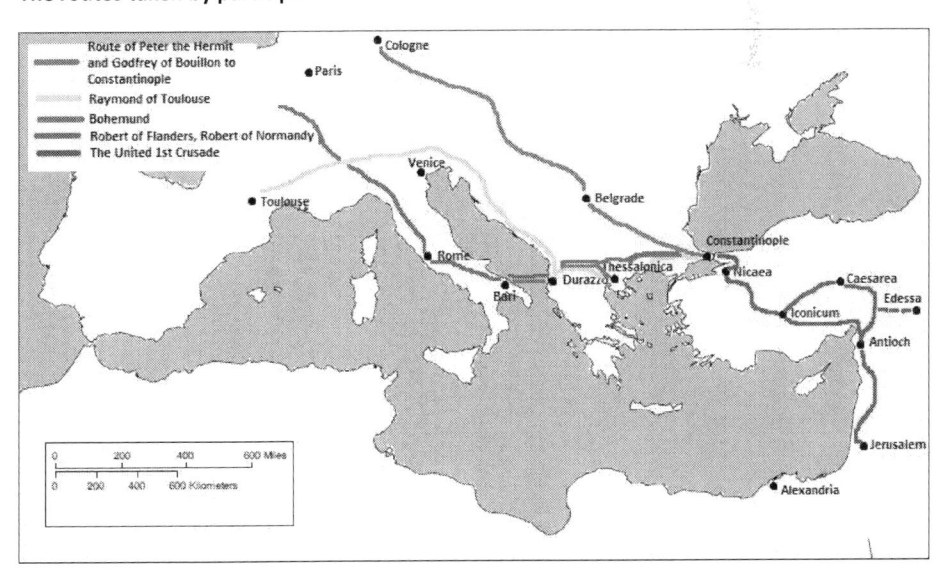

The Princes journeys to Constantinople

Hugh, Count of Vermandois

Hugh of Vermandois was the first Great lord to set out on the First Crusade. Aged about 40 years of age, Hugh was a well-connected noble who lacked the wealth and lands that his position may otherwise have been expected. Hugh was the brother of King Philip I of France and had acquired his lands, the County of Vermandois through his marriage. As we have seen, King Philip had been excommunicated by Pope Urban in 1095 due to adultery and perhaps one factor in Hugh joining the Crusade was due to pressure exerted by King Philip in order to have his excommunication lifted.

Hugh of Vermandois began his march to Constantinople at the end of August 1096 and travelled through Italy, visiting Rome and set sail across the Adriatic Sea from the southern Italian port of Bari in October 1096. Unfortunately a storm wrecked Hugh's fleet and caused the Count himself to be washed ashore. Local Byzantine authorities re-equipped Hugh and his small army and escorted him with no incident to Constantinople by early December 1096. Despite being a guest of the Emperor, it was clear to contemporary sources that Hugh was closely watched and kept under a form of house arrest. This house arrest may have encouraged Hugh of Vermandois to accept an oath of loyalty and allegiance to Alexius.

Godfrey of Bouillon, Duke of Lower Lorraine

Like Hugh of Vermandois, Godfrey of Bouillon set out for Constantinople by the end of August 1096. Godfrey was of a similar age to Hugh, around thirty six years of age and unlike Hugh, his lands had not been visited by the Papal tour. Godfrey was the Duke of Lower Lorraine and also Count of Antwerp and lord of Bouillon.

Godfrey, accompanied by his brothers Eustace (Count of Boulogne) and Baldwin (the future king of Jerusalem) had raised a large army partly funded by blackmailing the local Jewish community as well as selling some of his lands.

Godfrey took a different road to Constantinople than that of Hugh. Godfrey's army reached the Hungarian frontier in early October 1096 and was permitted to cross Hungary so long as he left his brother Baldwin as a hostage. Unlike the earlier attempts by the popular crusade expeditions, Godfrey's army crossed Hungary in peace and arrived at the border with the Byzantine Empire in late November.

Godfrey's army began to march across the northern provinces of the empire at a time when the locals were short of food and already embittered by the lawless passing of peter the Hermit's men, as a result food and supplies were in short supply and on the 12th of December, Godfrey's army attacked and seized the town of Selymbria, within a hundred miles of the Empire's capital city of Constantinople. It was not until the 23rd of December that Godfrey's army reached Constantinople and here relations between Godfrey and Alexius reached a low.

Godfrey refused to meet with the Emperor at first, perhaps he considered Hugh's house arrest as an insult to the dignity of the Crusaders. Alexius attempted to bend Godfrey to his will be reducing the food supplies that was reaching his army. In reprisal Godfrey's men began to pillage and loot the lands outside the city walls, the supplies were restored on condition that Godfrey moved his army away from the city, but Godfrey still refused to meet with Alexius and swear the oath of allegiance. By the end of March 1097 Alexius once again began to reduce the supplies being sent to Godfrey's army which again led to attacks (often orchestrated by Baldwin) on local civilians and imperial soldiers.

In early April, Godfrey led his army back towards Constantinople and after some provocation on the side of the Crusaders, Alexius decided to attack Godfrey's army. The Crusaders were rapidly defeated by the Imperial army in a short skirmish and this use of force finally made Godfrey swear the oath of allegiance to Alexius on the 5th April 1097. Thereafter the army of Lower Lorraine was transported across the Bosporus by the Imperial navy.

Bohemund, Prince of Taranto

Bohemund took the cross in the summer of 1096 and departed from the southern Italian port of Bari in October 1096, shortly after Hugh of Vermandois. Bohemund was tall, attractive and aged around forty years of age when he left for the First Crusade.

His small but well equipped army of Normans and Italians landed in the Byzantine Empire without incident and his march along the route of the Via Egnatia (with some detours) was peaceful with the exception of an attack for food and livestock on a village of Christian heretics living in the Pindus mountains, and even then he returned the livestock when he received supplies from the Byzantine authorities.

Bohemund made clear that he would seek the favour of Alexius at all opportunities and was more aware than the other crusade leaders of the politics of the empire, Bohemund also spoke some Greek so this may have helped him in his diplomatic endeavours. He arrived in Constantinople on the 9th April 1097 and swore the oath of allegiance to Alexius the next day. Bohemund was already known to Alexius as a former opponent and was suspicious of his efforts to be hailed by the Emperor as military leader of the Crusade forces in the Empire.

Raymond of St. Gilles, Count of Toulouse

Perhaps the largest army to set out on the First Crusade was led by Raymond of St. Gilles, the Count of Toulouse. At the time of his departure, Raymond was about sixty years old. Raymond was well connected, he himself came from a well-established noble house and his wife was a Spanish princess. His wife and legitimate son accompanied him on Crusade, his illegitimate son Bertrand remained in control of Toulouse on behalf of his father. It appeared that Raymond was planning to remain in the East. Bishop Adhemar of Le Puy also joined Raymond's expedition.

Raymond's large army left Toulouse in October 1096. His expedition did not march through Italy, perhaps the size of the force and the cost involved made it more practical to march thought he Balkans. Unlike other crusaders, Raymond did not march through Hungary but instead kept to the western coast; a mountainous and lawless region which they travelled in winter.

After a hard journey that seems to have involved some fighting with local Dalmatian tribes intent on raiding the army, Raymond reached the Byzantine Empire in February 1097. Perhaps due to its experience of the march through Dalmatia, Raymond's army was ill-disciplined and pillaged its way across the Empire. Imperial soldiers escorting the army attacked raiders and mistook Adhemar Le Puy as one such raider. He was wounded in a skirmish and forced to stay at the city of Thessalonica whilst he healed from his wounds.

As the army approached Constantinople, Raymond's army captured and sacked the Byzantine town of Roussa. Eager to make contact with the Emperor, Raymond left the army and went ahead to Constantinople. In his absence the army continued to raid until it was defeated in battle by the Imperial escort, thereafter the army made its way to Constantinople, arriving in April 1097.

Despite pressure from the other crusaders, Raymond refused to swear the oath of allegiance to Alexius. Perhaps this refusal was in part because Raymond saw himself as the secular leader of the crusade (a position he never really attained). Instead however, Raymond did agree to swear a modified oath that was not an oath of allegiance, but instead an oath to 'respect the life and honour of the Emperor'. Alexius seems to have been satisfied with this oath and thereafter relations between Alexius and Raymond appear to have been strong.

The two Roberts and Stephen

The two Roberts and Stephen of Blois all left Northern France on Crusade together in September of 1096. Combined their force must have been as great as any of the other expeditions, perhaps larger. Together they marched into Italy and met the Pope at Lucca in November 1096. Despite meeting the pope, they did not help him in his endeavours to return to Rome.

Whilst Robert of Normandy and Stephen of Blois wintered in Italy, Robert of Flanders crossed the Adriatic Sea in December and travelled along the Via Egnatia without incident, arriving at Constantinople in Early April 1097. Robert of Normandy and Stephen of Blois delayed, excessively long and some of his followers deserted or joined other expeditions. Their armies were the last of the Princes to reach Constantinople in early May and were transported across to Asia Minor in order to join the other armies now beginning to operate against the city of Nicaea. None of these leaders objected to swearing oaths of allegiance to Alexius.

How many people went on Crusade?

We have little information in the sources about how large the various contingents of the Princes expeditions were. The sources variously give numbers from the exaggerated (high tens of thousands) to the wildly fantastical (hundreds of thousands). Attempts have been made to arrive at estimated numbers of the various forces commanded by any given leader on the First Crusade. The numbers stated in this material are estimations based on those estimates provided by other historians. In his *'History of the Crusades'* Stephen Runciman (see Book I, Appendix 2) attempted to calculate the approximate numbers of cavalry (knights) and infantry soldiers.

According to Runciman, the approximate size of the armies of the lords was as follows;

- Hugh, Count of Vermandois

100-150 knights, 1000-2000 infantry

- Godfrey of Bouillon, Duke of Lower Lorraine

1000 knights, 7000 infantry

- Bohemund, Prince of Taranto

500 knights, 3000-4000 infantry

- Raymond of St. Gilles, Count of Toulouse

1000 knights, 10000 infantry

- Robert, Duke of Normandy

800 knights, 3000-5000 infantry

- Stephen, Count of Blois

200 knights, 1000-2000 infantry

- Robert, Count of Flanders

600 knights, 3000-5000 infantry

It is these numbers that we shall use here on in. As an approximate total, Runciman estimates that some 4,500 knights and 30,000 infantry with at least an equal amount of non-combatants, another 30,000, of which perhaps some 20,000 could fight or participate in military situations in certain situations.

2.4: The motives of the Crusaders in the First Crusade

In this topic we will;

- *Consider the various motives that might have encouraged people to join the First Crusade*
- *Understand why the Jews were targets or persecution by some in the First Crusade*
- *Explore the possible motives of the Princes*

Religious motives of the peasantry and poor to join the crusades

In April 1095 much of Northern Europe witnessed a meteorite shower that was visible in the skies. This phenomenon was interpreted by written sources as a future prediction that masses of people would shortly be on the move.

Urban's speech at Clermont and later pronouncements declared that sins committed would be forgiven by the act of pilgrimage.

Economic motives of the peasantry and poor to join the crusades

Towards the end of the 11th century, the peasantry could have had many reasons for joining the First Crusade that could not be considered to be religious or spiritual. The years preceding 1095-1096 had seen famine and crop failures across large parts of Western Europe. Food shortages led to malnutrition and encouraged disease. Crop failures would also have been compounded by nobles exerting pressure on the peasantry to meet their obligations of tax or face being ousted from their lands. Pope Urban's speech at Clermont hinted at economic opportunities in the Holy lands, peasants with little in the West could seek opportunity for economic betterment in the East.

The Crusades against the Jews May-July 1096

Peter the Hermit was not the only one who preached the First Crusade to the wider populace and their victims were not always to be Muslims. Other preachers in Germany found targets for persecution nearer to hand in the form of the Jewish community.

Jews had been present in Western Europe for centuries, establishing communities in mercantile centres; Jewish communities performed the important but somewhat unpopular functions of merchants and bankers.

Some of the Great lords who went on Crusade, notably Godfrey of Bouillon, exerted pressure on the Jewish communities in their areas in order to raise funds. Godfrey raised much money through a combination of threats and blackmail from Jewish communities in order to fund his expedition, but others, exceeded this exploitation.

Why were the Jews targets for persecution?

The Jewish communities of Western Europe were targets for persecution in the First Crusade because;

- They were a minority that were perceived to have kept themselves separate from the bulk of the population.

- The Jews in Palestine were held responsible for the execution of Jesus Christ in AD33.

- The Jews were thought to be wealthy in cash and served as money lenders to the nobility and those aspiring to be seen as noble. As a result many were in debt to the Jews.

- As a minority, the Jews were relatively few in number.

Jews had no civic rights explicit in law. They relied on the protection of local lords and the Church.

The motives of the Princes

The Princes all made the decision to go on Crusade. Genuine piety must have been at least a factor in all of their reasons to go, however each prince probably had additional reasons to go on the journey to Jerusalem.

Hugh, Count of Vermandois

Hugh of Vermandois was the first Great lord to set out on the First Crusade. Aged about 40 years of age, Hugh was a well-connected noble who lacked the wealth and lands that his position may otherwise have been expected. Hugh was the brother of King Philip I of France and had acquired his lands, the County of Vermandois through his marriage. As we have seen, King Philip had been excommunicated by Pope Urban in 1095 due to adultery and perhaps one factor in Hugh joining the Crusade was due to pressure exerted by King Philip in order to have his excommunication lifted.

Godfrey of Bouillon

Godfrey claimed descent through his mother to the idealised Christian rule of Western Europe, Charlemagne. Godfrey then was wealthy, had extensive lands and was well connected. However, he was Duke of Lorraine only through his allegiance to King Henry IV of Germany and his future position of Duke was in question due to his poor administration of these lands which he held on behalf of the king. It is not known whether Godfrey expected to return from the Crusade, certainly his elder brother, Eustace held much land in Northern France as well as in England returned from the Crusade as soon as he was able. His other brother however, Baldwin was landless in the West and set out with his whole family. He clearly never intended to return as his participation in the First Crusades demonstrated.

Bohemund of Taranto

Despite his grand sounding title of 'Prince of Taranto', Bohemund was the poor relation to his half-brother Roger Borsa of Naples and Southern Italy and Uncle Roger, who was king of Sicily. Bohemund had a reputation as a skilled warrior and general (he had led part of his father's attack on the Byzantine Empire in the 1080s), but he lacked wealth, land and his position was threatened by his periodic revolts against Roger Borsa. When he heard of the crusade being launched, Bohemund was not slow to see the potential opportunities that it offered him and when he was able, he took the opportunity to seize the city of Antioch for himself.

Raymond of St. Gilles, Count of Toulouse

Raymond was a very powerful lord who ruled much of what is today southern France. Raymond held more land than the King of France and it is therefore worth considering why such a powerful, wealthy and well-connected man might want to go on Crusade.

Raymond had a track record of fighting against Muslims. He had fought in Spain on several occasions against Muslim opposition and therefore Raymond may well have believed in the ethos of Holy War well before he went on Crusade. Genuine piety may also have been a key factor in Raymond's motivation to join the Crusade. He was one of the first Great lords to declare his intent and he also appeared to spend the remainder of his life in the Holy land.

Robert, Count of Flanders

Robert of Flanders family had connections with both the Byzantine Empire and pilgrimage. Robert's father had been on pilgrimage to Jerusalem and had also served the Empire as a soldier in 1086. Robert's father knew the Emperor Alexius personally and the pair had been friends until the death pf Robert's father a few years previously. It may therefore be that emulation of his father was a key motive for Robert of Flanders to take the cross.

Robert, Duke of Normandy

Robert of Normandy was the eldest son of William the Conqueror and aged about forty years of age. His brother, William Rufus was king of England and like many rich and famous brothers, they did not get along. Robert and William had been involved in a series of periodic wars until Pope Urban II encouraged them to reconcile. In part, William Rufus financed Robert's crusade with 10,000 silver marks and men from England came to join his army. Partly this reconciliation as well as piety might have been the motive for Robert to go on Crusade. Perhaps he sought to emulate his father, but given his lack of assertiveness during the Crusade, perhaps this was not a motive.

Stephen, Count of Blois

Stephen of Blois did not really have a large army, but we include him here because of his later actions. Stephen had a small County, but it was wealthy and he was able to raise a small force of knights. Stephen was married to Adela, daughter of William the Conqueror and so was brother in law to Robert of Normandy. Given that Adela made Stephen of Blois go back on Crusade after his disgrace at Antioch, it may be that Adela made him go on Crusade in the first place.

Task: Motives of the Princes

Why might each Prince go on Crusade?

Here is a list of possible motives to go on Crusade;

- To fulfil religious obligations
- To increase their own reputation
- To acquire land
- To acquire wealth
- To escape from troubles problems at home
- Consider each Crusade leader in turn and decide how important each factor was to them?

2.5 The First Crusade 1095-1100: From Nicaea to Jerusalem 1097-1100

In this topic we will;

- *Consider the progress of the First Crusade*
- *Understand the problems and challenges faced by the Crusade and how these were overcome.*
- *Explore the motivations and roles of the leaders of the First Crusade.*
- *Consider why the First Crusade succeeded in capturing Jerusalem*

Introduction

By May 1097 all the major contingents of the Crusade had departed from Constantinople and were beginning to gather outside the Turkish held city of Nicaea which they besieged. In addition to the crusaders there were a substantial number of soldiers from the Byzantine army who also organised food and equipment for the whole force. Nicaea surrendered in June 1097; a considerable achievement in itself which was later overshadowed by the other major events of the First Crusade culminating in the capture of Jerusalem in June 1099, some two years later.

The First Crusade in summary

- *June 1097 – Nicaea captured.*
- *July 1097 – Crusader victory of Seljuk Turks at the battle of Dorylaeum.*
- *October 1097-June 1098 – Siege and capture of the city of Antioch.*
- *June 1098 – Crusader victory of Kerbogha of Mosul at Antioch.*
- *June-July 1099 – Siege and capture of Jerusalem.*
- *August 1099 – Crusader victory over an Egyptian army at Ascalon.*

Nicaea

Accompanied by the Byzantine Army the Crusaders besieged the city of Nicaea. Nicaea was a large important city and was occupied by the Seljuk Turks. The Turkish Sultan, Kilij Arslan I was absent, away to the east on a military campaign against the Danishmend Turks. Kilij Arslan sent reinforcements, but they were too few and arrived too late to save the city.

The Crusaders reached Nicaea on the 6th May in waves until almost the whole crusader army was there by the end of May. The Byzantines sent engineers and food supplies and the Crusaders worked well together. A Council of the Crusade leaders organised and commanded the siege.

On the 21st May, Kilij Arslan arrived with his army and attacked, giving and receiving many casualties, but failed to break the siege. After the battle on the 21st Kilij Arslan withdrew and the victorious Crusaders demoralised those defending the city by catapulting the severed heads of the dead Turks over the city walls.

The city surrendered on the 19th June 1097, not to the Crusaders, but to the Byzantine Emperor Alexius. The Crusaders were not permitted to loot the city, but were rewarded; a good meal for the regular Crusaders, a large gift of gold for the leaders. The First Crusade had gained a major success, and news of this success was filtered to Europe, were further crusading forces were prepared.

Dorylaeum

After the capture of Nicaea, the crusaders planned the next stage of their journey. The route across central Asia Minor along the old Roman road network led through Dorylaeum, a small village which became known for the major battle that was fought there.

The crusade expedition left Nicaea on the 26th June 1097, accompanied by a small Byzantine detachment led by an experienced general named Taticius. The size of the expedition meant that travelling as one group appeared to be a strain on food supplies and road space, so the Crusaders marched in two roughly equal sized groups;

- Bohemund, Robert of Normandy, Robert of Flanders, Stephen of Blois and the Byzantines.

- Godfrey of Bouillon, Raymond of Toulouse and Hugh of Vermandois

On the 1st July 1097, Kilij Arlsan I attacked the group under Bohemund and the two Roberts near the village of Dorylaeum. Thanks to good scouting work, the Crusaders were not taken by surprise and deployed their force defensively whilst they waited the arrival of the other crusaders under Raymond and Godfrey. The Turkish soldiers used mounted archers to harass the Crusaders and inflicted heavy casualties with their arrows, while staying out of close combat, however Kilij Arslan thought he was fighting the whole force of crusaders, he was therefore surprised when he was attacked by Raymond and Godfrey. The Turks were defeated, in part by a detachment of crusaders led by Bishop Adhemar of Le Puy. The Seljuk camp was captured and much plunder was taken, but Crusader casualties were heavy. Kilij Arslan had also suffered heavy losses and decided that he would no longer oppose the Crusaders in their march across his territory.

Into Syria

The Crusade army continued its march as a united group on the 3rd of July across the barren regions of central Anatolia and many horses and livestock died before the Crusaders reached another Seljuk held city named Iconium (modern Konya) in mid-august. The crusaders found Iconium abandoned by the Seljuks and rested here for a time before continuing. The march continued and towards the end of August the Crusaders fought a small series of battles against the Danishmend Turks near the town of Heraclea near the Taurus and Anti-Taurus Mountains.

Crossing the Anti-Taurus Mountains in September and October caused much hardship for the Crusaders. Food was short and the poor weather encouraged disease and sickness. Losses from illness, starvation and desertion were heavy by the time the Crusade reached the border of Syria in mid-October 1097.

The rise of Baldwin and Tancred

Some Crusaders left the main force, not to desert the overall expedition, but opportunities were being identified that promised land and wealth for those with the desire to gain it. Bohemund's nephew Tancred left the main army on the 10th September 1097 and sought to occupy villages in the region known as Cilicia. Baldwin of Boulogne also left the army and travelled to the north of the main expedition and even went so far as to fight Tancred for control of some villages.

Tancred would return to the main crusade force and seek opportunities later on but Baldwin of Boulogne continued eastwards, returning only briefly to the Crusade force when he heard news that his wife and children were dying of disease. Baldwin would in time gain control of the large city of Edessa and establish the first Crusade state in the East.

The occupation of Edessa was important for the overall success for the Crusade. Edessa was strategically placed and blocked easy access of communication between the cities of Mosul, Aleppo and Antioch. By seizing Edessa from the local Christian Armenian leadership (which nominally held allegiance to the Byzantine Empire) Baldwin interposed a block between the Muslim leaders of Antioch and Mosul and prevented Kerbogha of Mosul from sending rapid help to Yaghisiyan who controlled Antioch.

Yaghisiyan of Antioch and Muslim disunity

The Crusader army approached the city of Antioch towards the end of October 1098. On the approach the Crusaders heard a rumour that the city was undefended. The rumour was false but Count Raymond dispatched 500 of his own knights to try and seize the city without the knowledge of the other leaders. Antioch was a great prize and a prize that would encourage division in the crusaders' ranks.

Antioch was one of the largest cities of the Roman Empire, although it had experienced its share of disaster and economic decline, Antioch was still a much larger city than London or Paris in size and population. Despite being ruled by a Turkish governor, Antioch was the seat of one of the five Patriarchs of the Christian faith, who remained in the city even after the capture of the city by the Turks in 1085 and the bulk of the population remained Christian.

The ruler of Antioch was Yaghisiyan, a Turk and *Atabeg* (military governor) of the Seljuk Sultan Malik Shah. Yaghisiyan however had been ruling as an independent lord who had played off the rival emirs in order to maintain his position as an independent ruler. This independent stance ensured that help would be slow in coming from the other Turkish ruled cities of Aleppo, Damascus and Mosul.

On hearing of the approach of the Crusaders, Yaghisiyan imprisoned John the Oxite, Patriarch of Antioch and exiled other leading Christians that were suspected of collusion and sent his soldiers out to harass the local Christian villages. Yaghisiyan also sought help from the rulers of Aleppo, Damascus and Mosul.

Duqaq, the emir of Damascus responded positively and began to organise an army, as did Kerbogha the *atabeg* of Mosul and the most powerful Turkish ruler in Northern Syria. But these efforts would take time. Ridwan, emir of Aleppo was in theory Yaghisiyan's superior, and the nearest source of help, but due to Yaghisiyan's acts of disloyalty (he had been conspiring with Duqaq of Damascus, Ridwan's brother and main rival), Ridwan hesitated to help at first.

The siege of Antioch (October 1097-June 1098)

The Crusader army reached Antioch on the 20th October, supported by many local Christians who ousted the Turkish soldiers in their villages and began to offer the Crusaders help in the form of information, supplies and probably some military assistance. The Crusaders were too few to besiege the entire city, which owing to the mountainous terrain was impractical anyway, so the Crusaders blockaded the gates of the city on the North, East and Western sides, but with the southern gates left open. Yaghisiyan likewise had too few men to defend all the walls of the city, which were over ten miles of circumference. Supplies could enter the city and the siege progressed very slowly.

At Antioch we can identity cracks in the unity of the Crusade leadership. Raymond of Toulouse wanted to attack the city straightaway; others recommended awaiting the arrival of the Byzantine field army under the Emperor himself. Bohemund on the other hand wanted to bribe his way into the city by making contact with soldiers who were willing to betray Yaghisiyan.

Reinforcements reached the Crusaders at Antioch, a fleet of Genoese ships arrived bringing several thousand men in mid-November 1098 and the nearby port of St.Symeon was captured which allowed easy communication to Cyprus and the West. Hearing that Duqaq of Damascus was approaching, Bohemund and Robert of Flanders led 20,000 men to meet the army of Damascus in battle at Albara on the 30th December 1098. Duqaq was defeated and forced to withdraw. Yaghisiyan attempted to break the siege in the absence of Bohemund and Robert of Flanders, but was unsuccessful.

In the winter months, the siege continued, despite much hardship for both sides. Many crusaders died of starvation and the horses of the army were decimated. Food was sent from Cyprus (organised largely by the efforts of Adhemar, Taticius and Patriarch Symeon of Jerusalem who was living in exile on the island). Local Christians also sold food to the crusaders, but at inflated prices which impoverished many Crusaders.

The Byzantine General Taticius travelled to Cyprus, to liaise with the Byzantine authorities there, but elements of the Crusade portrayed this as desertion, led by Bohemund these elements could argue that when Antioch was captured, it would not need to be returned to the Byzantine emperor. The Emperor was campaigning in Asia Minor, securing the gains made by the Crusaders. He was too involved here to easily join the Crusaders in Syria, though rumours reached them that he would join them in 1099. As winter progressed, desertion became a problem for the Crusaders. Many left to return home, and even Peter the Hermit attempted to flee in January 1099. He was forcibly returned by Tancred in disgrace.

In February 1099, the army of Ridwan of Aleppo marched to rescue Antioch. The Crusaders sent out all their available mounted knights to meet them. Only seven hundred in number, so great had been the loss amongst the horses, the Crusaders led Ridwan's army into a trap and defeated them. Yaghisiyan again attempted to break the siege, but was again unsuccessful.

On the 4th of March a large fleet arrived at St.Symeon. The fleet had come from England, Northern Europe, Italy and the Byzantine Empire and was led by the exiled English claimant to the throne Edgar Atheling. The Byzantine Empire had loaded siege engines onto the ships as well as reinforcements. These additions allowed the Crusaders to construct towers that provided greater protection against raids from the city. One tower called 'Malregard' was built earlier; another was called 'La Mahomerie'. During the siege, the Crusaders made contact with the Fatamid rulers of Egypt who were enemies of the Turks and made an unsuccessful offer of a ceasefire to Duqaq of Damascus.

In May 1099, two large armies were thought to be approaching; Alexius and the Byzantine army from the roads to the West, and Kerbogha of Mosul's forces. Kerbogha had been reinforced by soldiers from Baghdad but delayed his approach on Antioch by attacking Edessa for three weeks. This delay saved the Crusade. Baldwin of Boulogne provided a great service for the crusaders by holding onto Edessa, delaying Kerbogha and allowing the Crusaders to seize Antioch before Kerbogha arrived.

On the 2nd June 1099, fear of Kerbogha's approach encouraged Stephen of Blois to desert. As he fled he reached Alexius and his army and advised him that the Crusade was destroyed. This information encouraged Alexius to abandon his attempts to reach Antioch. Stephen of Blois however had misjudged his desertion. The same day Bohemund announced that his attempts to bribe his entry into the city were successful. A Muslim captain called Firouz helped the Crusaders onto the walls and to open the gates to the city. On the 3rd of June Antioch was captured by the Crusaders after a siege of eight months. Muslims within the city were massacred by Crusaders and local Christians. Though the Crusaders did not capture the Citadel, which remained in the hands of Yaghisiyan's son, they gained control of the rest of the city. Yaghisiyan himself did not survive the siege, attempting to flee, a local Christian killed and beheaded him.

Perils and miracles

Antioch had been captured, but the Crusade was still in danger. Although the Crusaders now had the protection of the city walls, they did not have control of Antioch's citadel and the food supplies in the city were exhausted. The Crusaders worked together, clearing the streets of bodies and restoring John the Oxite to his position as Patriarch.

Just four days after the capture of Antioch, on the 7th June1098, Kerbogha's army arrived outside the city and laid siege to the Crusaders in turn. He immediately replaced the former soldiers of Yaghisiyan in the citadel and tried to attack from this place on the 9th June. The Crusaders had expected this and built a wall to block off the citadel from the rest of the city. This attack almost succeeded but the Crusaders here, led by Hugh of Vermandois and the two Roberts managed to drive off the attack.

By the 10th of June, the whole city was blockaded and some Crusaders deserted, including Bohemund's own brother-in-law. The same day, a peasant pilgrim named Peter Bartholomew, who had nearly died in the fighting that day told Adhemar and Raymond of Toulouse that he had received visions from the Saints that provided him with the location of the Holy Lance; the Spear that had pierced the side of Jesus Christ whilst he was on the cross. This holy relic would be found buried in the floor of the cathedral of Antioch.

Adhemar rejected this story – he had already seen the Holy Lance, held as a relic at Constantinople. But Raymond was prepared to investigate. Another vision was revealed, a priest called Stephen impressed Adhemar that the Crusade was failing due to lack of resolution of the leadership. The Crusade leaders were all made to swear an oath that they would not desert the expedition. All did.

On the 15th June, with the siege continuing, Peter Bartholomew discovered a fragment of the Holy Lance in the floor of the Cathedral. Perhaps Peter had discovered this relic, perhaps he had planned the whole thing, but whatever the circumstance, the discovery was revealed in triumph to the rest of the Crusade, whose spirits rose as a result and Raymond of Toulouse and his Southern French all took particular pride in the Holy Lance.

The siege continued, Raymond fell ill and so Bohemund was appointed military leader of all crusade forces. Bohemund planned a full scale assault on the army of Kerbogha. Kerbogha had his own problems, his army was comprised of soldiers from across Syria and Iraq and some forces were already tired of the siege, and others did not want Kerbogha to have so much control and power. Desertions were to deprive Kerbogha of success. On the 27th June the Crusaders sent an emissary, Peter the Hermit, to Kerbogha it is not known what was said, but no deal was reached. Perhaps the emissary was sent to spy on Kerbogha's forces for the next day, the Crusaders attacked.

The Crusaders, led by Bohemund, marched out of the city and formed for battle in six divisions. Raymond, who was still ill, remained in the city and was tasked with its defence with a small force. The crusaders attacked and rapidly routed Kerbogha's forces, many of whom took the opportunity to withdraw without fighting. Kerbogha's army was shattered, he himself survived but his authority was ruined.

With victory secured, the Citadel surrendered to Bohemund and some of its soldiers even converted to Christianity and joined the Crusade army.

Delays in Northern Syria

The question of the possession of Antioch now arose. Who should control this large and important city? There were several candidates including the Emperor Alexius, Raymond of Toulouse and Bohemund of Taranto. Alexius in theory had the strongest legitimate case for possession of the city. It had long been a city of the Empire, much of the population were Greek Christians and the city had been governed by Alexius' brother before it was captured. Alexius too had ensured that the Crusaders were fed and supplied throughout their siege and allowed reinforcements to reach the Crusade.

However, Alexius was not close by. His main army was bogged down in central Anatolia and his representative with the Crusade Tacticius, had left the expedition for Cyprus. Alexius simply put, was too far away and too far removed from the action to be considered by the Crusaders. For the Crusaders, it was they who had captured the city so therefore it should be one of those that should govern the city. No local authority seems to have ever been considered. After the fall of Constantinople, it seems that Hugh of Vermandois wished to leave the Crusade. He was therefore chosen to go to the Emperor to explain the situation at Constantinople before headed home to France.

Raymond of Toulouse fancied himself as the secular leader of the First Crusade, his army was the largest and he was the most illustrious of the major lords, however he had been ill for much of the siege and other leaders had taken the lead in the siege of Antioch.

Bohemund had engineered the capture of the city by negotiating with the soldiers that would betray the city. He spoke Greek so could liaise easiest with the local inhabitants. He also had been at the forefront of the fighting throughout and it was his plan that had defeated Kerbogha. Bohemund backed up this reasons for his ownership with some more practical measures. He seized control of the city and the citadel, using his men to force out those of Raymonds. On the 14th of July he secured the assistance of the Genoese by granting them trading rights and property within the city walls.

The death of Adhemar

On the 1st August 1098, the whole expedition was disturbed by the death of Adhemar of Le Puy. Adhemar died probably of Typhoid fever in an epidemic that broke out in Antioch that summer. With his illness and death, much of the unity of the First Crusade was lost. Adhemar had managed to keep control of the lords and keep them directed towards their eventual goal. Adhemar had worked with the crusaders, local Christians such as the Patriarchs of Antioch and Jerusalem and the Byzantine Emperor and his efforts had ensured that supplies from Cyprus and the Byzantine Empire had kept flowing. Now with his death, this unity of effort was in danger.

Procrastinations

Whilst Typhus affected Antioch and Raymond and Bohemund squabbled over the city, several Crusaders began to seek out their own territory; control of towns and villages in the local area, or by travelling to Edessa to take up service with Baldwin.

Godfrey of Boullion joined Baldwin for a time and was granted the lordship of the towns of Turbessal and Ravendel in the County of Edessa. Robert of Normandy travelled to the port town of Lattakieh, but was forced out by the arrival of a Byzantine naval force when he attempted to fleece the local inhabitants of their wealth. Bohemund too left Antioch for a time to ensure the control of towns and cities to the North and West of Antioch in Cilicia.

The Crusade leaders gathered again in Antioch in September 1098 to plan, but accomplished little more than to appeal to Pope Urban II to send help and to inform him of the death of Adhemar. Meantime, the Crusade rank and file, the soldiers, humble knights and the non-combatants that still survived agitated for a march on Jerusalem, now only some 300 miles away. Threats were issued to destroy the walls of Antioch if the Crusade did not proceed. Still, nothing happened in that direction. The months of October, November and December 1098 all passed with the expedition remaining in Syria. Some towns were attacked and Raymond and Bohemund continued to squabble over Antioch.

Finally, a few days after Christmas 1098, Raymond of Toulouse announced that he would lead the expedition into Palestine. Admitting defeat in the contest of Antioch, Raymond now tried a new tactic, he would attempt to become undisputed leader of the Crusade. At a town called Rugia, Raymond offered bribes to the other lords of the Crusade in order to secure their leadership. The bribes were only partially successful. Robert of Normandy and Tancred, the nephew of Bohemund accepted Raymond's leadership. Bohemund was not approached and remained in Antioch. Godfrey and Robert of Flanders rejected the bribes and remained in Syria.

Raymond's march on southwards began on 13th January 1099. Portraying himself as a leader of a pilgrimage, Raymond left Syria barefoot and on foot at the head of a small army of less than ten thousand in total.

The march to Jerusalem

Events had transpired in Palestine whilst the Crusaders had besieged Antioch and remained in Northern Syria. Jerusalem had been captured by Egyptian forces in July 1098. The local Turkish rulers had been driven from the city, helped in part by the activities of the Crusaders in Northern Syria distracting those that may have otherwise have helped. Damascus for example, was the nearest major Turkish ruled city, but Duqaq's army had been engaged in attacking the crusaders at Antioch.

Raymond led his small group of crusaders into Palestine in January 1099. His progress at first was fairly rapid. Lacking the numbers to attack many places with any hope of success, local Arab emirs welcomed the opportunity that the Crusaders offered to become more independent of the Turks. The emirs of the towns of Homs, Shaizar and Tripoli paid off the crusaders with money and food supplies if they would pass through their lands in peace. Crusaders could even enter these towns in order to make purchases.

However, the town of Arqa was attacked by Raymond's men in mid-February 1099. The important port of Tortosa was also captured at the same time, which allowed for greater communication with Antioch, Cyprus and Europe. Arta remained uncaptured however, and Raymond delayed here in his attempts to capture the town. Godfrey and Robert of Flanders re-joined with Raymond and Robert of Normandy during this siege.

On the 13th May 1099 the siege of Arqa was abandoned and the Crusaders moved on southwards, through the territory of the emir of Tripoli (who supplied them) in peace and into Egyptian Fatamid territory. The Fatamids had no army in Palestine to oppose the Crusade and what forces were present were retained for the defence of Jerusalem. Meantime the Fatamids prepared to raise an army in Egypt. At the town of Tyre, some reinforcements reached the Crusaders under the command of Baldwin le Bourg (the future King Baldwin II of Jerusalem) who led some men from Antioch and Edessa.

On the 3rd of June 1099 the biblical town of Ramleh was occupied by Robert of Flanders and on the 6th June Bethlehem was occupied by Tancred and Baldwin Le Bourg. The next day, the Crusaders reached Jerusalem.

The siege of Jerusalem

Jerusalem was held by the Egyptian Fatamid General Iftikhar ad-Dawla. He had a small but professional army, his forces were well supplied and the defences of the city were in good repair. Iftikhar took further measures. Whilst permitting Jews to remain in the city he ejected all Christians from the city as untrustworthy and poisoned many sources of water in the area of Jerusalem. The Crusaders were thus attempting the siege of a large city with small numbers, uncertain supplies and in the heat of the summer. Iftikhar therefore could wait with some confidence for help to come from Egypt.

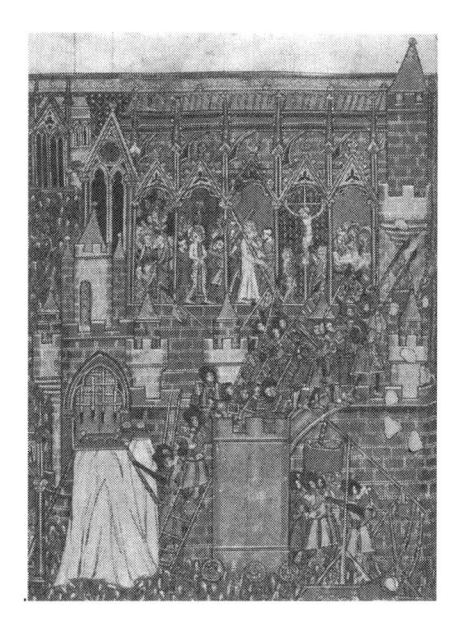

The Crusaders took up positions near the gates of the cities but could not afford to have a long siege like they had undertaken at Antioch. They lacked foods, numbers and water had to be transported from some 6 miles away. On the 13th June 1099 the Crusaders launched an attack which failed, but on the 17th June help for the Crusaders arrived by sea. A fleet of English and Genoese ships had captured the sea port of Jaffa and brought supplies and reinforcements for the siege of the city. Even this assistance did not at this late stage prevent some Crusaders from deserting. Perhaps they could argue that they had reached Jerusalem, perhaps the fear of an army from Egypt encouraged their decision. Time was spent in the construction of siege towers, weapons and ladders, and sermons were held on the Mount of Olives – where Jesus was crucified.

The Capture of Jerusalem

On the 8th July the Crusaders held a penitential procession around the city walls and proceeded to the Mount of Olives to hear sermons by the senior clergy remaining with the expedition.

The Crusaders, reduced now to a force of some 1200-1300 knights and some 12,000 infantry attacked again on the 13th of July 1099 in the middle of the night. The attacks continued relentlessly for over 24 hours. After severe fighting the city walls were stormed and the Crusaders, led by Godfrey's men entered the city.

What followed was a massacre of almost all men, women and children in the city of Jerusalem. In some particularly repugnant acts, the population of Jerusalem was slaughtered in their homes, in the streets and in the holy sights of the city. The temple mount was the scene of a massacre of Muslims, a synagogue was torched along with the Jews that had fled there. Only Iftikhar and a few of his men were saved from the slaughter by Raymond of Toulouse. Certainly, tens of thousands of people were killed in the capture of Jerusalem and for some months afterwards the streets of the Holy city were littered with the corpses of the victims of the Crusade.

Ascalon and the end of the First Crusade

The Crusade had achieved its goal. Like Antioch, the question now arose who would control the city of Jerusalem? There were four of the Crusade leaders remaining with the expedition; the two Roberts, Godfrey and Raymond. The two Roberts both ruled themselves out. They intended to go home now that they had fulfilled their Crusade vows. That left Raymond and Godfrey. It appears that Raymond was offered the crown, to be king of Jerusalem, but surprisingly, he refused. That left Godfrey. Godfrey too refused the kingship of the city of Jerusalem. However, Godfrey did accept the position of ruler, without the position of king. He became *'Advocatus Sancti Sepulchri'* or *'Dedicated defender of the Holy Sepulchre'*. This settled the Crusaders now had to fight the Fatamid army now approaching.

The Egyptian army was led by the vizier Al-Afdal and was large, but inexperienced. The Egyptian army gathered at Ascalon, a town on the coast. The Crusaders did not wait for the Egyptians, but marched out of Jerusalem on the 9th August 1099. On the 12th August 1099 the Crusaders launched a surprise attack and decisively defeated the Fatamid army. Ascalon was not captured, but Jerusalem was secured.

At the end of August, the two Roberts and Raymond all left Jerusalem, with most of the survivors of the First Crusade. Godfrey was left in charge of the city with precious few men, perhaps 300 knights and 2000 infantry. The two Roberts were leaving Palestine; Raymond would remain, but wanted to establish his own territory.

Stay or go? The leaders of the First Crusade

Peter the Hermit.

Returns to France in 1099 and established a monastery.

Hugh of Vermandois

Returns to France 1098. Joins the with failed Crusades of 1101 and dies of wounds at Tarsus in 1101.

Adhemar, Bishop of Le Puy

Dies at Antioch 1098 (probably of Typhoid fever).

Godfrey of Bouillon

Remains. First ruler of Jerusalem; Dies of illness in July 1100.

Baldwin of Boulogne

Remains. Ruler of Edessa 1097-1100 and King of Jerusalem 1100-1118.

Bohemund of Taranto

Prince of Antioch 1098-1100. Captured by Danishmend Turks. Released 1103 and returns to Italy 1105. Leads a failed invasion of the Byzantine Empire 1108. Dies in Italy 1111.

Tancred of Lecce

Remains. Prince of Galilee, Regent of Antioch then Prince (1105-1108). Dies in Antioch 1112.

Raymond of Toulouse

Remains. Attempts to capture Tripoli 1103-5; Dies in 1105 after injury.

Robert of Flanders

Returns home. Killed in battle 1111

Robert of Normandy

Returns home. Defeated and imprisoned by his brother Henry I in 1106 and spends rest of life as a prisoner, dying in 1134.

Stephen of Blois

Deserts Crusade June 1098 and returns home 1099. Joins failed Crusades of 1101, survives and reaches Jerusalem 1102. Dies in battle 1103.with an Egyptian army at Ascalon.

The arrival of Daimbert

Pope Urban II never heard of the capture of Jerusalem. He died in July 1099, after the capture of Jerusalem, but before news of its capture could reach him. He had sent a new legate to replace Adhemar; a bishop called Daimbert who sailed with a Pisan fleet. Daimbert's first act in the East was to lay siege to the Byzantine held port of Lattakieh, but he was deterred from this by the urgings of Raymond and the two Roberts who arrived on the scene. The two Roberts now left for home by sea, sailing in Byzantine ships via Constantinople.

Daimbert reached Jerusalem and was appointed Patriarch (Symeon, who had been exile at Cyprus having died). Jerusalem now had a Catholic European ruler and a Catholic European Patriarch which stood at odds with the bulk of the Christian population. Baldwin and Bohemund also arrived at Jerusalem in order to fulfil their crusade vows in December 1099, before they returned to Edessa and Antioch.

Godfrey, Bohemund and Tancred all paid homage to Patriarch Daimbert in return for acknowledged control of their territories.

By the end of 1099, the various leading Crusaders were based as follows;

- Raymond of Toulouse – Lattakieh and Tortosa
- Godfrey of Bouillon – Jerusalem
- Bohemund – Antioch
- Baldwin of Boulogne – Edessa
- Tancred – Galilee
- Daimbert – Patriarch of Jerusalem

The First Crusade was over.

Why did the First Crusade succeed?

The First Crusade succeeded in its aim of capturing Jerusalem. It had achieved this success through a combination of several factors;

- Huge numbers
- Muslim disunity
- The support of the Byzantine Empire
- The support of Christians in the East
- The liberal use of violence
- Continued reinforcements from Europe
- The general unity of purpose of the crusade command
- The exploitation of opportunity
- Military skill and organisation

Tasks

a) Consider each factor listed above.

Identify examples within the narrative of the First Crusade which you can use to illustrate each of these factors.

How important do you think each factor was in contributing to the success of the First Crusade?

Write this response in approximately 45 minutes

b) Write a response to the following exam style response;

To what extent did the First Crusade succeed in its' goal of capturing Jerusalem through the liberal use of violence?

Consider this factor in light of the other factors listed above

Write this response in approximately 50 minutes

PART THREE:

The establishment of the kingdom of Jerusalem to the Second Crusade 1101-1146

PART THREE: To the Second Crusade 1101-1146

3.1 - The failed Crusades of 1101

3.2 - The Establishment of the kingdom of Jerusalem

3.3 - The County of Edessa 1097-1144

3.4 – Fulk and Zengi

3.5 - The Second Crusade

3.1 - The failed Crusades of 1101

In this topic we will;

- *Understand why there were Crusades in 1101*
- *Consider the reasons why these Crusades failed*

Introduction

When news reached Europe of the capture of Jerusalem and the establishment of Outremer it inspired many to follow in the footsteps of the 1st Crusade. They were needed. The survivors of the 1st Crusade were few in number and many of those were determined to return home now that they had fulfilled the vows of pilgrimage. If the newly established states of Outremer were to survive, they needed a constant flow of reinforcements. Many were keen to emulate the heroics of the 1st Crusade and saw an opportunity to seek land and wealth in the new territories.

For others it provided a chance of redemption. Stephen of Blois and Hugh of Vermandois had left the 1st Crusade; Stephen through his desertion at Antioch and Hugh, because he had been sent on a diplomatic mission to secure reinforcements. Necessary this may have been, but his vow was still unfilled.

After the news reached Western Europe that the 1st Crusade had captured Jerusalem several armies set out to the East with great enthusiasm. All together, these armies may not have been much less in number as those of the 1st Crusade, and as we will see, they each met with disaster. Separately they comprised of three main groups;

- The Lombard Crusade
- The Nivernais Crusade
- The Aquitainian Crusade

We will discuss each of these separately.

The Lombard Crusade

The Northern Italian cities had not contributed much to the First Crusade. However, the success of the First Crusade encouraged many Northern Italians (sometimes known as Lombards) to take the cross and proceed to the Holy Land, led by a group of Bishops and Counts, including the Archbishop of Milan, Anselm of Buis, and

Albert, the Count of Biandrate. According to Albert of Aix (viii.i) the Lombard Crusade probably numbered around 20,000 in total. However, most of these were urban poor, untrained in arms and led by a small group of bishops and knights. The Lombards set out across Northern Italy and down through the Balkan peninsular to the Byzantine Empire. They were undisciplined and frequently caused trouble as they marched. Upon reaching Constantinople their indiscipline at the sight of the wealth and splendour of that city caused them to riot. Breaking into one of the palaces, they killed one of the Emperor's pet lions before order was restored through a combination of the pleas of their leaders and the force exerted by the Imperial Guard.

At Constantinople a small French army joined the Lombards. It was led by Stephen, Count of Burgundy and Stephen of Blois. Also joining the Lombard and French was Count Raymond of Toulouse who had been visiting Alexius in 1100. Together they restored order and took council with the Emperor Alexius. It was decided to retrace the steps of the 1st Crusade across Asia Minor with Raymond of Toulouse in overall command. Any conquests in Asia Minor were to be returned to the Empire and a contingent of the Byzantine army joined the Lombards to facilitate this.

Once ferried across from Constantinople the Lombard majority almost immediately rejected the plan of retracing the steps of the 1st Crusade across Asia Minor. The route was difficult, but given that the Seljuk Turks had been disrupted by the 1st Crusade the way may have been possible. Instead, the Lombards determined to rescue Bohemund who they learned was being held captive by the Danishmend Turks in North Eastern Anatolia. The Lombards voice, being the bulk of the army was loud and the leaders had little choice but to change their plans to suit the demands of the Lombard contingent. The French contingents were too small to fight their way across Asia Minor by themselves.

At first things went well and the Lombards were encouraged. In June 1010 the town of Ankara (now the Capital of modern Turkey) was captured and restored to the Empire. However it did not last.

The Seljuk and Danishmend Turks, both fearful of yet more crusaders united their strength and determined to attack any future crusades crossing Asia Minor. Resistance hardened and the Lombards soon had to fight as they marched. The Lombards failed to capture the fortress towns of Chakiri and Kastamuni. Soon the

Lombards were low on supplies of food and water and by marching away from the planned route could not be supplied by the Byzantine Empire.

At the town of Mersivan the combined Seljuk and Danishmend armies attacked the Lombards. The defeat was total. The Lombard and French leaders mostly survived due to the speed of their horses, the infantry and non-combatants were massacred, with perhaps only a quarter of the total army surviving. The leaders fought their way clear to the north and upon reaching the Black Sea coast took ship to Constantinople. From there they sailed on to the Holy land.

The defeat at Mersivan undid much of the work of the 1st Crusade in Asia Minor. It restored the military prestige and reputation of the Turks and the Seljuks were able to recover many of the towns and land that had been lost in the past few years. Moreover, the Turks did not rest after their destruction of the Lombard Crusade; they determined to attack the other Crusading expeditions even now attempting to cross Asia Minor.

The Nivernais Crusade

The Crusade led by William II, Count of Nevers left for the Holy land in February 1100. Unlike the Lombard Crusade the Count of Nevers led a well-equipped and disciplined army. It was however small. This lack of numbers would prove to be fatal. The Nivernais army reached Constantinople in May 1100.

Learning that the Lombard army was marching ahead, Count William chose to try and catch up with them. Presuming that the Lombards were following the route of the 1st Crusade William led his men to the South East, however learning in July that the Lombards had turned east and reached Ankara, Count William changed direction and followed the Lombards. Learning of the disaster that the Lombards had experienced at Mersivan, William turned back to his planned route and the road through Konya. Konya was a Seljuk possession and garrisoned by a force strong enough to repel the small Nivernais army. William therefore determined not to attack Konya but to continue his march to the South East.

The Seljuks and Danishmends fresh from their victory at Mersivan learned that the Nivernais were proceeding across Asia Minor and set off to meet them. The combined Turkish army, mostly cavalry moved much more quickly than the Nivernais and intercepted Count William and his men at the town of Heraclea.

Despite their better training and discipline the army of Nivernais fared no better than the Lombards and the bulk of the French army was destroyed, only Count William and a few of his horsemen escaping.

Count William was now, like the Lombard survivors, a General without an army. He reached a Byzantine fortress at Germanicopolis and was provided with a small escort to see him through to the Holy land. Even then insult was added to injury as Count William was robbed by his Byzantine escort and arrived in the Holy land, practically alone and with little more than the clothes on his back.

The Aquitainian Crusade

It may have been better for William of Nevers to delay a while at Constantinople. Soon after he left a larger French/German army arrived led by Duke William IX of Aquitaine and Duke Welf of Bavaria. Also accompanying the army was Hugh of Vermandois and Ida of Austria.

The crusaders left Constantinople and could have probably caught up with William of Nevers. However, the Nivernais force was marching rapidly and the Duke of Aquitaine was a bitter rival of Count William and so probably reluctant to join forces with him. The men of Aquitaine and Bavaria followed the route of the 1st Crusade but found supplies to be low along this route. The army captured Konya from the Seljuk Turks but found little food there. Continuing on the army deteriorated through lack of food and water and hurried to reach the town of Heraclea (modern Ereghli) in the hopes of securing food and water.

Approaching Heraclea the crusaders found a river and rushed in a mob to slake their thirst. It was a trap. The Turkish army was still in the area after crushing the Nivernais and had sabotaged all water resources in the area except the river where they lay in wait. Like the Lombards and the Nivernaism, the crusaders were no match for the well organised Turkish army and they were rapidly destroyed. Like the leaders of the other crusades of 1101, only the leaders survived in any numbers. The rest were massacred. Bishops were martyred and Ida of Austria lost; probably killed in the stampede. Hugh of Vermandois was badly wounded and although he escaped, he died of his wounds at Tarsus a few weeks after the battle. The Dukes of Bavaria and Aquitaine survived the defeat and made their way to the Holy land without an army.

The consequences of the crusades of 1101

Each of the crusading expeditions of 1101 was an unmitigated disaster. Of the tens of thousands who had set out, only a fraction made it to the Holy land in small groups or as individuals. The Latin states of Outremer had needed the manpower these crusades were bringing in order to really establish themselves. The surviving leaders were not needed in the East; their men were.

The Seljuk and Danishmend Turks had re-established themselves in Asia Minor and restored their military prestige which had been dented by the 1st Crusade. The land route across Asia Minor remained closed to most pilgrims and the Byzantine Empire was unable to use the crusades of 1101 to restore the territory lost after the battle of Manzikert. As a further consequence they were also unable to exert any great influence on the Latin states of Outremer and the Muslim cities of Syria.

However, the remnants of the crusades of 1101 were put to some use for the benefit of Outremer. Raymond of Toulouse would use the survivors to help him capture Tortosa before they fulfilled their vows of reaching Jerusalem and heading home. Some, like Stephen of Blois, would stay on and took service with King Baldwin I of Jerusalem. He would be killed in battle at Ramleh in May 1102.

Task: Exploring the reasons for the failure of the Crusades in 1101

In the earlier section we explored the reasons why the First Crusade succeeded. Look again at the factors that allowed the First Crusade to succeed;

- Muslim disunity
- The support of the Byzantine Empire
- The liberal use of violence
- The general unity of purpose of the crusade command
- The exploitation of opportunity
- Military skill and organisation
- Luck

Consider now these factors with reference to the Crusades of 1101. In what ways did these factors cause the Crusades of 1101 to fail? Having done this, write a response to the following exam style response;

To what extent did Muslim unity cause the Crusades of 1101 to fail?

Consider this factor in light of the other factors listed above

3.2 - The Establishment of the kingdom of Jerusalem

In this topic we will;

- Explore the priorities of the kings Baldwin I and Baldwin II
- Understand the major events of the reigns of Baldwin I and Baldwin II
- Consider the reasons why the Crusader states survived and prospered under Baldwin I and Baldwin II

Jerusalem: Introduction

Godfrey did not remain longer as ruler of Jerusalem, but while he lived he did attempt to extend and secure his newly founded realm. Godfrey managed to negotiate the surrender of the port town of Arsuf in March 1100 and fought several inconclusive battles with Duqaq of Damascus in the region around Tiberias.

In July 1100 Godfrey died of an illness, the bulk of the army of Jerusalem was on campaign and during the period of interregnum the Patriarch Daimbert attempted to seize control of Jerusalem for himself. In this he was thwarted by the knights of Godfrey's household. A new ruler was sought and Baldwin, Count of Edessa was summoned to take over Jerusalem.

Baldwin I (1100-1118)

When Godfrey died on the 18th July 1100, Baldwin, his brother, was Count of Edessa. He could not leave Edessa immediately and it was not until November 1100 that Baldwin reached Jerusalem. He wasted no time in demonstrating to all that he would be an energetic and aggressive ruler.

Within a week of his arrival at Jerusalem, Baldwin left the city to raid the lands south of the Dead Sea and also to make a demonstration at Ascalon to deter the Fatamid Egyptians. Baldwin returned to his kingdom soon after to be crowned king on Christmas Day at Bethlehem. Baldwin's decision to be crowned king was a departure from his brother's policy of ruling in name but not by title.

Baldwin found his new kingdom of Jerusalem to be vulnerable. Its borders were undefined, the neighbours were largely hostile and it had no adequate sea port through which communications with the West could be guaranteed. In comparison also to Edessa, Jerusalem was also a much poorer country. Only good communications and a measure of authority over its neighbours would enable the kingdom of Jerusalem to survive. Baldwin I's actions then must be seen as a concerted attempt to overcome these shortcomings.

In 1101 Baldwin raided Arab trading caravans; he demanded and received tribute from the still independent city states of Arsuf, Caesarea, Tyre and Acre. Baldwin also ransomed Muslim prisoners to Duqaq of Damascus for 50,000 much needed Bezants. With the assistance of a newly arrived fleet from Genoa carrying pilgrims Baldwin besieged and captured Arsuf and Caesarea, thenceforward these cities would become part of the kingdom of Jerusalem. The population of Non-Christian population of Caesarea was massacred; a deliberate policy demonstrating that Baldwin I was not to be opposed and that his kingdom was to be primarily a Christian one. In the autumn of 1101 Baldwin I defeated a Fatamid army at the 1st battle of Ramleh, sent to help the cities of the coast resist.

In May 1102 Baldwin was opposed again by the Fatamid armies. At the 2nd battle of Ramleh Baldwin was defeated, most of his army killed or captured. Baldwin managed to escape the disaster and the Egyptian army turned to besiege the port of Jaffa. Fortunately for Baldwin I, a newly arrived fleet of English, French and German pilgrims arrived at Jaffa allowed Baldwin to defeat the Fatamid Egyptians. Baldwin also faced opposition from the newly appointed Patriarch of Jerusalem Daimbert who aspired for Jerusalem to be ruled by the Church. Daimbert was implicated in a conspiracy and forced out of office. Baldwin I then had only to face Muslim opposition to his rule.

In 1103 Baldwin I laid siege to the port of Acre without success, partly due to the lack of a fleet. He was almost killed by bandits on Mount Carmel, despite this Fatamid policy seems to have faltered; the army sent to attack Jerusalem broke up through internal dissension.

In 1104 Baldwin I received a new naval fleet from Genoa and with their assistance captured Acre. Like at Caesarea in 1102, the non-Christian population was massacred. Acre was a great prize and a a city that would become the commercial heart of the kingdom. In 1105 Baldwin defeated a Fatamid invasion at the 3rd battle of Ramleh; however a small group of Egyptians managed to raid right up to the walls of Jerusalem and these raids continued into 1106.

At the end of 1108 Baldwin made a truce with Toghtekin of Damascus in order to re-establish trade and so that both parties could focus on other enemies. The Truce lasted until 1113.

In 1108 Baldwin I besieged the port city of Sidon but failed to take the city. In 1109 Baldwin I met with other leaders of the states of Outremer before the walls of Tripoli and was acknowledged the leader of all these states. In turn Baldwin helped Bertrand capture the city of Tripoli in 1110 and then used many of the same forces to capture Beirut. The population of the city was massacred. In the same year Sidon was also captured partly through the assistance of a Venetian and Norwegian fleet led by their respective rulers, the Doge of Venice and king Sigurd of Norway; the first royal visitor to the Holy Lands.

In 1111 Baldwin tried to capture the port of Tyre and the frontier fortress of Ascalon on the Egyptian border. In both these attempts Baldwin was unsuccessful. Until the end of his reign Baldwin focused his attention on Egypt. In 1115 Baldwin raided south of the Dead Sea and established the castle of Montreal, attempting to control communications into and out of Egypt. These raids continued into 1116 and in this year Baldwin led a small expedition to the Red Sea, reaching and fortifying the port of Aqaba. The result would be that the Fatamids of Egypt were less able to communicate with other Muslim states further East and less able to send raiders and armies against the kingdom of Jerusalem.

In 1118 Baldwin launched an ambitious attack on Egypt itself with a small army of 216 horsemen and 900 infantry. It proved to be his last act. Taking sick on the expedition Baldwin died on the return journey on the 2nd April 1118.

Baldwin I was an aggressive and energetic ruler. It was he, and not his brother who ensured that the kingdom of Jerusalem would survive its establishment. Baldwin established the frontiers of the kingdom and secured access to the sea through many ports. Baldwin I massacred many Muslims as a matter of policy, and these actions were remembered by his opponents, however Baldwin realised that the kingdom could not survive purely as a Latin Christian kingdom. He protected the rights of other Christian groups and allowed them to maintain their churches and practices. Despite being married three times Baldwin had no children to survive him and did not appoint a successor.

> **Task: The achievements of Baldwin I**
>
> Write a response to the following question in no more than 500 words;
>
> *Assess the view that success in battle was the most important achievement of Baldwin I?*

Baldwin II (1118-1131)

In 1118 Baldwin Le Bourg was appointed the second king of Jerusalem. Baldwin II was crowned in Jerusalem on the 14th April 1118. He was not appointed by his predecessor, but rather by a council of nobles led by Joscelin of Courtney, then Prince of Galilee. A potential rival was Eustace of Boulogne, the elder brother of both Godfrey and Baldwin I. After the capture of Jerusalem, Eustace had returned home to Boulogne. He appears to have not been keen on the idea, but when news reached him that his brother Baldwin had died, along with the suggestion that he should be the new king, he started out for Jerusalem, but in Italy he heard news that Baldwin Le Bourg had been crowned instead. Eustace returned to Boulogne rather than fight for the kingship.

Baldwin's qualifications

Baldwin II's qualifications for the position of king were that he was a cousin of Baldwin I, he was like Baldwin I a veteran of the First Crusade and the last surviving great lord of that expedition in the East. Baldwin had also been Count of Edessa ever since Baldwin I became king of Jerusalem. He was also supported in his claim by the majority of the Jerusalemite nobility, led by Joscelin of Courtney, then Prince of Galilee. As a reward, Joscelin would be appointed Count of Edessa in place of Baldwin II, despite the part not really getting along personally. Finally, Baldwin was at hand. He had arrived in Jerusalem on the day of Baldwin I's funeral.

Baldwin II was a religious man, genuinely pious and more likely to take the advice and religious leadership of the Patriarch of

Jerusalem. He was also, unlike Baldwin I, a happily married man. He had married an Armenian princess named Morphia and together they had four daughters. Baldwin II then was seen as something as a link between the Christians of West and East. Upon his accession Baldwin II was recognized as overlord without trouble by Joscelin of Courtney, now appointed Count of Edessa, Pons of Tripoli and Roger of Antioch. Baldwin II than was a figure of some respect and standing in the Crusader states and accepted as leader of the Latins in the East.

Challenges

Baldwin II was fortunate that he lacked opposition within the sphere of the Crusader States; for Muslim opposition was quick to test out the new king of Jerusalem. In 1118, an alliance of Damascus and Egypt led to a threatened invasion. Baldwin II led the army of Jerusalem to confront them and for three months both sides faced each other without fighting. After three months both sides went home. It was just as well. Disaster had struck in Antioch.

In June 1119, Roger, regent of Antioch faced an invasion by an army commanded by Il-Ghazi of Mardin; the leading Ortoquid Turkish ruler. Roger was massively outnumbered, but rather than await help from the other Crusader states, Roger rashly marched out to confront Il-Ghazi. The result was a slaughter. At the battle named thereafter as 'The Field of Blood' on the 28th June 1119, Roger was killed along with almost the entire Antiochene army of 700 knights and 4000 infantry.

Baldwin hurried north with from Pons of Tripoli and managed to secure the city of Antioch and safeguard much of the territory of the principality, but Antioch was essentially leaderless. Most of the knights and lords of Antioch were dead, the recognised heir was Bohemund II, then a child of 10 years of age growing up in Italy, and the city was controlled by the Patriarch.

Baldwin took over the regency of the city and appointed new lords of the lands left vacant by the deaths of their owners. He did this by forcing widows of the dead lords of Antioch to marry knights from the Jerusalem army. This way, he could provide territory for his men and ensure that the lands of Antioch were not unoccupied by owners responsible for their protection and upkeep.

The regency of Antioch was to concern Baldwin II for the bulk of his reign. Baldwin returned to Jerusalem in December 1119, leaving the Patriarch of Antioch as his representative in the city. In 1120 Baldwin II, perhaps still working to make good the damage of the Field of Blood, supported the establishment of the Military Orders. The Templars and the Hospitallers were granted lands and rights within the Crusader States and would grow in time to become major participants in events.

Capture

In the years 1120-1122 Baldwin II spent much time travelling to and fro between Antioch and Jerusalem. A truce was made with Il-Ghazi and Antioch was largely secured. However conflict remained almost constant in Northern Syria and on the 13th September 1123 Joscelin, Count of Edessa was captured in a raid by Balak, a nephew of Il-Ghazi. With Joscelin in prison, Edessa was leaderless, though the army of Edessa remained largely intact. Fortunately for Baldwin II, Il-Ghazi died in November 1122 and his sons and nephews set about squabbling over the inheritance. The death of Il-Ghazi gave Baldwin II the opportunity to take advantage and restore the authority of the crusader states in Northern Syria, unfortunately though Baldwin was defeated in battle and captured by Balak, now Emir of Harran. Baldwin joined Joscelin in captivity at a castle called Kharpurt.

Despite the death of Roger of Antioch and the capture of both Joscelin and Baldwin II, the Crusader states survived relatively intact during this period. The Patriarchs of Antioch and Jerusalem took over effective control of their respective lands and the administrative wheels continued to turn. A military leader of Jerusalem was appointed; Eustace Garnier who was lord of the towns of Caesarea and Sidon.

In August 1122 Baldwin II and Joscelin attempted to escape their captivity. A rescue team of some fifty Armenians loyal to the rulers of Edessa seized control of the castle of Kharpurt. It was decided that Joscelin would go and seek help, whilst Baldwin would defend Kharpurt with the Armenians. Joscelin reached safety and together with Eustace Garnier led the army of Jerusalem northwards. They were too late.

Baldwin II was unable to hold Kharpurt. After a short siege the castle was stormed and all the Armenians killed by Balak of Harran. Baldwin was kept alive and transported by Balak to a new prison.

Eustace Garnier was recalled to Jerusalem to defend the city when the Egyptians attacked again in 1123. Eustace defeated the Egyptians at Ibelin in May of that year, but died soon after. Help also reached Jerusalem in 1123. Hearing news of Baldwin's captivity, the Venetians sailed to Outremer with a large fleet. The Venetians defeated an Egyptian fleet around the same time as the battle of Ibelin and joined the army of Jerusalem in laying siege to the sea port of Tyre in February 1124.

Marriages

In May 1124 the Emir of Harran was killed fighting other Muslims and Baldwin II was ransomed by his new captor (who did not want the job), a son of Il-Ghazi named Timurtash for 80,000 dinars in June 1124. Baldwin returned to Jerusalem to find it stronger than he had left it. Tyre surrendered in July 1124, and after securing trading agreements and alliances which benefitted both sides, the Venetians returned home.

In May 1125 Baldwin II led the army of Jerusalem north to fight a new Muslim leader; Il-Bursuqi was master of both Mosul and Aleppo and was threatening Antioch. At the battle of Azaz in 1125, with both sides suffering heavy casualties Baldwin defeated Il-Bursuqi. A truce was made and Baldwin paid the ransom he owed to Timurtash to Il-Bursuqi instead. Il-Bursuqi did not long remain a threat, a shi'ite assassin killed him in November 1126 and the resultant power struggle brought chaos to the Muslim factions competing for power in Mosul and Aleppo. Turning his attention back to the south, Baldwin defeated Toghtekin of Damascus in battle in 1126. Damascus would remain a target for much of the remainder of Baldwin's reign.

In late 1126, Bohemund II, now eighteen years old, arrived with a fleet of supporters to take up his inheritance. Baldwin came to Antioch to meet him. A marriage between Bohemund and Baldwin's second eldest daughter, Alice was arranged. Measures were also taken to arrange for an heir to the throne of Jerusalem. The forty year of Count of Anjou, a wealthy territory in France, was selected to marry Melisende, the eldest daughter of Baldwin and Morphia. This marriage took place in 1129.

The death of Baldwin II

Baldwin II hoped to crown his reign by capturing the city of Damascus. Damascus had long been a rival of the cities of Mosul and Aleppo and its close proximity to Jerusalem made it an ideal base from which to launch attacks on that place.

In 1129 Toghtekin was dead and the arrival of Fulk coincided with an appeal for aid to Europe. The leader of the Templars was sent to Europe to recruit men and reinforcements poured in Jerusalem. It is estimated that Baldwin and Fulk led an army some 50,000 men against Damascus and its new ruler; Toghtekin's son Buri. However, the campaign was a failure and little was achieved.

In 1130 the new Prince of Antioch, Bohemund II repeated the mistakes of his predecessor and was killed in battle. He wife Alice attempted to keep control of the city on behalf of their two year old daughter; Constance. Baldwin once again had to come to Antioch, only to find that his daughter would rather seek assistance from Zengi, the Atabeg of Aleppo, than that of her father. Baldwin ousted his daughter from Antioch and instead appointed Joscelin, Count of Edessa as guardian of Antioch whilst a replacement could be found. This journey proved to be Baldwin II's last. He died in August 1131 in Jerusalem.

> **Task: The achievements of Baldwin II**
>
> Write a response to the following question in no more than 500 words;
>
> *Assess the view that success in diplomacy was the most important achievement of Baldwin II?*

Task: Jerusalem under Baldwin I, Baldwin II

Write a response to the following question;

To what extent do you agree with the view that military ability was the main qualification for a king of Jerusalem in the years 1100-1131?

In your response make sure that you consider points of challenge and support for the representation contained within this question.

Also consider other relevant factors including;

- Relationships with other Latin nobles
- Needs and demands of neighbouring Muslim rulers
- Relationships with local Christians
- The contribution of European fleets and armies

Try to write your response in no more than 750 words;

3.3 - The County of Edessa

In this topic we will;

- Explore the location and extent of the County of Edessa
- Understand the major events and challenges to the County of Edessa
- Explore the career of Zengi
- Consider the reasons why Edessa was captured in 1144

The County of Edessa: A timeline

1098 Baldwin of Boulogne seizes control of Edessa

1100 Baldwin of Boulogne becomes King of Jerusalem. Baldwin Le Bourg becomes Count of Edessa.

1104 The Battle of Harran. Edessan leaders captured.

1105 Regency of Tancred.

1106-8 Regency of Richard of Salerno.

1115 Battle of Tell Danith.

1118 Baldwin Le Bourg becomes King of Jerusalem.

1123 Joscelin of Courtney captured.

1131 Death of Joscelin of Courtney.

1138 Edessa joins Byzantine led attack on Shaizar.

1144 Edessa captured by Zengi.

Introduction

The County of Edessa was the first Latin state to be established by the First Crusade in March 1098, when Baldwin of Boulogne (later King Baldwin I of Jerusalem) detached himself from the 1st Crusade with a small retinue and seized control of the city of Edessa.

Geographical overview

Located far from the coast, the County of Edessa consisted of several fortified towns such as Turbessel (Tel Bashir), Ravendan, Aintab, Saruj as well as Edessa itself. The County straddled the Upper Euphrates river but had no other defined boundary. The population of the County of Edessa was mostly Armenian and Syrian Christians; however the town of Saruj was many peopled by Muslims. The County was a border country, but its land was fertile and its towns were prosperous. At the beginning of the 11th century, Edessa was wealthier than Jerusalem.

Edessa was strategically valuable; its possession helped secure the north of Outremer by preventing easy access of communication for Muslim armies to the coast of the Mediterranean. Because of its location, Edessa could also be used as a base from which to launch invasions down the banks of the Euphrates river into the heart of Iraq. The Romans had certainly used it for this purpose centuries before.

The needs and priorities of Edessa

Given its strategic position and lack of Crusader settlers, who favoured the coastal regions of Outremer, Latin settlers in the county were few and according to Runciman appealed only to;

"Adventurers ready to lead the life of a brigand chief"

Runciman II,p11

Edessa was a tempting target for Muslim armies seeking to reply to the success of the 1st Crusade.

As a Latin ruled sate, Edessa was dependent upon;

- The goodwill of the Armenian majority.
- A lack of unity amongst the Muslim rulers of Aleppo, Mosul and Damascus.
- A friendly relationship with the Byzantine Empire.

A Brief history of the County of Edessa

In 1100 Baldwin of Boulogne left Edessa to become King of Jerusalem. The rule of Edessa fell to Baldwin's cousin – Baldwin Le Bourg (later to become Baldwin II, King of Jerusalem). Baldwin Le Bourg married into the Armenian local elite by marrying Morphia of Melitene in 1102. He also devolved much responsibility to Joscelin of Courtney (a cousin of Baldwin Le Bourg) who was based at Turbessel.

Taking advantage of Muslim disunity after the death of the death of the Atabeg of Mosul Kerbogha, the County of Edessa was able to expand its territory in the north and south. This phase of expansion was cut short in 1104 however when a combined Edessan-Antiochene army was defeated near Harran. Both Baldwin Le Bourg and Joscelin of Courtney were captured and imprisoned until released in 1108.

Edessa then was without leaders; therefore Bohemund briefly installed Tancred as ruler in their absence until 1105 when Tancred was recalled to govern at Antioch after Bohemund was himself captured. Tancred was replaced by Richard of Salerno and for a time it looked like Edessa and Antioch would merge into a single territory.

In 1108 Baldwin Le Bourg was released and immediately called upon Muslim support to help him drive out Richard of Salerno; Joscelin of Courtney appears to have conspired against Baldwin Le Bourg and was exiled. Joscelin went to Jerusalem to become Prince of Galilee.

Latin unity in the North of Outremer was restored by 1113 be the threat of renewed Muslim attacks by Mawdud of Mosul in the years 1110-1113 and also by the death of Tancred of Antioch in 1112. To seal the improved relations, Baldwin Le Bourg's sister married Tancred's successor Richard of Salerno in the same year. A combined Edessan-Antiochene army defeated Bursuq of Hamadan in 1115 at the battle of Tell Danith.

> **The Rulers of Edessa**
>
> **(Regents in brackets)**
>
> - *1097-1100 Baldwin of Boulogne*
> - *1100-1118 Baldwin Le Bourg*
> - *(1105 Tancred)*
> - *(1105-1108 Richard of Salerno)*
> - *1118-1131 Joscelin of Courtney*
> - *1131-1150 Joscelin II*

In 1118 Baldwin I, King of Jerusalem died. His successor was Baldwin Le Bourg who entrusted Edessa to Josecelin of Courtney when he became king of Jerusalem. Holding Edessa as Baldwin II's representative Joscelin of Courtney soon became the most powerful lord in Northern Outremer when Richard of Salerno and almost the entire army of Antioch were destroyed at the battle known as the Field of Blood in 1119. However this did not prevent Joscelin being captured again in 1123 when he raided the territory of Balak of Aleppo. He was released in 1124 and Joscelin led a united Latin army to try to rescue King Baldwin II of Jerusalem when he was captured in 1123. Joscelin continued to lead an active policy of raids against his Muslim neighbours as he joined attacks on Aleppo in 1124/5 and Damascus in 1129.

Joscelin also had some good relations with local Muslim rulers and sought their assistance when he opposed Bohemund II of Antioch in 1127. So was clearly willing to seek assistance from anywhere he could. In 1131 Joscelin of Courtney died after repelling a Muslim raid. He had been in his death bed but when he heard of the raid he insisted on being carried out in a litter. The raiders fled and Joscelin died immediately after giving thanks to God for the success. He was succeeded by his son, Joscelin II.

Joscelin II succeeded his father in 1131, but despite his efforts he was unable to prevent the deterioration of the County. Joscelin was also faced with the first great Muslim threat to Outremer. In 1128 the atabeg of Mosul, a Turk named Zengi united the cities of Aleppo and Mosul under his control. This was a serious threat to Edessa as now two of the major cities neighbouring the County of Edessa were united and could act in concert. Zengi's advance against Edessa and the other Crusader states was slow but deliberate. In 1137 the Castle of Montferrand in the territory of Tripoli was captured and Zengi also united the cities of Homs and Baalbak further encircling the County from the rest of Outremer.

The fall of Edessa

In 1138 Antioch and Edessan forces combined with an army led by the Byzantine Emperor John. The army assaulted the city of Shaizar but failed to capture the place. This failure increased Edessan vulnerability and Joscelin II was unable to have harmonious relations with the Prince of Antioch Raymond. In 1143 the Kingdom of Jerusalem and the Byzantine Empire both were distracted by the deaths of their rulers in that year. In December 1144, whilst Joscelin II was away raiding the territory of Aleppo, Zengi attacked Edessa whilst it was stripped of defenders. After a siege of four weeks the city of Edessa surrendered on Christmas Eve. This event triggered the Second Crusade.

After the loss of Edessa, Joscelin's territory was much reduced, and the County was now ruled from Turbessel. The failure of the Second Crusade spelled the end of the County of Edessa as a Crusader state. Joscelin II was captured in 1150 and would spend the rest of his life as a prisoner in Aleppo, dying in 1159. Turbessel was sold by Joscelin's wife to the Byzantine Emperor Manuel I Comnenus in 1150 but Zengi's successor Nur Al-Din soon overran the remainder of the County in 1151.

3.4 – Fulk and Zengi

In this topic we will;

- *Consider the importance of the daughters of Baldwin II*
- *Explore the careers of Fulk and Zengi*
- *Consider the reign of Fulk alongside that of Zengi*
- *Explore why both Zengi and Fulk sought control of Damascus*
- *Consider the reasons why the Crusade states failed to deal with Zengi*

King Baldwin II and his daughters

Baldwin II and his wife Morphia had four daughters;

- Melisende
- Alice
- Hodierna
- Jovieta

As the eldest child of Baldwin II, Melisende was Baldwin's heir, but she would not be allowed to rule. Her husband, whoever he may be, would rule Jerusalem on her behalf. Of the other daughters Jovieta was destined for the Church; she would in time become the Abbess of Bethany. Hodierna would in time marry Raymond II of Tripoli (in 1137) and Alice was married to Bohemund II of Antioch. By marrying his daughters to the leading men of Antioch and Tripoli, Baldwin II sought to consolidate his position as leader of the Franks in Palestine and Syria. By doing this Baldwin managed to unite the crusader states, for the most part, under his leadership. Fulk, Count of Anjou was born in France. He was summoned to the Kingdom of Jerusalem in 1128 in order to marry the eldest daughter of King Baldwin II,

King Fulk became king towards the end of the year in 1131. As the third king of Jerusalem, Fulk had inherited a kingdom that his predecessors had spent much of their lives establishing with some measure of success. Those that had settled in Outremer in the aftermath of the First Crusade had managed to create a series of states in the East that were based in part on Western European societal models.

These settlers had managed to establish themselves and a second generation of Franks was now coming to the fore in Outremer. Many of these had been born in the East and saw themselves as integrated in the wider fabric of society. Some therefore saw Fulk, born in France as an outsider, a foreigner. Despite his selection by King Baldwin II, there was some resentment at Fulk becoming king.

Joscelin II, Count of Edessa saw himself as the leading Frank of Northern Syria and at first refused to acknowledge Fulk as his overlord, as did Pons, Count of Tripoli. At Antioch, Alice, now a widow, was also somewhat reluctant to view Fulk as her overlord. There were rumours that Alice desired a new husband and was willing to marry Manuel, the son of the Byzantine emperor John. If this marriage went ahead then Antioch would come under the control of the Empire. This plot by Alice was the most serious and the first that Fulk was determined to prevent.

Establishing control

Fulk's response to this insubordination was to lead the army of Jerusalem north. In 1132 Fulk headed north, primarily for Jerusalem, but in order to do so he would need to travel through the County of Tripoli. Pons refused access to the army of Jerusalem and a somewhat embarrassed Fulk therefore had to sail to Antioch.

Arriving in Antioch, Alice was quickly abandoned by the nobles of Antioch. Fulk assumed the regency of the Principality and placed trusted men in control of Antioch when he returned to Jerusalem. This show of force also ensured that both Edessa and Tripoli acknowledged the supremacy of Fulk. This was welcome, but Fulk faced problems at home, potentially in his own household.

Returning to Jerusalem in 1132, Fulk heard rumours that his Queen was having an affair. A local noble, Hugh of Jaffa had grown up with Melisende as her friend and, some said more. Scared for his life (and perhaps providing some evidence of his guilt), Hugh of Jaffa gathered a party of knights to protect him at court, but this did not prevent his own step son (he had married an heiress) from accusing Hugh of plotting to kill King Fulk. Hugh denied this and it was agreed that a trial by combat between Hugh and his step-son should be held to decide who was right.

Hugh refused to fight and, found guilty was to be exiled for three years and stripped of his lands, but before he could go into exile, he was nearly killed by a knight newly arrived from Europe who hoped to ingratiate the king to himself for this service. The attempted assassin instead was executed and Hugh was exiled from Outremer, dying shortly after.

Pons of Tripoli was also finally brought to heel in 1133 when he was defeated in battle by Muslim forces from Damascus and besieged in a castle. Fulk led an army to rescue him this time, but Pons was killed in battle against the Damascene army in 1137.

In Antioch, Alice had returned to power in Antioch in 1135, but she still needed marrying in order to provide a military leader in Antioch. She still preferred Manuel Comnenus, but Fulk instead decided on a different plan. Alice was technically a regent for her daughter, Constance, who had been born in 1128 and had been two years old when her father Bohemund II was killed.

Fulk invited a French noble, Raymond of Poitiers to marry Constance, but he made Alice believe that it would be she who married Raymond. So when Raymond arrived in Antioch in 1136, the marriage of Raymond of Poitiers, aged thirty seven and Constance, then aged nine, was performed without the knowledge of Alice. Distraught and thwarted in her plans, Alice would die shortly afterwards

This series of affairs demonstrates that Fulk was resented as ruler by some of the established, indigenous Franks of the Crusader states, who saw him and those others who travelled East as intruders. It was through rapid action that Fulk was able to assert himself as the leading man of the Crusader states, as well as an appreciation by those in Antioch, Edessa and Tripoli that they would need to be united if they hoped to prosper in the face of increased Muslim unity.

Fulk's reign 1137-1143

In 1137 Pons of Tripoli was killed by an army from Damascus. His son Raymond II of Tripoli succeeded him and was married to the sister of Melisende, Hodierna. Fulk joined Raymond of Tripoli in a campaign against the invaders of Tripoli but was surprised and defeated by the arrival of Zengi's army from Aleppo.

Raymond was captured by Zengi and Fulk besieged in the castle of Montferrand, surrendering soon after in order to secure the release of himself and Raymond in return for the surrender of the castle.

In 1139 Fulk attempted to extend his kingdom with an invasion of the territory of Unur of Damascus. Aided by Crusaders newly arrived from Europe commanded by Thierry, Count of Flanders, Fulk and Thierry achieved some success against Damascus capturing lands and fortresses before agreeing to a ceasefire and alliance with Unur; both Unur and Fulk realised that Zengi was ultimately a greater threat to both of them. After 1139, Unur and Fulk worked together to help thwart Zengi's efforts to seize control of Damascus.

In 1141, Fulk turned his attention to the south of his kingdom. The frontier shared with Egypt was long and open. In order to have greater security, Fulk authorised the construction of several new castles in the south. We will discuss these in more detail in Part four.

Fulk's end

Fulk then had achieved some measure of success. He had secured his position over the other Crusader states; he had brought Raymond of Poitiers to oversee Antioch and gained the good will of both Pons and Raymond of Tripoli. Fulk had made efforts to make alliance with Muslims who shared their fear and hostility to Zengi, and he had made efforts to further secure his kingdom by the construction of castles in the south.

In 1143 the Byzantine Emperor John II died, and along with his death the Christian position in Northern Syria became less stable and secure. It was therefore doubly unfortunate that Fulk would die in the same year; horribly injured during a hunting expedition, Fulk died soon afterwards leaving two male heirs to his kingdom, Baldwin III and Amalric, both however were children. Fulk's death created a power vacuum in the Crusader state, and the state most exposed was Edessa.

> **Task: The achievements of Fulk**
> Write a response to the following question in no more than 500 words;
>
> *Assess the view that success in diplomacy was the most important achievement of Fulk?*

Zengi

We turn our attention now to Zengi, the first Muslim ruler to really begin to unite the various cities and factions of the Muslims in Syria against the Crusader states.

Who was Zengi?

Zengi, or to give his full name; Imad al-Din Zengi was military governor (atabeg) of the cities of Mosul and Aleppo. In theory Zengi owed his allegiance to the Turkish Seljuk Sultan and the Caliph at Baghdad in Iraq. In practice Zengi was an independent ruler.

Zengi had a consistent policy of expansion. He spent much of his career attempting to expand his area of authority in Northern Syria and spent much of his later years warring against other Muslim powers; notably the city of Damascus, but it is his capture of the Crusader state of Edessa for which he is best well known in European history.

Zengi's background

Zengi's father was a former atabeg (military governor) of the city of Aleppo who died whilst Zengi was a child. Much of Zengi's early life and career was spent in attendance of the Seljuk Sultan in Iraq and also in service to the atabegs of Mosul; Kerbogha and his successors.

In 1122, Zengi became an official, overseeing the Iraqi towns of Wasit and Basra. His administration was found to be successful and in 1127 he was appointed a senior official at Baghdad briefly before being posted to Mosul as atabeg. On arrival in Mosul, Zengi rapidly made a military truce with Count Joscelin of Edessa so that he could concentrate on attacking the Ortoqid Muslims. This policy of focusing on the Ortoqids soon bore fruit. In 1128 the inhabitants of Aleppo invited Zengi to take control of their city; driving out the Ortoqids who had so misgoverned the city. Zengi had united both Mosul and Aleppo. He was recognised by the Sultan as governor of 'The West'; and tasked with recovering authority from the lands of the Crusader states and those Muslims who were opposed to the Seljuk Sultan.

The dangers to the Crusader states of Muslim unity

By uniting the cities of Mosul and Aleppo under a single energetic ruler; the Crusader states of Northern Syria would be threatened; especially Antioch and Edessa. They would need to work together in the face of this Muslim unity; unfortunately for them they did not.

In 1129, the then king of Jerusalem launched an ambitious attack on the city of Damascus. Damascus was an independent Muslim held city; but if the Christians could gain control of the city they may secure a permanent hold in Palestine and Syria. Soon after the failure of the Christian attempt on the city; Zengi attempted to assert his control over Damascus. In this he was unsuccessful, despite a number of attacks on the city, combined with rigorous diplomacy. The pressure he did exert on Damascus through the years 1138-1143, however did ensure that the then ruler of Damascus, Unur, made an alliance with Fulk of Jerusalem in 1139.

Zengi sought out opportune moments to increase his own power. We have already mentioned the truce with Joscelin of Edessa. In 1137 Zengi attacked the County of Tripoli; trying to drive his way to the coast after Pons of Tripoli was killed in battle with the Damascene army. In the same year Zengi defeated a combined force commanded by Fulk of Jerusalem and Raymond II of Tripoli and laid siege to Fulk when he took refuge in the strategically positioned castle of Montferrand.

At Montferrand, in July 1137, Fulk surrendered to Zengi. Zengi could have held Fulk prisoner or even had Fulk executed; instead Fulk and his men were released on condition that the castle be surrendered. This generosity surprised many – for Zengi had a reputation for bloodthirst; it was rumoured that he had once scared someone to death just through the fear he generated. Instead though Zengi needed to prioritise other threats; the Byzantine army under the Emperor John II was entering Northern Syria.

John Comnenus and Northern Syria

The Emperor John had succeeded his father Alexius in 1118. He was an experienced general and had spent almost his entire life engaged in military campaigns. In 1137 John and his army were determined to reassert Byzantine control over the city of Antioch.

John captured many towns in Cilicia (a region contested by the Antiochene Princes and the Byzantine Emperor) and even laid siege to Antioch itself. The siege was brief and one-sided. Receiving no help, the Prince of Antioch; Raymond of Poitiers, surrendered to John on condition that he could rule the city under the authority of the Emperor.

In 1138, the Byzantine army commanded by the Emperor returned to Northern Syria and together with the forces of Antioch and Edessa laid siege to the Muslim held city of Shaizar. The city of Shaizar held out for Zengi was coming to confront the Byzantine army. Rather than meet that confrontation however John decided he must withdraw. He had other problems in other parts of his Empire and therefore made a truce with Zengi.

Zengi too was somewhat relieved by the withdrawal of the Empire; it was by no means certain that he could defeat the Byzantine army and Zengi was still eager to gain control of Damascus and other places. In 1138, Zengi captured the city of Homs and in 1140 he captured Baalbek; both from other Muslim rulers.

The capture of Edessa

The rulers of Antioch and Edessa continued to squabble. Both made alliances with local Muslims that would harass each other and the two Crusader states even fought each other on occasion. In late 1144 the main Edessan army commanded by Count Joscelin II was away raiding to the West when Zengi launched a surprise attack on the city itself. The city was besieged in November 1144. Joscelin tried to get help; but Raymond of Antioch refused to assist the Count of Edessa; partly through mutual dislike, but mostly through an acknowledgement that he could achieve little.

King Fulk had died the year before in 1143 in a hunting accident, as had the Byzantine Emperor John (his death was also due to a hunting accident). Jerusalem was ruled by Queen Melisende. An army was dispatched north but arrived too late. Edessa was captured by Zengi after a four week siege.

Edessa was captured and sacked on Christmas Eve 1144; whilst the local Christians which survived the attack were spared, the Franks, the Christians from Europe, were slaughtered or enslaved.

Zengi's death and succession 1144-1146

Zengi was at the height of his power; but did not survive to consolidate his success. In 1145 Zengi had to return to Mosul to subdue a revolt there. He achieved this, but on 14th September 1146, whilst campaigning against a minor Muslim ruler who still rejected his authority, Zengi was murdered by one of his own slaves; a Frank who murdered him whilst Zengi was drunk on wine.

Zengi had several sons who now divided his inheritance amongst themselves. One son; Saif al-Din, took control of Mosul, another Nur-Al Din took control of Aleppo. Whilst Zengi's sons were distracted, Joscelin II attempted to recapture Edessa. In November 1146, Edessa was regained briefly by Joscelin, but was soon driven out again. Joscelin was defeated and soon relinquished all claims to what was left of his County, but for Edessa the unsuccessful revolt was much worse. The city was recaptured by the sons of Zengi, the walls were destroyed and the entire Christian population either killed or sold into slavery. The city of Edessa never recovered from this devastation.

Task: Comparing the careers of Baldwin I and Zengi

Using the information contained in this course; write a response to the following essay style question;

Compare and contrast the careers of Zengi and Baldwin I. To what extent could it be argued that they have much in common?

Write your response in no more than 750 words.

3.5 - The Second Crusade

In this topic we will;

- *Explore the reasons for launching the Second Crusade*
- *Consider the motives of Louis VII and Conrad of Germany for going on Crusade*
- *Explore the role of Pope Eugenius III and Saint Bernard in launching the Crusade*
- *Understand the major events of the Second Crusade*
- *Consider the reasons why the Crusade failed to achieve its goals*

Introduction

Edessa was captured by Imad al-Din Zengi on 24th December 1144. The immediate response by the other Crusader states appears to have been somewhat muted. Raymond, Prince of Antioch did little, partly through his hostility to Joscelin II of Edessa, partly through his own lack of military strength. The new Byzantine Emperor Manuel was still trying to secure his own position at Constantinople. The kingdom of Jerusalem too lacked an established ruler; Fulk had died the year before leaving his son Baldwin III, now aged around thirteen years old, under the supervision of Queen Melisende as regent.

The response of Jerusalem was not to send an army north to recover Edessa. Instead it was decided to send an embassy to the Pope and request that a new crusade be dispatched. This appeal reached the Pope in Italy in September 1145; some nine months after the capture of Edessa.

A New Pope

The new Pope was Eugenius III who had only been appointed a few months before the Jerusalem embassy reached him. Eugenius was not based in Rome, but rather in the town of Viterbo. His predecessor, Pope Lucius had been killed in rioting by the people of Rome and likewise Eugenius too had been ejected from Rome. The King of Sicily was likewise hostile to the Pope and his own position in Italy was uncertain whilst the Sicilian king maintained his hostility. It is fair to say then that Eugenius had his own problems when the appeal arrived.

However, the Pope saw in the appeal opportunity. Pope Urban II had used the popularity engendered by the launching of the Crusade in order to re-establish himself at Rome. Eugenius could use the same method in order to reassert and consolidate his position.

The Pope evolved a plan. Whilst he would encourage the French to undertake the crusade, he would likewise encourage the Germans to assist him in dealing with Sicily and help to restore him to his rightful place in Rome. The Sicilian king, Roger II, had offered to help with the crusade. His help was rejected by Eugenius III. In addition to his hostility to the Pope, Roger II; as a cousin of Bohemund, had a claim on the city of Antioch that he would like to assert. The Pope requested help from the kings of France and of Germany.

The French: Louis VII's motivations and response

The embassy sent from Jerusalem continued in its journey to France. The French king, Louis VII was young, aged about twenty five. On one hand he was a good choice to lead the crusade. He was pious. He was the overlord of many of the nobles of the Crusader states. He was also rumoured to be suffering guilt from his earlier actions. Louis VII had a feud with the Count of Champagne and during a raid had apparently burned down a church in Vitry, killing those inside. Louis VII was also willing to go and had announced a few months before news of Edessa that he wished to go on pilgrimage to the Holy lands.

Louis VII summoned his vassal lords to a meeting at Christmas 1145. At this meeting he told them he desired to go on crusade and urged the lords to join him. The response was somewhat muted however. Disappointed, Louis VII announced he would appeal to them again in three months' time. In the meantime he requested assistance from the leading Churchman of Europe; not the Pope, but Saint Bernard, Abbot of Clairvaux.

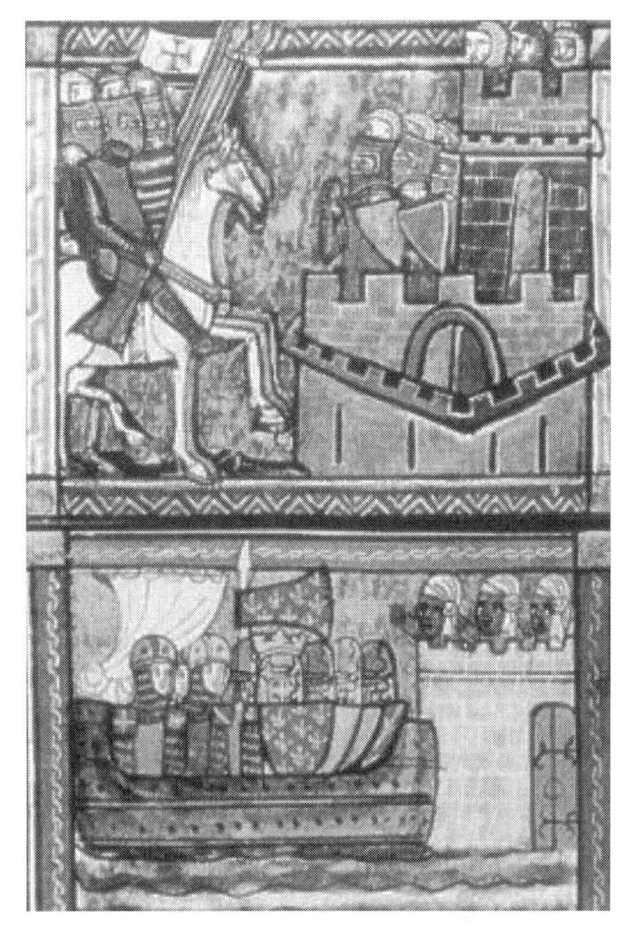

The role of Saint Bernard

Saint Bernard of Clairvaux was a legend. He had solved Churchly disputes in Europe and intervened in secular matters. He had encouraged the establishment of monasteries and churchly foundations far and wide. He had helped to write the rules of the Military Order of the Templars. His teachings had inspired a new wave of students in the Christian faith; including one pupil of his, the Pope himself.

Saint Bernard welcomed the opportunity to preach the Crusade. At Vézèlay on the 31st March 1146, In the presence of the French king and many of his lords, Saint Bernard encouraged people to take the cross and join the Crusade in return for the promise of remission of sins. The response was huge. Many thousands of French took the cross then or soon after including;

- Louis VII – the King of France

- Robert, Count of Dreux – the brother of Louis VII

- Alfonso-Jordan, Count of Toulouse – son of Raymond of Saint Gilles, born in the East in 1105

- William, Count of Nevers – son of William of Nevers killed in the 1101 Crusade

- Thierry of Flanders – who had already been to Jerusalem in 1139

The entire French expedition probably numbered some between 15,000-20,000 soldiers. Not all who went were soldiers. Pilgrims accompanied the crusade in large numbers and also several noble women. The wives and families of many great lords accompanied them; including Queen Eleanor of Aquitaine.

The Germans: Conrad III's motivations and response

News of the crusade call reached Germany. Saint Bernard decided to continue his recruitment tour through Northern France and into Germany. In Germany the fervour encouraged by the Crusade had already found victims. Like in the First Crusade, mobs of Germans were encouraged to attack the Jewish community in the towns and cities along the Rhine River. One Monk named Rudolf incited mobs to conduct massacres of the Jews in Cologne, Mainz, Strasbourg and other places. Hundreds, if not thousands were killed. Some local bishops sought to protect Jews but it took Saint Bernard to confront Rudolf himself and force him to return to his monastery.

Conrad III was king of the Germans. He was aged in his late fifties, had been king of the Germans since 1138. He had experience of the Holy land, having travelled there in 1124 to take part in the fighting of that year at the siege of Tyre. Conrad's sister was also married to the Byzantine Emperor Manuel; therefore it could be argued that Conrad would be a very useful figurehead for the crusade.

Conrad thought was faced with problems at home. Several of his lords and family members contested his position in Germany and, despite being king of the Germans, he had not as yet been crowned by the Pope as Emperor, which further reduced his authority (indeed, he would never be crowned Emperor).

The Pope also did not want Conrad to go on Crusade. He wanted Conrad instead to come to Italy and deal with Roger II of Sicily. In turn he would be crowned Emperor. Unfortunately, this plan was not shared by Saint Bernard. He urged the Germans to join the crusade – either to Palestine, or to wage war on the pagan tribes of Eastern Europe and the Baltic.

Initially, Conrad showed some reluctance to go on the crusade, but this was probably a façade. Saint Bernard visited Conrad in October 1146 and again on Christmas day 1146 and urged him to join the crusade and the Abbot of Clairvaux continued to recruit in Germany in 1147 encouraging Germans to go East – either to the Holy lands or to Eastern Europe and the Baltic to crusade (unsuccessfully) against the Pagan Slav tribes.

Conrad officially took the cross on the 27th December 1146. His chief political rival in Germany, Welf, Duke of Bavaria had taken the cross, three days earlier, on the 24th December 1146. Conrad's nominated heir, his nephew Frederick of Swabia, likewise took the cross at the same time as Conrad. With both his heir and his rival as crusaders, Conrad had ensured that his kingdom would be secured in his absence. By taking part in the Second Crusade, Conrad had help to unite his kingdom in the face of internal division.

Conrad's army was larger than the French, at least 20,000 soldiers with many pilgrim non-combatants in attendance. It would leave in May 1147, some months before the French. If Conrad announced that he would go on crusade only five months before, then it would have been near impossible to raise such an army and fund it in such a short period of time. Conrad must have planned to join the Crusade much earlier, before he met Saint Bernard.

The role of the Pope

Pope Eugenius III did not conduct a papal tour like his predecessor Pope Urban II. Eugenius preferred to remain for much of the years 1145-1147 in Italy. Perhaps he was preoccupied with a return to Rome. He did succeed in this briefly over Christmas 1146, but was forced out again by the people of Rome soon after. In 1147 however, Eugenius did travel north of the Alps in 1147. He did not meet Conrad III, but rather spent several months in France meeting with King Louis VII and Saint Bernard at Clairvaux in April 1147 and King Louis again in June 1147 at Saint Denis. Louis was officially appointed as leader of the Crusade, given a papal banner and a relic to wear around his neck by the Pope himself.

The *Quantum praedecessores*

On the 1st December 1145 the Pope Eugenius III announced his declaration for a new crusade. The *Quantum praedecessores* was a Papal Bull; a commandment and instruction for those Christians who accepted the Pope as their leader. By issuing such a commandment, the Pope was laying claims to secular as well as spiritual leadership.

The Pope based his authority as leader of the Christian faith; his authority was absolute in this matter as he himself states *'by the authority given us by God'*.

Eugenius III argued in the *Quantum praedecessores* that the loss of the city of Edessa was a threat and challenge to all of Christianity and that Western Europeans should seek to aid in the defence of the Eastern Church. The Crusade was both a holy and necessary work that Christians should undertake.

In turn the Pope offered certain benefits to those who undertook this service. All confessed sins would be forgiven. Those who went on this crusade then were guaranteed a place in heaven if they died attempting this duty. The loss of Edessa was due to lack of faith; therefore those luxuries that distracted people from their faith were also discouraged. Luxuries such as colourful or fur lined clothes were frowned upon, as were weapons and armour that were ostentatious in their decoration, hunting dogs and hawks were also considered to be demonstrations in the love of the world over the love of God.

More practical assistance was also provided. Those who had debts would be exempt from paying interest on these debts. Likewise any loan taken out to finance a crusader would be guaranteed interest free. These loans could be obtained by loaning land and property to the church in return for money. The families and properties of those on crusade would likewise be under the protection of the Church in their absence and no crusader could be prosecuted in a law court once that had taken the cross. The crusade then offered an opportunity to those in trouble with the law or those heavily in debt to escape from these problems.

> **Task: essay style response**
>
> Write a response to the following question;
>
> *To what extent do you agree with Pope Eugenius' stated views that the loss of Edessa was due to the sins of Christians and 'a threat to all Christianity?'*
>
> Write your response in no more than 750 words

Departures

We shall now trace the journeys of the major Crusade forces to Palestine. All left in 1147 and arrived in the Crusader States in 1148, approximately a year after they set out.

The English, Flemish and Frisian Fleet

The French and the Germans were not the only people to go on crusade. During the spring of 1147 and shortly before the armies of Conrad and Louis marched, a fleet of ships from England and Northern Continental Europe set sail for Palestine. The fleet was commanded by a variety of minor lords and bishops and sailed south along the coasts of France and Spain before landing in Portugal.

The Count of Portugal was Afonso-Henry and he aspired to create a Christian kingdom. The important city of Lisbon was held by Muslim forces, and in order to achieve his aim of founding a Kingdom, Alfonso-Henry desired to capture this city. Alfonso-Henry requested the help of the Crusader fleet, and for five months the Portuguese along with the Crusaders laid siege to Lisbon.

Towards the end of September 1147, after a siege of five months the city of Lisbon surrendered, refusing to abide by the terms of the surrender the Crusaders undertook a massacre of the Muslim garrison, despite the wishes of Alfonso-Henry. This did not prevent Alfonso-Henry inviting many of the Crusaders to remain as settlers in Portugal. Of the approximately ten thousand crusaders in the fleet, only about half continued their journey to Palestine, arriving there around April 1148.

The expeditions march to Constantinople

Conrad and his large army left Ratisbon in Germany in late May 1147 and marched slowly across Europe to Constantinople. The slowness of the march suggests that the expedition was huge, as Conrad's forces only travelled at a rate of approximately ten miles a day; much slower than the largest contingents of the First Crusade, and along much the same route. Additional evidence for the size of the expedition can be found in the almost constant struggle to find food whilst on their journey. Lack of food may have provided an additional motive for the common rank and file of the crusade to take part. Europe was suffering from food shortages caused by crop failures in the years preceding the expedition. The German force was probably over 20,000 strong, not including non-combatant pilgrims that travelled with the expedition for security.

The German Crusade crossed through Hungary with little trouble, but on arrival in the Byzantine Empire around the 20th July 1147, the Crusaders soon began stealing from local villagers and even murdering those that tried to prevent them. The German leadership swore an oath of non-injury to the Byzantine Emperor but in practice this oath accomplished little, as did the knowledge that Conrad's sister was the Empress of the Byzantine Empire.

At the town of Philippopolis the Germans burned down a large part of the town in part caused by their reaction to a local juggler. Near Adrianople a German lord was murdered by Byzantine bandits that preyed in turn on the crusaders. In reprisal Frederick of Swabia led a force that destroyed a nearby monastery, killing a large number of local monks.

The Emperor Manuel demanded that the crusaders cross into Asia Minor away from Constantinople. The Germans refused. It was therefore in a bad temper that the Germans arrived outside Constantinople in early September 1147.

King Louis VII left Saint-Denis with papal blessing on the 8th June 1147. His army was smaller than the German army, but it was more professional and more disciplined. It was also accompanied by a force of knights Templar. Following in Conrad's footsteps, the French travelled to Ratisbon, arriving there on the 29th June 1147 and travelled through Hungary in August, arriving at the border of the Byzantine Empire at the end of August.

The French marched quicker than the Germans, but found that the Byzantine peasantry were hostile to them, for the most part because of the behaviour of the Germans. Louis VII's army however avoided any major incidents on their march, arriving at Constantinople on the 4th October 1147.

The march across Asia Minor

The Germans had squabbled with the Byzantines, they had squabbled amongst themselves and they squabbled with some advance units of the French army that caught up with them at Constantinople, refusing to share food or even let them join their expedition.

Manuel used a combination of bribery and threat to get the Germans transported over the Bosporus in September 1147 and advised them to keep to the coastal roads and delay the continuation of their journey until the French could join them. Manuel had recently fought several inconclusive wars against the Seljuk Turks and realised that the bulk of the crusade forces would suffer in a fight with the Seljuk Turks. The Germans travelled to the city of Nicaea in early October but instead of following the advice of Manuel the Germans determined to follow the more dangerous central road that the First Crusaders had followed. The German pilgrims would take the coastal road and these forces would later join the French.

Disaster was not long in coming. Near the town of Dorylaeum on the 25th October 1147 the Seljuk Turks attacked. In the days that followed the Germans were slaughtered. Defeated in battle, around ninety percent of the German army was lost. Those with good horses and good armour; Conrad, Frederick and other lords managed to escape, but not unscathed. Conrad was shot twice with arrows, once in the head. He was seriously injured but would survive.

King Louis VII reached Constantinople on the 4th October 1147, some of his men suggested that Manuel should be attacked, his city captured. Louis refused, though later events made him regret this decision.

The French were ferried over to Asia Minor and hurried to catch up with the Germans, as rumours were reaching the French that the Germans were in danger. Louis arrived at Nicaea to meet the shattered remnants of the German army straggling back at the beginning of November. The advice of Manuel was now heeded. The combined armies marched south along the coast to the city of Ephesus. Here Conrad was taken ill and, still suffering from his wounds was collected by the Byzantine Emperor himself who transported him back to Constantinople. As a result of this enforced leave of absence, other Germans too deserted.

The Crusade continued, again heading inland, the Crusaders suffered from constant Turkish attacks, possibly aided by local Byzantines. In January Louis himself was almost killed in battle and losses amongst the French were heavy. Early in February 1148, the crusade reached the port town of Attalia – a Byzantine city surrounded by hostile Turkish groups. Here still suffering from attacks the decision was made by Louis to use all available ships to transport as much of the army to Outremer.

In practice this meant that the King, his household knights and other picked forces were transported. The infantry and poor were abandoned to march as best as they could to Antioch where they would join the king. Louis VII reached the Antiochene port of Saint Symeon on 19th March 1148. When he was re-joined by his infantry in May, only about half of them had made it.

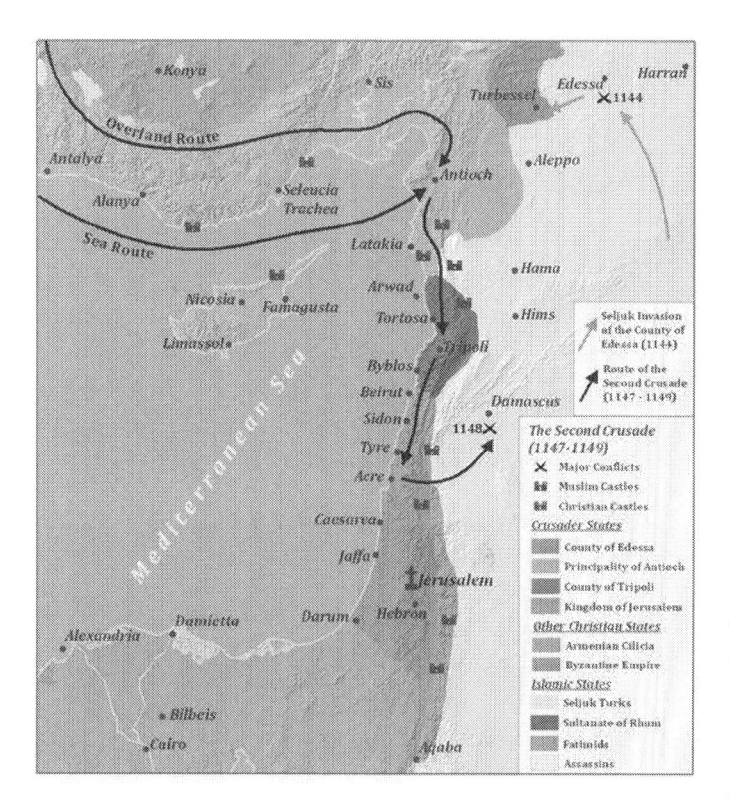

Hesitation in the North

Louis VII arrived at Saint Symeon in March 1148 he travelled to Antioch and there awaited the other French elements that remained. All told Louis had perhaps two thousand knights and perhaps an equal amount of infantry. This was a small army, but the large numbers of knights meant that it could still be powerfully effective in battle, especially when used for attack.

The Prince of Antioch, Raymond of Poitiers welcomed Louis and his entourage. He was a French noble in his own right and uncle to Queen Eleanor. Raymond urged Louis to fight here in the north – against Nur-Al Din of Aleppo who was even now attacking the territories of Antioch as well as what was left of the County of Edessa. Other lords in Northern Syria also appealed to Louis for aid, both Joscelin, Count of Edessa, now holed up in Turbessel and Raymond Count of Tripoli sent requests for assistance.

Three main strategic choices were presented to Louis VII;

- To attack Nur Al-Din at Aleppo (Raymond of Antioch)

- To attempt to recover Edessa, the loss of which why the Crusade was called; (Joscelin of Edessa)

- To recover the lost castle of Montferrand (Raymond of Tripoli)

King Louis VII however hesitated. None of these plans really appealed to him. He could raid with his knights, but sieges were out of the question given his lack of infantry. Louis instead argued that as a crusader and pilgrim it was his duty to go first to Jerusalem and pray at the holy places. King Conrad had been transported by sea to Jerusalem in March 1148 and an embassy was sent, headed by the Patriarch of Jerusalem, summoned Louis to come to Jerusalem. This embassy, along with Louis' pilgrim duties gave him just the excuse he needed to leave Antioch.

It was rumoured that Raymond of Antioch was having an affair with Queen Eleanor. These rumours gained weight when Eleanor refused to travel to Jerusalem, declaring instead that she would remain in Antioch. Louis had to forcibly remove his wife from Antioch.

Towards fiasco

Louis and his French army travelled south to Jerusalem, reaching the Holy city in May 1148. Raymond of Antioch refused to journey with him. Perhaps he had been having an affair with Queen Eleanor, but it is probably more likely that Raymond was needed to defend his own lands. Likewise Joscelin, Count of what was left of his territories. By Louis headed south it appeared that the recapture of Edessa would not be attempted.

Raymond of Tripoli also remained absent from the assembly at Jerusalem. He faced a potential rival in the form of Alfonso-Jordan, count of Toulouse. As the legitimate son of Raymond of St. Gilles he had a better claim to the County of Tripoli than did Raymond himself; who was grandson of Raymond of St. Gilles' bastard son Bertrand. Alfonso-Jordan did not have time to press his claim however. He died soon after his arrival in Palestine; perhaps of appendicitis but Raymond was accused of poisoning his rival. This claim was loudly broadcast by many including Alfonso-Jordan's son Bertrand who too had come on Crusade and this claim encouraged Raymond of Tripoli to absent himself from the crusade.

A great assembly was held in June 1148 at Jerusalem. Louis and his French army joined with Conrad, his remnant and the Germans, Flemish and English who had come by sea from Lisbon joined with the army of Jerusalem and those knights of the military orders. All together the force was large, perhaps twenty thousand strong. The decision was made to attack Damascus.

Some argue that the decision to attack Damascus was mystery. In fact, there were many good reasons to attack Damascus;

- Damascus was wealthy

- Damascus was close to Jerusalem and a threat to the long term security of the Holy city

- The ruler of Damascus, Unur lacked Muslim allies

- Damascus had often been a target of conquest for Jerusalem in the 1120s and 1130s

- By capturing the city, the Muslims of Egypt and Northern Syria could not easily communicate and work together

However, there were also many good reasons to not attack Damascus;

- Damascus, as a large and wealthy city would be a difficult place to capture

- The main threat to the Crusader States was Nur Al-Din, not Unur

- The Crusade had been launched to deal with the loss of Edessa and the threat to Northern Syria, Unur of Damascus had not been involved in the capture of Edessa

- By attacking Damascus, Unur would be sure to seek allies; including Nur Al-Din

Damascus

Damascus was indeed a prize worth taking. A large city wealthy in its own right, the crusaders and Jerusalemites could not agree on who would control the city after it had been captured.

One faction; the Kings Louis, Conrad and Baldwin III all favoured the city being granted to Thierry, Count of Flanders for him to rule as a semi-independent state. The other faction was composed of the majority of the nobility of Jerusalem, who wanted Guy of Briseberre, Lord of Beirut to rule the city as part of the Kingdom of Jerusalem. Divisions were apparent in the commanders then before the army left Jerusalem.

The Crusade began its attack on Damascus in late July 1148. It would last for five days. Upon realising that he was the target, Unur did what was expected and called upon Nur Al-Din for assistance. Nur Al-Din agreed and sent reinforcements to Damascus.

The crusaders began to clear the suburbs of Damascus and fought several skirmishes with the Damascene army. The crusade army approached Damascus from the south and here found access both to food supplies and water. Attacks continued as reinforcements entered Damascus from the north and immediately continued to attack the crusaders. But on the 27th July the decision was made to move the entire Crusade army to the East of Damascus. Here the crusaders found themselves opposite the strongest parts of the city walls and also had no easy access to water.

This position was soon found to be totally unsuitable. The Crusaders were also disheartened by rumours of the arrival of Nur Al-Din with a large army from Aleppo, the continued harassment by the army of Damascus and the lack of food and water. Rumours also spread that the Jerusalem nobles were bribed to mislead the Western leaders. The decision was made to retreat. The crusade army left Damascus five days after arriving before the city walls. They retreated back to Jerusalem, harassed all the way by Muslim soldiers who killed and injured many.

The expedition had ended in complete failure. Conrad left Jerusalem almost immediately, leaving the port of Acre by ship in early September 1148, he stayed at Constantinople for Christmas, ensuring good relations with Manuel and forming an alliance against Roger II of Sicily, who had invaded the Byzantine Empire whilst the Second Crusade was in progress.

King Louis remained in Jerusalem for a few more months. He stayed for Easter 1149 and left soon after, then returned home in Sicilian ships offered by Roger II of Sicily. These ships were attacked by a Byzantine squadron on the return leg and by the time Louis reached Italy, he was ready to make an alliance with Roger II against the Byzantine Empire. Increasingly, he had blamed the Byzantines for the failure of the crusade. They had not been particularly helpful in the march across Asia Minor it is true. But the decision to attack Damascus had nothing to do with Manuel.

Only Bertrand, the son of Alfonso-Jordan remained in Outremer after all the others had gone home and he soon had cause to regret this decision. Bertrand decided to attack Raymond of Tripoli. Seizing control of a castle, he repelled Raymond's attacks and threatened Tripoli. Raymond sought allies, namely Unur of Damascus, who with the assistance of Nur Al-Din destroyed the castle in a short siege and captured Bertrand. Bertrand would spend the next twelve years as a prisoner in Aleppo.

Task: Essay style response

Write a response to the following question;

The Historian Sir Steven Runciman used the word 'fiasco' to describe the Second Crusade. To what extent do you think this view is accurate?

Write your response in no more than 750 words

PART FOUR: The Crusader States

PART FOUR: The Crusader States

4.1 Antioch and Tripoli

4.2 The rulers of Jerusalem 1143-1185

4.3 Administering Outremer

4.4 The Defence of the Holy Land – Castles, Sea power and ports

4.5 The Defence of the Holy Land – Military Orders

4.1 Antioch and Tripoli

In this topic we will;

- Understand an overview of major events that took place in the states of Antioch and Tripoli
- Explore the challenges Antioch and Tripoli faced during their foundation to 1150
- Consider the view that the problems faced by the rulers of Antioch and Tripoli were largely self-inflicted

Antioch: Introduction

Interventions at Antioch by the kings of Jerusalem

Baldwin I (1100-1118)

- 1109/1110
- 1111
- 1115

Baldwin II (1118-1131)

- 1119-1126
- 1130-1131

Fulk (1131-1143)

- 1131/2
- 1133

Baldwin III (1143-1163)

- 1149
- 1150
- 1152
- 1157
- 1158
- 1161

Antioch was established as a Latin principality in June 1098 when the 1st Crusade captured the city after a long siege lasting from October 1097 to June 1098. Antioch was a small principality, but it was wealthy and well-populated. In addition to being a Patriarchal Seat, Antioch was renowned for its silk and textile production. The Principality comprised of the Lower Orontes Valley, the Plains of Antioch and the Amanus Mountains. It had several ports including St. Symeon, Lattakieh and Alexandretta.

Like the neighbouring county of Edessa, Antioch's population was largely comprised of Muslims, Armenians and Greeks. Unlike in other parts of the Holy land, the indigenous population was called upon to provide leaders as well as manpower. Antioch thrived through a policy of combining local and Latin institutional practices. Antioch also had an internal cohesion which was often lacked by the other Latin states. In 1135 for example the Antiochene barons refused to accept Byzantine authority despite the will of Alice, widow of Bohemund II. Despite this unity, Antioch often required external assistance from the kings of Jerusalem as disasters and tragedies often left Antioch without a ruling Prince.

However, the city of Antioch had been part of the Byzantine Empire until its capture by the Turks in 1084. Many of its inhabitants still therefore saw themselves as part of the Empire and after the occupation of the city by the crusaders, the Byzantine Emperors Alexius, John and Manuel all made attempts to assert their overlordship of the city; with some success. The Princes of Antioch accepted Byzantine overlordship in 1137,1145 and 1158-9.

Antioch was defended by a series of castles controlling the borders of the principality and important strategic points such as the Orontes valley. Despite a great deal of warfare, Antioch also had some good relationships with their Muslim neighbours. Local alliances were made between lords of the border regions of Antioch and their Muslim neighbours in the territories of Damascus and Mosul. These local agreements were vital for the continuation of trade in northern Syria as Antioch thrived on trade that passed through it on its way to the ports of the coast.

Antioch under Bohemund (1098-1101)

It is fair to say that the prize of Antioch was for Bohemund greater than his vow of completing his vow as a crusader. When the 1st crusade left Antioch for Jerusalem, Bohemund refused to go, only journeying to Jerusalem after the city had been taken. Instead Bohemund focused on establishing a new principality.

Basing his new state on the city of Antioch, Bohemund sought to extend the extent of his territories, not by attacking Muslim held territories, but by attacking Byzantine possessions in Cilicia. In this however Bohemund was not successful. Seeking to aid the Armenians of Melitene against the Danishmend Turks, Bohemund could not fulfil his planned occupation of Cilicia and instead ended up being captured by the Turks. Imprisoned from 1100-1103Bohemund did not long remain in the East. Associated with the defeat of Edessa at the battle of Harran, Bohemund left Antioch in 1104 and never returned to the Holy land.

With the death of Godfrey in 1100 the Patriarch of Jerusalem, Daimbert called upon Bohemund to seize power. Daimbert wrote Bohemund a letter instructing him to waylay Baldwin and prevent him leaving Edessa; with force if necessary. This letter never reached Bohemund and eventually fell into the hands of Baldwin, who used it to oust Daimbert from his Patriarchal seat. In the event, when Baldwin marched southwards to Jerusalem to become king, Bohemund was on the campaign that saw him captured and imprisoned.

The Battle of Menbij, 1108

The battle of Menbij in 1108 is a prime example of the willingness of both Christians and Muslims to make alliances across religious divides.

On one side Baldwin Le Bourg of Edessa and Jawali, sometime Atabeg of Mosul fought against an army led by Ridwan of Aleppo and Tancred of Antioch.

Each army numbered about 2000 soldiers. After a hard fought battle and heavy casualties on both sides Ridwan and Tancred were victorious. Baldwin and Tancred were only reconciled after Jawali was withdrawn from Mosul and replaced by a new atabeg, Mawdud.

Antioch under Tancred (1101-1103 & 1104-1112)

According to one historian, Tancred was 'the real founder of the principality of Antioch' (Tyerman, 2007 p190). Tancred ruled as regent during Bohemund's captivity (1101-1103) and as ruler from 1105-1112 and there is much justification for Tyerman's assertion. Tancred recovered Cilicia from Byzantine control and extended the territory of the principality eastward after victory at the battle of Artah in 1105. Tancred was also *de facto* ruler of Edessa from 1104-1108 when the county was governed by Richard of Salerno, Tancred's appointee. Tancred continued Bohemund's policy of hostility to the Byzantine Empire. Throughout his career as ruler of Antioch, Tancred followed Bohemund's policy which was;

> *"Internally to consolidate the administration of the principality and to Latinize the Church, and externally to enrich himself at the expense of the Byzantines and of the neighbouring Muslim princes."*

Runciman 1954, Book II, p33

In 1101 Tancred captured Raymond of Toulouse and released him only after Raymond promised to withdraw his army from Lattakieh. In the same year conquered Cilicia, managing to detach the region from Byzantine control. With the help of a Genoese fleet, Tancred seized Lattakieh from the Byzantines 1103. In 1103 when Bohemund was ransomed through the efforts of Baldwin I and Bernard, the Patriarch of Antioch, Tancred who had not lifted a finger to help his uncle nonetheless remained in Antioch. Tancred and Bohemund were evidently reconciled by 1105, when Bohemund left Antioch never to return and left Tancred in charge.

Tancred resumed his lordship of Antioch at a dangerous time for the principality. Cilicia had been lost to the Byzantine Empire in 1104 and in the same year Ridwan of Aleppo led a raid that penetrated Antioch almost to the city walls. However, Tancred enhanced his reputation as a feared battlefield leader when he decisively defeated Ridwan at the battle of Artah in 1105, soon after Tancred and Ridwan agreed to a truce which allowed Tancred to focus on extending his principality by capturing the city of Apamea in 1106 and reconquering Cilicia from the Byzantine Empire between the years 1107-1109

Tancred also managed at the end of his rule to repel the Muslim counterattacks led by Mawdud of Mosul in the years 1110-1113.

Antioch under Richard of Salerno (1112-1119)

In 1112 Tancred died, possibly of Typhoid at the age of 36, Richard of Salerno became Prince of Antioch. He was helped in his first days as Prince of Antioch by the deaths of both Ridwan of Aleppo and Mawdud of Mosul in 1113. Ridwan died of an illness, Mawdud was murdered by an assassin in Damascus. Their immediate successors were distracted and allowed Richard to go on the offensive.

Despite some alliances with local Muslim lords, Richard of Salerno is principally remembered for two battles; Tel Danith, which he won, and the Field of Blood, in which he and almost the entire Antiochene army was destroyed.

In 1115 Richard won a major victory over Bursuq of Hamadan at the battle of Tel Danith, which marks the final attempt of the Seljuk Sultans of Baghdad attempting to recover Northen Syria. However this victory was overshadowed by Richard's defeat and death at the *Ager Sanguinis*; The Field of Blood in 1119 by Il-Ghazi of Mardin. According to Runciman, Il-Ghazi wasted his victory by retiring with his spoils and his captives (most of whom were tortured to death) and leaving the city of Antioch unmolested.

Tyerman disputes this however;

> "Even this (defeat) revealed the principalities strength…..Baldwin II contrived to retrieve the situation through the continued resistance of the frontier garrisons buying him time and the efficiency of the general mobilization he ordered at Antioch".

Tyerman 2007,p191

Ager Sanguinis, the Field of Blood 1119

The Field of Blood was a great disaster for the principality of Antioch and resulted in decades of regencies for the state and for years after required the presence of Baldwin II of Jerusalem in the city to oversee the principality when he should have been overseeing his own kingdom.

Il Ghazi the Ortoquid, Atabeg of Aleppo made alliance with Toghtekin Atabeg of Damascus and the emir of Shaizar and invaded the principality of Antioch with an army between 30-40,000 strong. Richard of Salerno refused to await reinforcements coming up from Jerusalem and Tripoli and led the Antiochene army of 700 cavalry and 4000 infantry out to defend his lands. On the 28th June 1119 the Anticohenes were surrounded by Il Ghazi and were massacred. Richard died on fought underneath his battle standard.

The regency of Baldwin II 1119-1126

The death of Richard of Salerno and almost all of the Antiochene aristocracy caused a great succession crisis at Antioch. The rightful heir, Bohemund II was aged ten and living in Italy. Until he came of age Baldwin II would act as regent in his stead when present, or when absent, the Patriarch of Antioch Bernard would be regent.

Baldwin II also selected eligible men from his own retinue and from those others at hand, including western pilgrims and married them to the widows of the knights killed at the Field of Blood. This was necessary to ensure that the lands of Antioch should have leaders again as soon as possible. Baldwin II also fought Il Ghazi and Toghtekin to a draw in 1119 at the battle of Hab and forced them to withdraw from the principality of Antioch, a truce being made in 1120.

In 1125 Baldwin II led a combined army from all the states of Outremer against Il-Bursuqi atabeg of Mosul and Aleppo to victory at the battle of Azaz. Il-Bursuqi had united the Muslims of Northern Syria and this unity presented a grave threat to the Christian states of Outremer.

Antioch under Bohemund II (1126-1130)

The short lived reign of Prince Bohemund II (Son of Bohemund) had at first promised so much. His untimely death in battle in 1130 however cut short his life as well as his reign and resulted in an unwelcome and untimely regency. At the age of eighteen, Bohemund II left Italy with a small army and fleet and journeyed to Antioch to assume his title. On his arrival Bohemund was met by the then regent Baldwin II and cemented ties with the King of Jerusalem by marrying Baldwin's daughter Alice.

Bohemund II began as Prince of Antioch well. In 1126 he captured the town of Kafartab and raided the territory of Aleppo in 1127. However, Bohemund II refused to co-operate with Joscelin of Edessa in 1130 and lost his life in battle against the Danishmend Turks. Bohemund's head was embalmed and sent to the Caliph at Baghdad as a trophy. Bohemund's death left his young widow Alice and their baby daughter Constance. Alice tried to maintain her independence but was forced to abandon this stance by both her father Baldwin II and the Antiochene elite.

The Regency of Fulk 1131-1136

In the five year period of 1131-1136 Baldwin II's successor King Fulk acted as regent in Antioch. During this period the principality suffered some erosion of its territory to both its Muslim neighbours and Armenian princelings seeking the independence of Cilicia. The Byzantine Empire was also increasing its authority in Cilicia during the reign of the Emperor John (1118-1143). It was clear that the Byzantine presence would soon be felt in Antioch. Alice offered to marry her daughter Constance to the Byzantine Prince Manuel (and future Emperor 1143-1180). It was clear to Fulk, who had his own kingdom to govern, that Antioch needed a new Prince. Following his own example, Fulk determined that Constance should be married to a well-connected noble from the West.

Antioch under Raymond of Poitiers (1136-1149)

Raymond of Poitiers journeyed from France, summoned to assume the title of Prince of Antioch. On is arrival he married the young daughter of Bohemund II, Constance. Raymond of Poitiers was connected by birth to both the royal families of England and France. His arrival was resented by many however, including the Emperor John of the Byzantine Empire. In 1137, John besieged Antioch and only lifted the siege when Raymond paid homage to the Emperor and recognised him as the overlord of Antioch. In 1138 Raymond and Joscelin II of Edessa accompanied the Imperial army in an attack on Shaizar. The attack was unsuccessful and Raymond was only allowed to remain in control of Antioch if he continued in his allegiance to the Emperor.

In 1142 the Emperor John returned to Antioch and demanded that Raymond hand the city over. Raymond refused and the Emperor raided the territory of the principality before retiring to winter in Cilicia. Had the Emperor returned in 1143 it is unlikely Raymond would have succeeded in his resistance, however this was averted by the death of the Emperor John in 1143 as a result of a hunting accident. Raymond participated in the Second Crusade but was killed in battle at Inab in 1149.

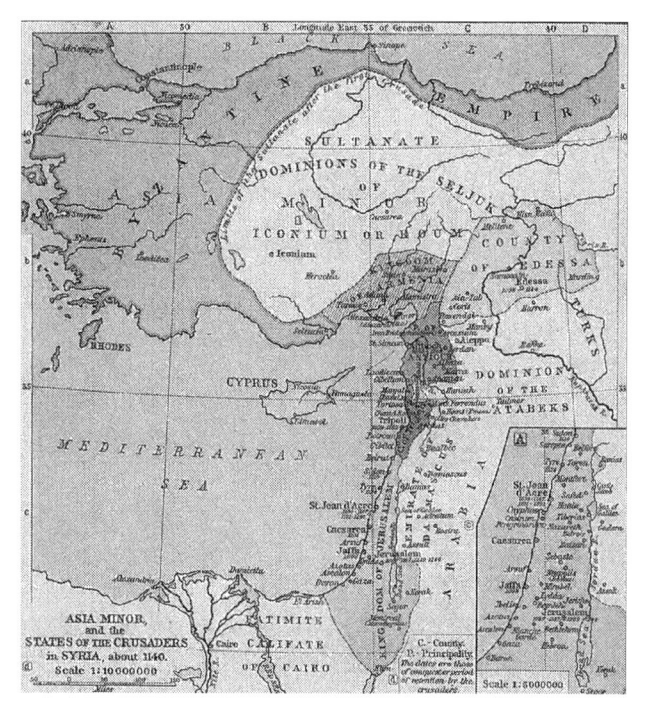

The County of Tripoli

Despite dying before the conquest of the new county was complete, the County of Tripoli was established by Count Raymond of Toulouse. Before setting out on the 1st Crusade, Raymond had sworn that he would never return to his wealthy lands in Southern France. The establishment of Tripoli therefore was a deliberate act consistent with both Raymond's intent as well as the reality that the Lords of the 1st Crusade were establishing Latin ruled states in the Holy Land.

The Rulers of Tripoli

- *1102-1105 Raymond of Toulouse*
- *1105-1109 William-Jordan*
- *1109-1112 Bertrand*
- *1112-1137 Pons*
- *1137-52 Raymond II*
- *1152-1187 Raymond III*
- *1187-1233 Bohemund of Antioch*

Raymond had experienced some difficulties and frustrations in his plan after the capture of Jerusalem. He was unsuccessful in holding onto Antioch in 1098. Despite being offered the post, he was realist enough to realise that he was not popular enough to be ruler of Jerusalem. He had been ousted from the port of Lattakieh by Tancred and his association with the disastrous Lombard crusade of 1101 had damaged his prestige with the Byzantine Emperor Alexius. He managed to capture Tortosa in 1102 but this port was too small in itself to establish a state.

Tripoli was the principal port for the city of Damascus and it was this city that Raymond determined to capture. The Emir of Tripoli, Fakhr al-Mulk Abu Ali, had supported the advance of the 1st crusade and also the march of Baldwin from Edessa on his way to claim the throne of Jerusalem but had been forced into an alliance with the Fatamid Caliphate. The naval support that the Fatamids provided ensured that the city resisted Raymond of Toulouse. Raymond and his 300 men built a castle called Mt Pilgrim close to the city. Placed under blockade by land in 1103, Raymond died in 1105 with the city still uncaptured, despite defeating a large Muslim army from the cities of Damascus, Homs and Tripoli that tried to break the siege.

Since Raymond's legitimate son Alfonso-Jordan was still a child, Raymond was succeeded by William-Jordan, Count of Cerdagne. Another son, Bertrand was an adult and had been in charge of Toulouse since the launching of the 1st Crusade but he was illegitimate. Alfonso-Jordan was sent to Toulouse and replaced Bertrand, who came East to Outremer with a substantial army numbering 4000. Bertrand followed his father's policy of favouring the Byzantine Empire and went first to Constantinople to pledge his allegiance to the Emperor Alexius.

Somewhat conveniently, William-Jordan died soon after Bertrand arrived therefore leaving the way clear for an orderly succession. Tripoli held on until 1109 when almost the whole of the Latin East joined in the siege of Tripoli and, allied with naval assistance from the Italian city state of Genoa, finally the city of Tripoli surrendered. Although the surrender was largely peaceful the Genoese sailors rioted and burned the library of Tripoli as well as conducted a slaughter of some of the inhabitants of the city.

The county of Tripoli was finally established and Bertrand ruled the county until his death

---

The County of Tripoli A timeline

1102 Capture of Tortosa

1103 Capture of Jubail

1103-1109 Siege of Tripoli

1105 Death of Raymond of Toulouse

1109 Death of William-Jordan

1110 Work begins on Krak Des Chevalier

1112 Death of Bertrand

1144 Krak Des Chevalier granted to the Knights Hosptialler

1149 Unsuccessful attempt of Bertrand, Son of Alfonso-Jordan to oust Raymond II

1150 Tortosa granted to the Knights Templar

in 1112. The County of Tripoli was the smallest Latin state of the Holy land. It was primarily a coastal province stretching from Beirut in the south to Maraclea in the north. The famous castle Krak Des Chevaliers was in this county protecting the inland frontier.

Bertrand was succeeded by his son Pons who ruled from 1112-1137. Tripoli almost consistently followed the lead of the kingdom of Jerusalem, occasionally adopting a more independent stance. However Tripoli was the weakest of the states of the Holy lands and often required assistance from her neighbours. Aware of the danger presented by Zengi, in 1144 the Knights Hospitaller were granted large tracts of land and towns in the county. These possessions included Krak Des Chevaliers, whilst the Templars were granted control of Tortosa in the 1150s. Another town, Jubail (captured in 1103) was controlled by a Genoese family named Embriaco.

On the death of Pons, Raymond II became count of Tripoli. He ruled until 1152 when he was murdered by the Ismaili Sect called the Assassins. Raymond II had the dubious honour of being the first important Latin murdered by the Assassins. The response to this murder was horrific, in an attempt to find the killers, the Latins massacred all non Latins in Tripoli. The killers escaped.

The son of Raymond of Toulouse, Alfonso-Jordan returned to Tripoli during the 2nd Crusade, but he died suddenly in 1148. In 1149 Alfonso-Jordan's son Bertrand attempted to oust Raymond II and in response Raymond II called in Muslim assistance from Nur Al Din and Unur of Damascus to help him. With their help Bertrand was captured and spent the years 1149-1159 in captivity in Aleppo.

Task: Essay style response

Write a response to the following question;

To what extent do you agree with the view that the problems faced by the rulers of Antioch and Tripoli were largely self-inflicted?

Consider;

- The deaths in battle or by other misadventures
- *The need for regencies*
- *The threat posed by Muslim rulers*
- *Dealings with neighbouring Crusader states*

Write your response in no more than 750 words

4.2 The rulers of Jerusalem 1143-1185

In this topic we will;

- Understand the major events of the reigns of Kings Baldwin III, Amalric and Baldwin IV
- Consider the challenges presented to Jerusalem and responses to these challenges during these reigns

Introduction

In this section we will consider the major events of the reigns of three kings of Jerusalem who reigned from 1143-1185. These rulers; Baldwin III (1143-1162), Amalric (1162-1174) and Baldwin IV (1174-1185), had several common problems. All three died relatively young, all three faced challenges both within and from outside Jerusalem and all three attempted to evolve strategies to deal with these challenges. Despite their efforts in the face of increasing Muslim unity, all three kings all tried to seek assistance from Europe in the form of military assistance.

It is notable that the kings of Jerusalem received only sporadic assistance from individual lords and from crusades, the exception being the Second crusade, at the start of Baldwin III's reign, which ended in failure. The reigns of these kings did however see the military orders became increasingly important and influential throughout their reigns. We will explore the military orders more fully later in a later section.

Baldwin III (1143-1162)

Baldwin III had become king in 1143 at the age of thirteen. During the Second Crusade Baldwin III took part in the counsels and decision making, but we can safely query how much weight his opinion as an adolescent carried. Until the age of twenty two, Baldwin III shared his rule with his mother Melisende, who continued to act as regent for six years after Baldwin III officially came of age when he turned sixteen. Baldwin's early reign therefore was overshadowed by others.

After the combined armies of Jerusalem and the Second Crusade withdrew from Damascus in 1148, the kings of France and Germany made plans to return home, their reputations having taken a severe denting through the failure at Damascus. Like in the First Crusade, most of those crusaders who had travelled to Outremer had no desire to remain in the East and no large scale influx of settlers occurred. The manpower problems of the Crusader states would remain chronic, it was therefore less than ideal that Baldwin, now aged nineteen, would be required to deal with a crisis in Antioch.

Problems in Antioch

In Northern Syria, through 1148-1149, Raymond of Antioch had been attacked by Nur Al-Din. Raymond sought help were he could (including from the Shi'ite Muslim sect of the assassins) and fought back. At the battle of Inab on the 28th June 1149 Raymond and almost his entire army was surrounded and killed. Raymond's skull was set in a silver case by Nur Al-Din and sent as a gift to the Caliph of Baghdad. Joscelin, the Count of what was left of the County of Edessa was also captured in 1150. He would die in captivity, un-ransomed and forgotten in 1159.

Like his predecessors, Baldwin III therefore was faced with the problem of what to do with Antioch after its prince had been killed in battle. Baldwin III went to Antioch in the company of a group of Templar knights and managed to establish a truce with Nur Al-Din.

Antioch needed a new lord. The widow of Raymond of Antioch, Constance had four children. The eldest boy, Bohemund III was an infant, only five years old in 1149. Constance desired to rule as a regent, much like her aunt Melisende, but pressure remained strong for her to take a new husband who could provide the military leadership so needed for Antioch. Constance rejected several suitors from both Jerusalem and the Byzantine Empire but eventually settled on her choice in 1153. The controversial and troublesome Reynald of Chatillion, a relatively humble knight from France who had remained in Outremer after the Second Crusade. Perhaps it would have been better for the Crusader states if Constance had married someone else.

What was left of Edessa was sold off by Joscelin's wife to the Byzantine Empire – but lost to a combination of Muslim rulers including Nur Al-Din and Mas'ud, the Seljuk Sultan of Rum.

Problems in Tripoli

Another challenge presented itself in 1152. The crisis this time was in Tripoli. Whilst Baldwin III was on a visit to Tripoli that year, Raymond was suddenly killed by an assassin. The motive for this murder was never established. Baldwin's immediate response was to order a massacre of all Muslims in the walls of Tripoli in an outburst of latent racism that never succeeded in finding Raymond's killer. Like at Antioch, a regent was needed for Raymond of Tripoli's twelve year old son (also somewhat confusingly called Raymond). This son would be Raymond III of Tripoli, and Baldwin III undertook to become regent for Tripoli himself, along with his aunt Hodierna. Baldwin III could more easily be regent for Tripoli than he could be for Antioch. Tripoli was much closer to Jerusalem and its success or failure was more intertwined with that of Jerusalem. Baldwin III himself was also now twenty three in 1152 and king in his own right, having managed to assert his kingly authority over his mother Melisende.

Baldwin and Melisende

In 1152, Baldwin now aged twenty two, had still not been crowned as king of Jerusalem. In theory Baldwin shared power with his mother, the regent Queen Melisende. Melisende had a faction of Jerusalem nobility supporting her and Melisende was reluctant to surrender her position. Baldwin III had come of age when he reached sixteen, but Melisende managed to keep practical control of the kingdom with the assistance of the Patriarch of Jersualem and the constable of the kingdom, Miles de Plancy, however, the question of Baldwin's coronation could not be longer delayed.

An agreement was made that control of the kingdom of Jerusalem would be divided. Melisende would hold possession of Nablus, Jaffa (for Amalric, her younger son) and Jerusalem itself. Melisende would also be crowned alongside Baldwin III as Queen Mother.

For Baldwin and his supporters this was impractical as well as intolerable. Baldwin III could not effectively govern or finance his kingdom without possession of Jerusalem so Baldwin acted. He forced the Patriarch of Jerusalem to crown him in a private ceremony and along with the people of Jerusalem had to forcibly remove Melisende from the city. Melisende was pensioned off into political retirement with just the territory of Nablus.

Ascalon

Ascalon was a large and important port in southern Palestine. Despite many attempts, Ascalon had so far remained uncaptured and was held by Fatamid Egypt. However, Egypt was entering into a period of political instability as the Caliphs tried to reassert control over the powerful officials that had been effectively ruling Egypt in the name of the Caliph. In 1150 Baldwin III took advantage of this political instability to refortify the port town of Gaza in southern Palestine and close to Ascalon. From 1150 onwards both the Christian kings of Jerusalem and the Turks of Syria became increasingly involved in the battle to control the fate of Egypt as the Fatamid Caliphate deteriorated and collapsed.

The fortification of Gaza placed increasing pressure on Ascalon and by 1153 Baldwin III was ready to attack. Baldwin III Baldwin gathered a large army and gathered a wide range of siege engines. The siege began at the end of January and no help was able to arrive to relieve the port. Ascalon surrendered in August 1153. The final port in Palestine was now under Christian control. However, the capture of Ascalon hastened the breakdown of the integrity of Fatamid controlled Egypt.

Baldwin and Nur Al-Din

The capture of Ascalon strengthened the kingdom of Jerusalem in the south, but this victory was more than counterbalanced by the surrender of Damascus to Nur Al-Din in 1154. Nur Al-Din now controlled all major Muslim cities along the eastern frontier of Outremer; Edessa, Aleppo, Damascus and also was overlord and effective ruler of Mosul. This unity of these cities and territories was a serious threat to the Christian crusader states. However, Nur Al-Din was more interested with fighting against another Muslim rival, the New Seljuk Sultan of Rum, Kilij Arslan II and this fighting would keep Nur Al-Din busy through the years 1155-1156.

In 1157 Baldwin III was engaged with raiding Nur Al-Din's territory close to Damascus and helped the assassins to capture the fortress of Banyas on the Tripoli-Damascene border. Nur Al-Din attacked and partially burned Banyas, but further fighting that year was limited by a series of powerful earthquakes that devastated many towns and fortresses. Baldwin however, reinforced by Thierry of Flanders, on his third expedition and Reynald of Chatillion to the East attacked the town of Shaizar and tried to detach it from Nur Al-Din's control.

However no one could agree on who would control the place once it was captured.

Due to Nur Al-Din's illness and the damage caused by earthquakes, much time was spent rebuilding these places. Nur Al-Din was also taken seriously ill in 1157 and nearly died. This illness, along with the earthquakes prevented Nur Al-Din from attacking Outremer and although raids were exchanged in 1158, both Baldwin III and Nur Al-Din were keen to agree upon a truce agreed later in 1158.

Reynald of Chatillon and Manuel Comnenus

In 1156, Reynald of Chatillon, now Prince of Antioch, decided to launch an attack on the Byzantine island of Cyprus. One of the ways in which he raised funds He raised funds by beating the Patriarch of the city, smearing him with honey then leaving him exposed on a rooftop in the summer heat. Cyprus was attacked and devastated. Men were killed, women raped and children and old people murdered. Those that survived the three week attack had to ransom themselves and their livestock. The island would take decades to recover, and the act enraged Manuel, the Byzantine Emperor.

Manuel retaliated, seizing control of the neighbouring region of Cilicia and then in 1159 occupying the city of Antioch with his army. Manuel forced Reynald to submit to his authority and reasserted his overlordship of the city of Antioch.

The Franks of Outremer hoped that Manuel would now march on Nur Al-Din and break his power in Northern Syria. However, Manuel had other different priorities. He was more interested in dealing with the Seljuk Sultan of Rum and Nur Al-Din was an natural ally against Kilij Arslan II. Nur Al-Din was not a threat to the Byzantine Empire, however, the Sultan of Rum was. Together they would wage war on Kilij Arslan II and force him to agree to a peace treaty in1160. Despite the release of some six thousand Christian prisoners of war held by Nur Al-Din (mostly Germans captured over a decade ago in the Second Crusade), this alliance however enraged some of the Franks, who saw this alliance as a betrayal. The Kings of Jerusalem would be more pragmatic and see that Manuel had other priorities to the Franks in Outremer. Indeed, Baldwin III sent an embassy to Manuel in 1157 and requested an imperial bride in order to strengthen their relations. Manuel was willing and in September1158 Baldwin III married Manuel's niece, Theodora Comnenus.

THE CRUSADES 1095-1204

Nur Al-Din had a truce with both the Byzantine Empire and Jerusalem by 1160. This truce however did not include Antioch and in 1160 Reynald was captured whilst on a raid near Aleppo. No-one wanted to ransom him and Reynald would spend the next sixteen years in prison.

This situation suited most parties (except for Reynald). Baldwin did not see the need to replace Reynald with a regent. Bohemund III was now fifteen years old and came into his inheritance, and anyway, Antioch was now under the authority and protection of the Byzantine Empire. Nur Al-Din had no desire to fight the Empire for Antioch and could turn his attention elsewhere.

Manuel's first wife, Irene had died in 1159 and in 1161 Manuel requested a bride from among the Franks of Outremer. Baldwin III suggested his cousin Melisende of Tripoli, however she was rejected by Manuel in favour of Maria, sister of Bohemund III of Antioch. This action pleased the rulers of Antioch who could look forward to improved relations with the empire, but bitterly disappointed Raymond III of Tripoli. The marriage took place in Constantinople in December 1161.

We do not really know of Baldwin III's response to this rejection of his choice, for soon after Manuel's marriage to Maria, Baldwin died of a sudden illness, in February 1162, aged thirty two.

Task: Assessing the reign of Baldwin III

Consider Baldwin III's reign. What do you think was Baldwin III's most important area of success – either Military or Diplomatic?

In no more than 250 words explain your choice

Amalric 1162-1174

Since Baldwin III died childless, it fell to Amalric, Baldwin's brother to become king. Amalric was twenty five in 1162 and the Count of Jaffa. His coronation as king however was conditional; the barons of Jerusalem insisted that he divorce his wife Agnes (despite having two children) on the grounds that she was too closely related to him. In actuality, Agnes and Amalric were third cousins and at the time there were many lords who had married much closer relatives, she was however older than Amalric and scandalous rumours surrounded her. Amalric agreed to the divorce on condition that his children Sibylla and Baldwin were to be recognized as legitimate. This situation indicates that the nobility of Jerusalem were pressing for a greater say in the running and authority of the kingdom.

Amalric consistently pursued a policy of friendship with the Byzantine Empire and worked with the Empire in order to stabilise the situation at Antioch. Both the Emperor Manuel and Amalric recognised the young Bohemund III as Prince of Antioch. Amalric and Manuel agreed to work together with regards to Egypt.

The contest for Egypt

With the apparent irreversible decline of the Fatamid Caliphate in Egypt, Jerusalem and the Byzantine Empire both considered that by intervening in Egypt, they could help to secure the lucrative trade links that existed and increase the security of the Crusader states. Both Manuel and Amalric also had to consider Nur Al-Din; who was also known to have design on Egypt.

In 1163, Amalric raided into Egypt but was soon forced to withdraw. Whilst Amalric was in Egypt, Nur Al-Din attacked Tripoli, but was opposed by a coalition of forces from Tripoli, Antioch, Crusader-pilgrims from France and an army from the Byzantine Empire. At the castle of Krak de Chevaliers in 1163, Nur Al-Din was heavily defeated and forced to retreat.

In 1164 Nur Al-Din sent an army into Egypt. This army was commanded by the general Shirkuh and was sent in order to help a former Fatamid official named Shawar take control of Egypt. With Shirkuh went his lieutenant, a twenty seven year old named Saladin. Shawar was rapidly restored to power, but once installed Shawar wanted Shirkuh to leave. Shirkuh refused and seized control of several forts and towns in Egypt. Shawar appealed in turn to Amalric to help him. Amalric led an army into Egypt in 1164 and together with the army of Shawar, forced Shirkuh to surrender and leave Egypt. As Shirkuh left, so too did Amalric, for once again, Antioch needed assistance.

The battle of Artah 1164

Whilst Shirkuh operated in Egypt, Nur Al-Din invaded the territory of Antioch in August 1164. Bohemund III was defeated in battle at Artah and captured. Once again, Antioch was leaderless and stripped of defenders, and once again Nur Al-Din was reluctant to attack the city of Antioch itself, the Byzantine Empire would come to occupy the city if he did.

Bohemund III was not the only notable leader captured at Artah, so too was Raymond III of Tripoli. Amalric travelled to Tripoli and assumed control of the County, in this he was helped by Thierry, Count of Flanders, now on is fourth pilgrimage/crusade to Palestine. Bohemund III was ransomed soon after by Nur Al-Din, but Raymond was not. Nur Al-Din probably preferred a weak independent Antioch to an Antioch that was part of the Byzantine Empire, Tripoli was governed as a part of the Kingdom of Jerusalem.

Shirkuh and Saladin in Egypt

In early 1167 Shirkuh and Saladin once again invaded Egypt with an army on the behalf of Nur Al-Din. Shawar once again appealed to Amalric to come to his help and paid him well to persuade him. Amalric protected Shawar, at the cost of occupying the city of Cairo for a time. Shirkuh was attacking towards the coastal city of Alexandria and in March 1167, Amalric was defeated by Shirkuh and had to retreat to Cairo. Shirkuh followed this victory up capturing Alexandria. Here Shirkuh left Saladin in command of a small garrison and then moved on. Shawar and Amalric besieged Alexandria in May 1167 and Saladin was forced to surrender. He and his men were escorted out of Egypt, whilst Shirkuh moved to the far south of Egypt. In return for Amalric leaving Egypt he was paid tribute. Shawar was left in charge of Egypt, for a time.

Alliances and endings

Amalric returned to Jerusalem and, after requesting a bride from the emperor Manuel, Manuel sent his great niece Maria Comnenus. With the wedding also came a new alliance between Byzantine Empire and the kingdom of Jerusalem. Together, they would invade Egypt; Amalric by land and the Byzantines with a large fleet. A plan was made to attack in 1168. For the moment, the Byzantines could not help, but Amalric did.

In October1168 Amalric marched on Cairo, not to help Shawar, but to overthrow him. He was reinforced by a number of French crusaders who demonstrated their independence when they massacred the surrendered garrison of the town of Bilbeis against the wishes of Amalric. In desperation Shawar appealed to Nur Al-Din for help. Nur Al-Din responded by sending a large army under Shirkuh, however the help Shawar wanted was an attack on Jerusalem, not an invasion of Egypt by yet another army. Shawar warned Amalric that Shirkuh was on his way and encouraged Amalric to retreat from Egypt in January 1169. Shawar was taken by Shirkuh and executed only a few days after Amalric retreated. In March 1169 Shirkuh himself died. Command of the army in Egypt passed to Saladin.

In October 1169 Amalric and the Byzantines together attacked Egypt again. Their target was the coastal port fortress of Damietta. Nothing however went right. The land forces under Amalric made little headway, the Byzantine fleet was undersupplied and the army of Jerusalem refused to send food to the ships, despite their own food supplies being ample. By December the siege was broken off and retreated. From Egypt, Saladin attempted to retaliate and invade the kingdom of Jerusalem, but he was defeated in early 1170.

In March 1171 Amalric undertook a state visit to Constantinople. Here he renewed his friendship with the Emperor Manuel, Amalric also managed to secure a truce with Nur Al-Din that would lead to peace until 1172. As part of the truce, Raymond III of Tripoli was released. Not all was good news however.

In the same year Amalric received the horrifying news that his son and heir, the nine year old Baldwin, was diagnosed with leprosy. This disease would be fatal and prevented Baldwin from having children. Amalric then needed to secure the longevity of his line through his daughter Sibylla. A husband would need to be found for the teenager.

In 1173 the truce with Nur Al-Din ended and fighting renewed. Together Nur Al-Din from Damascus and Saladin from Egypt attacked the southern region of the kingdom of Jerusalem known as Oultrejourdain. The invaders laid siege to the massive castle of Kerak, but Saladin abandoned the siege; to the great anger of Nur Al-Din who threatened to attack Egypt and drive Saladin out. This threat was never acted upon however as Nur Al-Din died on the 15th May 1174. Amalric could not take advantage of Nur Al-Din's death. He died soon afterwards, of dysentery in July 1174, aged thirty eight.

Baldwin IV (1174-1185)

Baldwin IV was only thirteen of years old when he became king. His elder sister Sibylla was still also unmarried, yet in spite of his age and his diagnosed leprosy, Baldwin was crowned king by the Patriarch of Jerusalem and no one was officially appointed as his regent. However, Count Raymond III of Tripoli did claim to act in this capacity. Raymond had wide support as regent but was opposed by a faction led by the former constable of the kingdom Miles of Plancy; Miles however was soon removed; he was assassinated.

The regency of Raymond of Tripoli

In addition to his position as Count of Tripoli, Raymond was also a high noble of the kingdom of Jerusalem, as he was the Prince of the fiefdom of Galilee through his marriage to the heiress of that fiefdom. Raymond could also support his claim as regent through his relationship to Baldwin IV; he was cousin to Amalric and therefore first cousin, once removed to Baldwin IV.

Raymond was thirty four in 1174. He had been a prisoner of Nur Al-Din for several years and in this period of captivity Raymond had acquired high ranking Muslim contacts, an understanding of Islamic culture and knowledge of Arabic language. He was therefore well suited to deal diplomatically with the neighbours of Outremer. For Raymond the most important factor in his diplomatic strategy was that the Christian states of Outremer must survive.

Raymond was supported in Jerusalem by several leading families of nobles, including the Ibelin family and also the Hospitaller Military Order. He was however opposed by the Knights Templar, newcomers from Europe who hoped to settle in Outremer and also by Reynald de Chatillion who had now been released from captivity. No longer welcome in Antioch, Reynald had come to Jerusalem and become lord of Outre-Jourdain and the castle of Kerak.

Raymond III of Tripoli was regent from 1174-1177 and these years were mostly a period of peaceful relations between Jerusalem and Saladin. This truce suited Saladin, as after the death of Nur Al-Din, Saladin was intent on capturing Aleppo and Damascus.

Baldwin's challenges

Baldwin IV came of age in 1177 and now aged sixteen took over the control of the kingdom of Jerusalem. Baldwin was disadvantaged from the start. In addition to the leprosy that would kill him in 1185, Baldwin could no longer count on the military and effective political support of Byzantium. In 1176, Manuel had led the Byzantine Army to a disastrous defeat against the Seljuk Sultan of Rum, Kilij Arslan II at the battle of Myriocephalum. Manuel was now also reaching the end of his life and Saladin would be unlikely to consider the Empire as a potential threat in the same way that Nur Al-Din had done.

Another task was to find a husband for his sister Sibylla. Sibylla had married William Montferrat; a western knight in October 1176, but he died shortly afterwards. Sibylla gave birth to their son Baldwin shortly after William's death, but given the king's leprosy, a new husband to step in as regent in the event of Baldwin III's death was a matter of urgency. Despite this urgency no husband would be found until 1180. The husband that Sibylla selected was Guy of Lusignan, a French adventurer who managed to offend the powerful Ibelin family; one of whom wanted to marry Sibylla instead.

In 1177 a large crusade expedition arrived in Palestine under the command of Philip of Flanders, son of the crusading addict Thierry. The crusaders united with other forces at Acre and planned to attack Egypt. Baldwin IV joined these forces as well as a Byzantine naval force. However, Baldwin IV became ill with his leprosy and no substitute leader could be found. The expedition broke up. Philip took his men north to raid Muslim towns, but was defeated near Hama and departed for home.

Baldwin IV and Saladin

In late 1177, Baldwin IV had recovered from his illness and led his army to fight Saladin. Saladin had attacked Ascalon and at Montgisard on 25th November 1177, Baldwin IV won a stunning victory over Saladin. Saladin's army suffered heavy losses, Saladin himself was almost killed and his army routed.

In order to secure his eastern frontier, Baldwin ordered the construction of a castle at Jacob's Ford in 1178. This castle was to be built in a sensitive position astride Damascus' main route to the Mediterranean coast, and Saladin offered Baldwin IV money to not construct the place. Baldwin refused and raided the territory of Damascus, but was defeated. This provocation led to Saladin besieging the castle in 1179 and capturing it in August of the same year. During this year of conflict many Jerusalemite lords had been captured including Balian of Ibelin and the Templar Grand Master Odo of Saint-Amand. Balian was ransomed, but Odo died in captivity.

This war in 1178-9 cost Baldwin IV much in manpower and money. Appeals were sent to the west for a new crusade. However, the response was poor. Many of those that did come East came to Jerusalem to visit the holy sites on pilgrimage and then returned home. Those that stayed included Guy of Lusignan.

Fortunately, in 1180 Saladin and Baldwin agreed to a truce which would last for two years. Saladin wanted a truce because he wanted to capture Aleppo and Baldwin needed to recover the fortunes and manpower of his kingdom. Both sides were also suffering from a famine that ensured that food supplies were limited and neither side wanted those crops that had grown to be burned and trampled in a series of mutual raids.

Factionalism

In 1180, Sibylla married Guy of Lusignan. It was not a popular choice amongst the nobility of Jerusalem. One of the people behind the marriage however was Baldwin and Sibylla's mother Agnes, whom their father had divorced under pressure from the Jerusalemite nobility.

Agnes was a power behind the throne. She helped to arrange the marriage of Guy and Sibylla, she arranged for a weak willed and barely literate monk to become Patriarch of Jerusalem, and she disliked the Ibelins. It had been the Ibelins that had pressurised Amalric to divorce Agnes and she was determined to ensure that the Ibelins did not further their own ambitions by allowing one of their own to marry Sibylla. Balian of Ibelin had already married Maria Comnenus, the step mother of Baldwin IV. Baldwin attempted to adopt a neutral stance. But in practice this neutral stance was overlooked. Both factions; the Ibelins (supported also by Raymond of Tripoli) and the faction of Guy (now Count of Jaffa and Ascalon) realised that Baldwin IV would not long survive with his leprosy. Both sides were determined that when he died, they would control the regency of his heir, Sibylla's son Baldwin V.

Factions seeking control under reigns of Baldwin IV and V (1177-1185)

Ibelin family, Raymond of Tripoli and Hospitallers

Lusignan family, Reynald of Chatillon and Templars

Towards war

In 1181, Reynald of Chatillon and now lord of Oultrejourdain attacked a Muslim merchant travelling between Damascus and Mecca in an open violation of the truce with Saladin. Saladin, now in Egypt, complained to Baldwin IV in line with the truce but despite being instructed to compensate Saladin; Reynald refused. In reply Saladin held 1500 pilgrims hostage – still Reynald refused to comply with the order to compensate Saladin.

In May 1182 Saladin left Egypt for the final time and travelled to Damascus with an army. On route Saladin raided Palestine and at the battle of Belvoir in July 1182, Baldwin IV and Saladin fought a battle. Despite heavy losses, the battle ended as a draw, however Saladin continued to attack the kingdom of Jerusalem by both land and sea. Raymond of Tripoli maintained a truce with Saladin so that his lands of Tripoli were safe from attack. For this Raymond was banned from entering the kingdom of Jerusalem; weakening the Ibelin faction and strengthening the Lusignan faction. Saladin broke off the attacks on Jerusalem when he was provided with the opportunity to capture Aleppo (which he did in 1183).

Baldwin's health declined rapidly after the battle of Belvoir and it was clear that he would soon die. In 1182 Guy of Lusignan was appointed regent, Raymond of Tripoli was excluded from Jerusalem and Reynald of Chatillion once again provoked war with Saladin by launching a pirate raid onto the Red Sea, attacking merchant shipping there and even threatening Mecca itself. A furious response by Muslims saw Reynald escaping but the bulk of his men being captured and executed. An army sent into the territory of Jerusalem by Saladin was confronted by an army led by Guy of Lusignan, however he failed to bring Saladin to battle and Guy was heavily criticised in this command. Baldwin attempted to reassert control and Guy was rejected as regent.

Saladin was determined to punish Reynald of Chatillion and attacked him at his castle of Kerak in 1183 and in 1184. Baldwin IV managed to leave his sick be and lead his men to rescue Kerak but these exertions were too much for Baldwin. Early in 1185, Baldwin IV succumbed to his leprosy. In his will he expressly forbade Guy of Lusignan from being regent to his nephew, the child Baldwin V. According to Baldwin IV's will, in place of Guy, Raymond III of Tripoli would be regent. Baldwin died in March 1185, aged only twenty four.

In conclusion we have examined the careers and reigns of three kings of Jerusalem; Baldwin III, Amalric and Baldwin IV. All three kings died at a relatively young age and all three experienced difficulties with the succession.

All three also faced challenges such as;

- increased Muslim unity
- the policies of the Byzantine Emperor Manuel
- factionalism in the nobility of the crusader states
- attacks on the states of Outremer
- instability in Antioch
- tensions with newcomers from Western Europe
- lack of manpower
- lack of large scale crusades

Task: Three kings and three challenges.

Construct three spider diagrams that summarises the challenges faced by the kings Baldwin III, Amalric and Baldwin IV during their reigns. Also consider what the responses were (if any) to these challenges.

Once you have created these diagrams, compare the spider diagrams and identify common challenges faced by the three kings and see if there were any common strategies evolved by these kings to respond to these challenges.

Task: The sickness of Baldwin IV

Consider the following statement;

Baldwin IV's reign was primarily dominated by his leprosy.

Write summary points that provide evidence that challenge and support the representation contained within this statement.

Write no more than 75-100 words that expresses your view on this statement.

4.3: - Administering Outremer

In this topic we will;

- *Understand how the Crusader states were organised and run*
- *Understand the main institutions and offices of the kingdom of Jerusalem*
- *Consider the extent to which the Franks integrated with the indigenous peoples*

Introduction

In this section we will consider how the Franks ruled the Crusader States of Outremer.

Outremer as a colony of Western Europe

The Crusader states of Jerusalem, Edessa, Antioch and Tripoli were known collectively in Western Europe as 'Outremer'; which literally means the 'Land beyond the Sea' and it could indeed be argued that the Crusader states were an early example of European colonisation.

To varying extents the culture, customs and outlook of the Franks was imposed by force on the native populations of Greeks, Syrians, Arabs, Armenians and Jews that comprised the bulk of the population of the Crusader States. However, some integration was inevitable and beneficial to their survival; Many Franks learned to speak Arabic for example.

However, even this limited level of social integration was resented by many European visitors to Outremer, who had come to Outremer to fight for the cross and instead found the local rulers dealing with their neighbours in an environment of mutual interdependence. The visiting crusader to Outremer; such as those taking part in the Second Crusade may have considered with some shock that the local Franks to have *'gone native'*.

The size of the colonial population

The Frankish colonists of Outremer were never numerous in proportion to the indigenous inhabitants. Some historians such as Tyreman argue that it is impossible to accurately calculate the numbers of franks in Outremer at any given time. Others such as Runciman attempt to provide very approximate estimates.

The nobles

According to Runciman, there were unlikely to be more than 1000 knights and nobles of a fighting age living in the kingdom of Jerusalem. The King could call upon his subjects to raise a fighting force of about 650 knights for his army amongst the knights and nobles of the kingdom, with this number excluding the knights of the Military Orders and crusaders.

Runciman also estimates that perhaps another 2000 noble Franks were resident in the kingdom of Jerusalem. These were the families of the nobles and knights, including women, children and non-combatants as well as large numbers of monks and priests. Taken together, the other states of Outremer could probably equal Jerusalem when considered together. So for Runciman the combined resident Frankish noble population of all states of Outremer numbered around 6000 nobles and knights, of whom perhaps 2000 could be called upon to fight. This was a small number that relied upon a constant influx of immigrants in order to counteract the losses inflicted by battle, disease and natural causes.

The powers and position of the King

The king of Jerusalem was appointed in some ways that a visitor from Western Europe may have found unusual. For a start the king of Jerusalem was a recent invention, rulers in Western Europe could point to Charlemagne and families of great ancestry. The first kings of Jerusalem, Baldwin I and Baldwin II, however were appointed primarily because of their ability. Given the precarious nature of the kingdom of Jerusalem in the early years of its foundation, the experienced veteran fighters of the First Crusade were selected primarily because of their track record and their standing amongst their peers. This however was not a policy that was continued. With the appointment of Fulk as king of Jerusalem an outsider was positioned at the head of the state, he had to earn his position amongst the nobles of Outremer.

The authority of the king of Jerusalem was typically considered the highest authority in Outremer. However, the relationship of the king of Jerusalem was never clearly or formally established with the rulers of Antioch and Tripoli. Edessa was slightly different in that both Baldwin I and Baldwin II had been Count of Edessa before becoming king of Jerusalem; this being the case Edessa was largely seen as technically subordinate to Jerusalem. Antioch and Tripoli however were more politically independent in theory. In practice though, the succession of enforced regencies at Antioch through the premature deaths of its Princes in battle meant that in practice the kings of Jerusalem were called upon to ensure that the Principality of Antioch remained viable.

Non Noble Franks and the extent of Frankish integration

The Franks of the noble classes did not tend to intermarry with the Non Frank population. Most male nobles who chose to settle in the states of Outremer elected to seek marriage to Frankish women either from established family groups or from those of fellow settlers. There were some exceptions however, such as Baldwin II who married an Armenian princess, Joscelin I of Edessa who also married an Armenian wife or Balian of Ibelin who married the Byzantine Greek Maria Comnenus, widow of Baldwin III.

Non-noble Franks who settled in Outremer did intermarry and integrate more with the native population, some settling in distinct communities or living in small communities alongside the local population. It is likely however that the majority of the Frankish population established themselves within the towns and cities. Although the majority of the Frankish population in Outremer came originally from Northern France, the port cities of Outremer housed communities of Italians, mostly merchants from the trading cities of Venice, Genoa, Pisa and Amalfi.

In addition to those who settled in Outremer after participation in crusade or pilgrimage, others were attracted to settle in the Crusader states in the prospect of better employment or living conditions. Stonemasons and Carpenters were attracted to Outremer by high pay offered for the construction of castles and other building projects. Latin blacksmiths, herdsmen, gardeners, butchers and bakers are all attested in the historical sources.

A recognised social group emerged in Outremer, 'the Bourgeois'; comprised on non-noble Frankish settlers, the Bourgeois had their own law courts and settled in towns mainly, but also in the countryside. Kings Fulk, Baldwin III and Amalric all offered attractive settlement terms around the city of Acre which included legal protection and good tenancy prospects such as low tax charges and/or large amounts of land. For the urban and rural poor of Western Europe, the ideal of pilgrimage could be combined with the prospects of a life more attractive than that they had previously known in Germany or France.

The Non Frankish population of Outremer

The vast majority of the inhabitants of Outremer were not settlers from Europe, but rather an admixture of native peoples. Many were Christians; of Greek Orthodox faith that spoke Arabic, Coptic Egyptian Christians, Armenians but many non-Christians remained in the states of Outremer; Jews and Muslims; both settled and nomadic. It is fair indeed to describe the states of Outremer as a cultural melting pot.

In the sources the non-Frankish people were known by the following distinctions;

- Suriani – Syrians - that were Christian inhabitants living in Outremer

- Saraceni – Saracens – Muslim inhabitants living in Outremer

- Arabi – Bedouin – Nomadic Muslims that travelled into and out of Outremer

- Turci – Turks – a term collectively used to describe Muslims beyond the boundaries of Outremer that were to a greater or lesser extent hostile to the Franks

Note that the inhabitants of Outremer did not tend to distinguish between Shia and Sunni Muslims. Non-Frankish populations possessed their own leadership hierarchy and had their own courts to settle civil cases and issues of minor crimes. Muslim inhabitants of Outremer were liable for an individual tax – a poll tax, but were not encouraged to change or adapt their own customs.

The question must be asked to what extent were the states of Outremer accepting of integration with Muslims? The answer is varied. In some locations; such as Jerusalem and Jaffa, local Muslims were forbidden to live in the walls of these places, however in the port towns of Sidon and Tyre Muslims were permitted to remain after they had been captured by the Crusaders. On the other hand at Antioch, Muslims were encouraged to return to the city shortly after the city was captured. In the fiefdom of Caesarea for example on the Plain of Sharon, the settlement of Caco is known to have been inhabited by Franks, Muslims and Syrians in a single commune.

Upon the arrival of the Franks during the First Crusade many Muslim rulers were deprived of their estates and property and replaced. Non-Muslim communities however were often left undisturbed by the changeover of power. Villages and communities retained representatives to communicate their concerns and business with their local lord through an appointed headman; a *'Rais'* in Arabic, or in Latin a *'Regulus'*. In turn a local lord would communicate with these local communities either directly, or if language was a barrier, through a *'Dragoman'* a kind of Arabic speaking secretary.

Task: Inhabitants of Outremer

'Cultural Melting Pot' or 'Apartheid State'?

In your opinion which of these phrases best describes the Crusader states?

Write your response in no more than 500 words.

The powers of the king

Given the distance of Outremer from Europe and the authority of the Pope, as well as the continued potential and actual threat to the existence of Outremer by the neighbouring peoples; the King of Jerusalem had a level of independence that the kings of Europe could only envy;

- The king was Commander in Chief of the armies of Outremer

- He was the direct ruler of crown lands, not contested by another potential Christian overlord

- The king had great power on the appointment of bishops (something that particularly posed a problem for the German Emperor)

- The king held the tax monopolies of revenue raised from 'crown industries' such as dyeing, tanning, fishing and copper working

- The king received revenue from port taxes, taxes on pilgrims and taxes on merchants

- The king of Jerusalem ruled several towns and cities directly; including Jerusalem, Acre, Nablus and Daron.

The Organisation and Administration of the Kingdom of Jerusalem

The kingdom of Jerusalem and the other crusader states were organised in part using as a model the societal organisation of Western European kingdoms. The king of Jerusalem ruled several towns and cities directly; including Jerusalem, Acre, Nablus and Daron. The king also possessed many royal estates throughout the boundary of the kingdom and could grant these lands to other knights and lords in return for direct service.

The remainder of the kingdom was divided into fiefdoms ruled by lords and knights directly, but who were still required to provide military service to the king when required to do so. There were 4 major fiefdoms and 12 lesser fiefdoms such as Nablus and Caesarea.

The 4 major fiefdoms were;

- The County of Jaffa
- The Principality of Galilee
- Lordship of Sidon
- Lordship of Oultrejourdain

The County of Jaffa was often held by a relation or heir to the king. Amalric, before he was king, was Count of Jaffa as was Guy de Lusignan for example. Lords holding these fiefdoms were obliged to provide a fixed numbers of soldiers and knights for active service when required. The great fiefdoms are known to have been required to provide the following numbers of knights;

- The County of Jaffa – 100 knights
- The Principality of Galilee – 100 knights
- Lordship of Sidon – 100 knights
- Lordship of Oultrejourdain – 60 knights

The king also could grant portions of his own land to individual knights and nobles to hold either permanently or for a set period of time. Towns could also be granted to a given knight or noble as a 'money fief', a knight who held a town as a 'money fief' could as the name implies raise money from the town in the form of taxes in order to provide themselves with an income. The 'money fief' was often used as a motivator in order to encourage knights and lords stay in Outremer after they had come on pilgrimage or on crusade. Reynald of Chatillion was probably granted a money fief by Baldwin III before he became Prince of Antioch through marriage in the early 1150s.

Law and Order

The lords of the fiefdoms of Jerusalem; both major and minor, were together with leading church officials such as the Patriarch and bishops came together with the king in order to form the high court of the land. The High Court settled disputes between lords and the crown and considered major crimes as well as formed an advisory body for the king and his officials. The High Court could issue punishments and fines and on at least one occasion the decision of the High Court was to settle disputes through trial by combat as in the case of Hugh of Jaffa.

Offices of the State

The king relied on a select body of people to help him run and administer his kingdom and household. The king and major lords required a *Secrète* (Treasury) and a *Chancery* (Records Office) in order to provide and oversee his wealth and property.

Below is a selection of some of the major offices of the king's household, his lands, towns and castles. Lords of fiefdoms also used these official titles to help them run and oversee their own lands, towns and castles.

- Seneschal – Master of ceremonies and head of the civil service as well as head of the *Secrète*.

- Constable – The head of the army or armed forces of the fief in absence of the king or lord. The Constable was responsible for ensuring the soldiers of the land were recruited, equipped and trained. The Constable also paid for and commanded any mercenaries.

- Marshall – The deputy for the Constable.

- Chamberlain – governed the King's household and dealt with his personal finances and *Chancery*. The Chamberlain was by custom recruited from the Church.

- Viscounts – were chosen representatives of the king or great lord in towns, cities or castles. They dealt with local affairs; were responsible for collection of taxes, overseeing local law courts and peacekeeping and security duties.

The religious institutions of Outremer

As a deliberate matter of policy, many bishops were appointed to towns and cities in Outremer that came from the Latin Catholic faith rather than the religious beliefs of the majority of the resident population. Even at Antioch, were many of the local population looked to the Greek emperor as their political leader, the Patriarch of Antioch was often a Catholic. In Jerusalem in 1099 it was considered a matter of urgency to install a Catholic Patriarch. Orthodox Greek priests and bishops ousted during the turmoil of the last years of the 11th century were not permitted to return to their posts after the success of the First Crusade.

However, Syrian and Armenian Christians, particularly in Edessa and Antioch were allowed to keep their clergy and Christians of all churches were permitted to access the Holy sites at Jerusalem.

4.4 The Defence of the Holy Land – Castles, Sea power and ports

In this topic we will;

- *Understand the role and function of castles; civil and military*
- *Consider the extent to the necessity of castle building for the Franks of Outremer*
- *Explore some case studies of castles*
- *Evaluate the extent to which castles preserved the integrity of the states of Outremer*
- *Understand the contribution of sea power to the establishment and security of Outremer*
- *Consider the extent to the necessity of acquiring sea ports*
- *Explore a case study of a port city*

Introduction

In this section we will explore some of the main techniques used by the rulers of the Crusader states to control and safeguard their newly acquired lands; Castles, Sea ports and naval power.

Krak de Chevaliers

What are Castles?

Castles are fortified locations, places of safety where the inhabitants could take shelter in the event if an attack by an enemy. But they also fulfilled additional functions. Perhaps the first function of a castle that comes to mind was that of **defence**. A Castle with strong walls and towers provided a place of safety to which those who lived nearby could retreat to with their families and their property in the face of an attack by an enemy.

They were centres of **administration**, places where documentation and records could be kept safe. They would be central places from which local villagers and farmers could deliver their taxes to. They also could be used as places where courts could meet and settle disputes.

Castles were also centres for **observation and control**. This is perhaps the greatest role of a castle. By building a castle at a strategic location, for example on a hill overlooking a river crossing, or controlling a mountain pass in terrain which would be difficult or impossible to cross elsewhere, a castle could oversee who was passing through the area and soldiers from the castle could interrogate, oppose or harass any undesirable passing through the area.

A castle was also a **home** for a lord or his representative. The castle was an imposing construction that overarched and dominated the local area by its very appearance. It was therefore a suitable location for a lord to live. Some castles could be quite uncomfortable places to live for the majority of their inhabitants; however other castles could be opulent, even luxurious places to live. Difficult to access and secure; they also provided a safe haven for a lord to deposit his wealth in.

Castles in Outremer

There were many castles constructed in the Crusader states. Given that the Frankish population of Outremer was never large it was a sensible decision to construct castles at the earliest opportunity. In constructing castles the Crusaders were following a well-established tradition. The Norman conquerors of England after 1066 established castles throughout the country in order to keep themselves safe and to ensure that they could control their newly acquired lands. Indeed, on landing at Pevensey in 1066 the first act of William of Normandy was to construct himself a castle.

We should expect therefore the Crusaders to construct castles in abundance.

In the County of Edessa there were at least eight major castles;

- Turbessel
- Ravendel
- Al-Bira
- Samosata
- Aintab
- Duluk
- Birejik
- Rum Kalaat

The Principality of Antioch too had a number of castles in its territory including;

- Chastel Rouge
- Al-Atharib
- Marqab
- Baghras
- La Roche de Roussel
- La Roche Guilliaume

The County of Tripoli was home to several famous castles;

- Krak des Chevaliers
- Tortosa
- Montferrand
- Chastel-Blanc
- Mount Pilgrim
- Arqa

The Kingdom of Jerusalem also had many large well-fortified castles;

- Aila
- Beaufort
- Montreal
- Kerak
- Krak
- Jacob's Ford
- Tiberius
- Gaza
- Ibelin

Castles built by various kings of Jerusalem

There were lots of castles in Outremer as can be seen by the list provided above. Most kings of Jerusalem used castle construction in attempts to increase the security and control of the kingdom of Jerusalem.

Baldwin I constructed several castles in his newly founded kingdom, but many of his policies of defence were focused on fortifying and controlling pre-existing towns and cities such as Jerusalem itself and Hebron, both places were strongly defended under Baldwin I. In addition, much of Baldwin I's focus was on control and acquisition of sea ports along the coastline. These towns were also fortified and made secure. Aila, positioned on the gulf of Akaba was built to control access to the Red Sea and to deny easy communication between Egypt and Syria.

Case Study: Montreal

Montreal also known as 'Le Krak ds Montreal' or 'Royal Mountain' was one of the most important castles in Oultrejourdain. Montreal was built in 115 to control an oasis in the desert east of the Dead Sea and commanded a key caravan route. At first it was ruled by Roman of Le Puy until approximately 1132 when, after his death the castle was granted to an ally of King Fulk called Pagan the Butler. Pagan moved from Montreal to the larger and newer castle of Kerak around 1142. In 1172 Saladin attempted to capture Montreal but was unsuccessful at this time, he did manage to force Montreal to surrender in 1189, two years after he captured the city of Jerusalem after a long siege.

Montreal

Castles under King Fulk anticipated to some extent the need for greater security along the southern borders of his kingdom and the need to be able to exert his control and authority over communication and transportation of people and goods between Syria and Egypt. Unlike Baldwin I who prioritised access and control of the coastal regions, Fulk's castles were built primarily in the desert further inland.

Fulk not only ensured that existing castles were held and defended where possible, he also introduced a deliberate policy of constructing castles in the southern areas of the kingdom of Jerusalem. Around 1140 castle construction began on the castles of Ibelin, Blanchegarde and Bethgibelin. Bethgibelin would be constructed but soon handed over to the Hospitaller Military Order, but Ibelin became important because of the family that ruled it.

Ibelin was constructed at a strategic location; the site of a crossroads and at a site well supplied with water. The location of this castle ensured that whoever possessed it would become wealthy. Indeed, the Ibelin family; originally knights of Italian origin in the service of the Count of Jaffa would become one of the most prominent noble families of Jerusalem in the 1170s and 1180s.

Other castles built during Fulk's reign also included Kerak. Both these castles were in the territory of Oultrejourdain. Kerak, also known as *Petri Deserti* or the 'Stone of the desert' was a huge castle that dominated the roads between Egypt and Western Arabia that connected to Syria.

Case Study: Kerak

Kerak also known as *Petri Deserti* or the 'Stone of the desert' was a huge castle that dominated the roads between Egypt and Western Arabia that connected to Syria.

Construction began in 1142 on this large and impressive castle that controlled the roads that connected Damascus in Syria to Egypt. Its first ruler was Pagan the Butler, but its most famous owner was Reynald de Chatillion who came into ownership of the place when he married the widowed heiress of Oultrejourdain.

In the 1180s the castle was the target of numerous attempts by Saladin to capture it. In 1183 the castle was besieged by Saladin during the marriage of Reynald's step son which was held there. In deference to the newlyweds Saladin is purported to have asked which tower the newly wedded couple were staying in and on learning the location ensured that his siege artillery did not bombard that tower.

The castle withstood another siege in 1184 and was the site from which Reynald led an attack on a Muslim caravan despite there being a truce between Jerusalem and Saladin. This action led to the outbreak of war and the loss of Jerusalem for the Christians.

In 1188 after a siege of nearly a year, Kerak surrendered to Saladin.

Sea Power

Sea transportation was crucial to gaining and establishing the Crusader States of Outremer. Without sea power; the use of fleets and the resources they could bring to the Crusader States in the form of manpower, supplies and specialised siege equipment it is highly likely that the Crusader States of Outremer would never have been established. In previous topics we have established that Outremer was essentially a collection of Western European colonies established in the Islamic held East, and that one of the primary aims and chief policies of King Baldwin I (1100-1118) was to seize control of the port towns and coastal regions of the lands that they aspired to rule.

Likewise, as we shall see in Part Five, after his victory over the army of Jerusalem in 1187; Saladin focussed his military operations in conquering the coastal castles and ports that were still held by the Christians. The Third Crusade fought from 1188 to 1192 was largely fought along the coastlines of Palestine. Control of sea ports therefore was instrumental to ensure either a successful conquest of Palestine or to maintain the security of Palestine once it had been conquered.

The role of sea power in the First Crusade

In 1097, overlooked by almost all the contemporary sources that chronicled the First Crusade, the ports of Saint Symeon and Lattakiah in Northern Syria were already occupied by fleets of English and Genoese Italians. Likewise, before the siege of Antioch, when Baldwin of Boulogne arrived in the town of Tarsus, he met a fleet of pirates from the Rhine and surrounding regions that appear to have had been engaged in piracy for the previous eight years, these pirates were used by the Crusaders in order to occupy strategic points in the area around Tarsus.

These fleets provided a stream of reinforcements, brought supplies of food as well as specialised equipment in the form of siege artillery (probably loaded aboard by the Byzantine authorities) and without these vital reinforcements, it is likely that the First Crusade would have ended outside the walls of Antioch in disaster. Greek ships were also instrumental in bringing aid to the First Crusade outside Antioch. Greek shipping brought food supplies over from Cyprus as well as soldiers that occupied the port of Lattakiah in the Emperor's name.

In 1099, another fleet brought much need help to the First Crusade. A fleet of Italian Genoese arrived at the port of Jaffa and setting up a base, sent substantial help to the First Crusade that was laying siege to Jerusalem. The Genoese fleet sent reinforcements by the thousand as well as siege artillery, both of which were instrumental in capturing Jerusalem.

The First Crusade succeeded in part because it received a constant stream of reinforcements from Europe by sea. Supplies such as siege artillery (and the specialised engineers required to construct and operate these machines) were also critical. What is also noticeable is the timing of the arrival of these fleets; they seem to appear in the sources just as and when they were required. Although not stated in the chroniclers, it is indeed possible that the expedition of the first Crusade was in regular communication with reinforcements arriving from Europe (via Constantinople). These fleets were then being sent on to particular locations were they knew the Crusaders would need them, with the additional resources and reinforcements that had dribbled into Constantinople whilst the main expedition forged its way overland.

The establishment of the kingdom of Jerusalem and Sea Power

Sea Power did not just help the First Crusade however. Between the years 1099-1124 several European fleets, mainly Italian but including ships from Scandinavia, France as well as England travelled to Palestine on an annual basis bringing with them pilgrims of both the combatant and non-combatant variety, merchants and settlers as well as trading goods. These fleets would increase the wealth of their occupants and owners through trade, but they were also instrumental in ensuring that the coastal region of Palestine was ruled by Christians.

Below is a table of dates locations and factions who commanded fleets used in successful sieges of sea ports;

Date	Port	Faction commanding the fleet
1099	Jaffa	Genoa
1100	Haifa	Venice
1101	Caesarea	Genoa
1102	Tortosa	Genoa
	Jubail	Genoa
1103	Lattakiah	Genoa
1104	Acre	Genoa
1109	Tripoli	Genoa and Provence
1110	Beirut	Genoa and Pisa
	Sidon	Norway
1124	Tyre	Venice

Italian communities in ports

Several of these ports were besieged at other times (notably Tyre) however, the sieges conducted of these ports without the help of sea power failed. As can be seen in the table above, the Genoese provided many fleets that were used to successfully establish Christian European control of the coast. Each time they brought pilgrims and trade to Outremer but the naval fleets also received something in return for their military contribution and service.

The Italian city states in particular received trading privileges within the settlements they were granted within the territory of the ports they helped to capture. They had a reduction of, or no taxation on trade within their enclaves, possession of streets, churches and oversight of their own law courts, and some Italian merchant families became established as nobles in their own right within Outremer; for example the Genoese Embracio family at Jubail. These Italian communities enhanced the trading links between Europe and Outremer and helped to provide regular transportation and communication through their ships.

The Second Crusade and sea power 1146-1148

Like the First Crusade, the leaders of the Second Crusade decided that they would not sail to Outremer; instead they would follow in the tradition established by the First Crusade and march by land. This was a sensible decision on the one hand; it was much cheaper to travel overland in large armies. Most French and German noble had little or no experience of the sea and the French Louis VII had no direct control over the ports of Southern France. Most importantly, if it was decided to travel by sea, only a comparatively few would be able to travel.

Some however did travel by sea, in 1146 a fleet of Northern Europeans from the Rhine, Flanders and England did set sail for Outremer. It was this fleet that was involved in the siege of Lisbon in 1147. Perhaps 10,000 pilgrims and combatants travelled in this fleet, however with losses at Lisbon in battle, and the decision of many to subsequently settle in Portugal, perhaps only half of this total managed to arrive in Palestine in 1148. Some nobles sailed directly to Outremer including Alfonso Jordan of Toulouse.

The Third Crusade and sea power 1188-1192

Whereas the Second Crusade did not rely on fleets in order to transport the bulk of their crusading forces, the Third Crusade succeeded in part because of its use of sea transportation. The only major expedition that did not utilise sea power; the German expedition of the Emperor-King Frederick Barbarossa broke up upon the death of its leader.

The kings of France and England, Philip II and Richard I both decided to travel to Palestine by sea. With fleets paid for largely out of the *Saladin Tithe*, these rulers could afford to transport large armies by sea. Philip personally paid for 650 knights, 1300 squires and all their armour and horses, whilst Richard I raised more money and so could afford to transport a Royal army of around 6000 soldiers with their equipment in a fleet of over a hundred ships. With other nobles likewise paying for their forces initially, Richard I spent liberally on ensuring he also commanded some of these forces too. In the event Richard I probably commanded a total army of some 17,000 soldiers by the time he left Sicily.

Other nobles, such as Duke Leopold of Austria sailed from Venice in 1190 and arrived at Acre in early 1191, whilst fleets of merchants and minor nobles, landed in Palestine much earlier than the Royal contingents, such as a fleet of 50 Danish ships arriving in Palestine in September 1189 at about the same time as a small German fleet carrying some 1500 crusaders. These early arrivals ensured that there was still a portion of Christian Outremer resisting Saladin when the large Royal armies arrived in later years.

Unlike in earlier Crusades, the power of sea transportation ensured that the bulk of these armies arrived in Palestine not worn down by fighting their way across the Byzantine Empire, Turkish held Asia Minor or suffering from food shortages brought on by the long journey.

THE CRUSADES 1095-1204

The outcome of the Third Crusade was not only influenced by large naval forces. In 1187 a single ship of knights commanded by William, Count of Montferrat arrived in the nick of time at the city of Tyre, then under siege by Saladin. His arrival, with perhaps only 20 knights provided leadership and encouragement to the defenders and prevented the capture of the port. By safeguarding Tyre in Christian hands, the port of Tyre was therefore retained as a place of arrival for other Crusade fleets bringing much larger armies.

Task: Sea Power

Assess the contribution made to Outremer's establishment and survival in your own words between the First and the Second Crusades. To what extent do you think that sea power was more important than governmental administration and castle building.

Write your response in no more than 750 words

4.5 The Defence of the Holy Land – Military Orders

In this topic we will;

- *Understand the role and function of the military orders*
- *Consider the extent to the necessity of the military orders*
- *Explore the organisation and rules of the military orders*
- *Evaluate the extent to which military orders preserved the integrity of the states of Outremer*

Introduction

In this section we will explore the role, function and origins of some of the most prominent Military Orders of Outremer; the Templars and the Hospitallers.

The Military Orders

The Military Orders were according to Christopher Tyreman *'a unique institution in the Catholic Church'* (2006, p253). They were a combination of religious piety and secular violence; a solution to the problem posed by the demands of Outremer. Given the lack of manpower in the Christian States of the East, the Military Orders provided in themselves a trained soldier, a religious organisation and the wealth required to support themselves and others.

The Military Orders were not pilgrims and they were not in themselves crusaders; rather they were professional organisations whose members dedicated themselves to the service of the ideals of the order. These orders were inspired by the ideals of pilgrimage and holy war and therefore a product of their times.

Not all approved, at least one Abbot Guigo of Chartreusse argued that the Military Orders should not combine the ideals of monasticism and knighthood, however despite some opposition the Templars and Hospitallers grew to prominence and success. They became among the wealthiest institutions of Medieval Europe and did so in a relatively short period of time, by 1187 some 55% of land in the kingdom of Jerusalem were owned or overseen by religious institutions. Most of this 55% was owned by the two Military Orders of the Templars and the Hospitallers. This pattern was also reflected across Western Europe, in France the Templars would come to possess over 9000 individual grants of land, in England many place names that contain the word 'Temple' were Templar possessions and in 1134 King Alfonso I of Aragon (in Spain) bequeathed to the Military Orders almost all of his lands.

The Military Orders were also widely imitated; in Spain with the Orders of Calatrava and Santiago, in Germany and the Baltic with the Teutonic Knights. Most of these orders were dedicated to fighting, but they had additional functions; the Order of Saint Lazarus for example was established in order to provide a brotherhood for knights that were afflicted with leprosy.

The Templars

Origins and purpose

The Templars or to give them their full name 'The Order of the Temple of Solomon', were organised from the outset as a militarised, fighting order. They seem to have originated in Jerusalem in 1119 when a small company of just nine knights led by Hugh de Paynes and Godfrey of St. Omar dedicated themselves to protecting the pilgrims on the roads between Jerusalem and the port of Jaffa. Evidentially they were required; the roads were dangerous for pilgrims with raiders and bandits eager to take advantage of them.

The Templars attracted a lot of support very quickly. In 1120 Count Fulk of Anjou spent time living with them when he arrived in Jerusalem on his pilgrimage. They seem to have received royal and religious patronage from the outset. They were granted leave by King Baldwin II to headquarter themselves in the heart of Jerusalem next to the Al-Asqa Mosque and the palace of the King and in 1120 a meeting of leading churchmen in Outremer at Nablus reinforced the earlier approval of the Patriarch of Jerusalem.

'De laude novae militiae'

In 1126 King Baldwin II wrote to St Bernard of Clairvaux (whose uncle was also a Templar) in order to request that he construct official rules for the order. St. Bernard published these rules in the *'De laude novae militiae'* (In praise of the new knighthood). In addition to the rules of the Templars associated with monastic rules like when the Templars should eat and pray, the Templars swore vows of poverty, chastity and obedience to the rules of the order.

The *'De laude novae militiae'* also praised the military orders and called for knights to go to Outremer to fight for the holy places. It promised salvation for those who undertook armed pilgrimage and praised the idea of martyrdom. The *'De laude novae militiae'* became a manual for those undertaking pilgrimage and influenced those that led the Second and Third Crusades.

The *'De laude novae militiae'* was issued to coincide with a recruiting tour of Europe undertaken by the first Grand Master of the Templars, Hugh de Paynes which lasted from 1127-1129. Hugh de Paynes recruited knights of his new order, but also recruits for a military campaign against Damascus. In the course of this grand tour, Hugh de Paynes received land, money and equipment for the Templars and in 1129 High de Paynes, along with St. Bernard met the Pope and his order was officially endorsed by the Catholic Church. The Templars, like the Hospitallers were officially independent of any secular authority and needed only to answer to the Pope himself.

Fighting and politicking

The Templars began as a fighting order. Their initial duty was to escort pilgrims and patrol the roads between Jerusalem, the coast and other holy sites. In this role the Templars functioned as a kind of police force. By the late 1120s and into the 1130s the Templars accompanied the army of Jerusalem on many campaigns; most conspicuously in attacks on Damascus.

During the Second Crusade the Templars acted in many roles and functions for the expedition of French King Louis VII. The then Templar Grand Master Everard des Barres acted an emissary to the Byzantine emperor in order to negotiate the passage of the French army through Byzantine territory. The Templars also acted as bankers, providing money for Louis VII to borrow once his own funds ran out and providing food and supplies to needy crusaders on the march through Anatolia in 1148. Another Templar commanded a portion of a fleet of crusaders that launched from Dartmouth, England in 1146-7.

In 1153 the Templars joined others in besieging the port of Ascalon. During the siege the Templars managed to break into the city, however, rather than seek the help of the rest of the Christian army, the then Templar Grandmaster Bernard de Tremelay ordered that the bulk of the Templars prevent others from entering the city, whilst he led some 40 Templars to attack alone. The result was a slaughter; Bernard and his men were all killed and their bodies hung from the walls.

The Templars did not join in every military campaign however. In 1168-9 the Templars refused to accompany Amalric's army in attacks on Egypt. Perhaps they refused to join in because they had close financial relationships with Italian merchant communities that also had close trading links to the Fatamid Caliphate of Egypt.

The Templars also meddled in the politics of the kingdom of Jerusalem, in 1173 a Templar knight, Walter of Mesnil ambushed and killed an assassin embassy to Amalric, probably because any treaty between the assassins and Jerusalem would impact on the Templar ability to tax assassin villages. Walter was forcibly seized and imprisoned by Amalric and relations between the king and the Templars had not improved by the time of his death a year later.

By 1187 the Templars, together with the Hospitallers provided the major proportion of the army of Jerusalem that was defeated and massacred at the horns of Hattin. Surviving knights of the Military Order were given the choice of conversion to Islam or death; all except the captured Grandmaster of the Templars; Gerard de Ridefort were slaughtered by the army of Saladin after the battle in a deliberate policy of extermination.

Castles of the Templars

By 1150, the Templars already possessed much land in Western Europe, in the same year the Templars were granted control of the fortress port of Gaza by King Baldwin III. Thereafter they were granted many castles in the stats of Outremer as it became increasingly clear that they could afford to provide the finances and manpower required that the secular lords of the Crusader states increasingly could not afford. Castles such as Tortosa became Templar property in 1152 and Baghras in 1155.

There were many castles owned and occupied by the Knights Templar, below is a selective list and the dates they were captured or surrendered;

- Gaza (1187)
- Sahyun (1188)
- Safad (1266)
- Tortosa (1291)
- La Roche Guillame (1299)
- Bahgras (1188)

The Hospitallers

Origins and purpose

Whereas the Templars had fighting and warfare in mind from their foundation, the 'Order of the Hospital of Saint John of Jerusalem' had as their origins care for the sick. Originally the order was dedicated to the Saint John the Almsgiver; a 7th Century Saint, but soon adopted instead John the Baptist as their patron saint.

The Hospitallers origins can be traced to between 1070 and 1080 when monks from the Italian city of Amalfi were allowed by local Muslim officials to establish a hospital in Jerusalem in order to care for sick and infirm visitors and locals. In 1098 the Amalfitan monks were expelled from the city of Jerusalem along with other Christians when the First Crusade arrived in Palestine, they probably provided service to the Crusaders in the form of information as well as their original purpose of caring for the sick.

In 1113 the Hospitallers were recognised by Pope Paschel II for their services and in turn recognised only the Pope as their superior. King Baldwin I also granted the Order property in the same year and it is likely at this time that the Hospitallers became a Military Order. Perhaps the basis for this militarisation was that sick and wounded knights and pilgrims could find food and accommodation with the Order whilst they recuperated and perhaps reciprocated the Order's assistance by being prepared to fight on their behalf.

The Hospitallers had militarised by the 1120s, but they still retained as a duty care for the sick as their prime focus. The Hospital at Jerusalem was huge, it could accommodate several hundred sick at any given time and would not refuse to treat any individual on the grounds of religion or on the kind of ailment that they were suffering from; the only exception being those affected by leprosy. The Hospitallers also regularly gave charity in the form of food and money to the poor and destitute in Jerusalem. This too was a valued duty as many pilgrims who made it to Jerusalem were penniless by the time they arrived.

It is no surprise then that the Hospitallers became an influential and powerful institution. They were granted land and property in Outremer in abundance and by 1180 the Hospitallers were probably the largest and wealthiest landowners in Outremer; with more wealth even than the Templars. This wealth was used to pay a good part of the ransom of Raymond II of Tripoli in 1172.

A fighting Order

The Hospitallers are first identified as a military Order in their own right in 1126 when a number of them accompanied King Baldwin II's attack on Damascus. By 1136 the Hospitallers were in possession of several border fortresses as well as some settlements in Outremer. The Hospitallers joined the Second Crusade on the failed attack on Damascus in 1148 and also in the capture of the port fortress of Ascalon in 1153.

In 1158 some 500 Knights Hospitaller accompanied the attack on Egypt and again joined in attacking Egypt in the campaigns of 1167-8, however like the Templars the Hospitallers were not compelled to join in any military campaign. They could pick and choose which campaigns to join.

Some battles were best left unfought. On 1st May 1187 the Grand Master of the Hospital, Roger of Moulins was killed during the battle of Cresson when a handful of Military Order and local knights fought an unnecessary battle against 7000 Muslim cavalry. Likewise the Hospital sent several hundred of its members to fight and die at the battle of Hattin in July 1187. Thereafter the Hospitallers took part in the military campaigns of the Third Crusade, participating in the siege of Acre as well commanding Richard III's rear-guard in his march from Acre to Jaffa in 1192.

The castles of the Military Orders

As the Military Orders became increasingly well established and wealthy in Europe, they also took over increasing responsibility for the safety and security of areas of the Crusader states of Outremer. The cost and expense of building and maintaining a castle was huge and since each Crusader State required a large number of castles in order to help control and safeguard their territories, the Lords of Outremer all sought ways to relieve themselves of this burden through a policy of outsourcing.

The Military Orders offered the provision of this security, they would provide the manpower and wealth required to maintain an effective castle based defence system. In turn they would receive revenues from the immediate surroundings. The Hospitallers had many castles in Outremer including;

- Krak Des Chevaliers
- Belvoir
- Arqa
- Ibelin

Case Study: Krak Des Chevaliers

Krak Des Chevaliers also known as the 'Mountain of the Knights' or 'Hisn al_Akrad' is one of the most famous and best preserved castles of Outremer, Krak is a huge castle that dominated the plains and road network on the edge of the County of Tripoli, is close to the city of Homs and controls access through hilly country to the sea.

Krak Des Chevaliers was a strategically important site before the arrival of the First crusade, a castle known as the 'Hill of the Kurds' was located here and captured by the First Crusade. Today it is one of the best preserved and photographed castles in the Middle East.

Krak Des Chevaliers was controlled by the Count of Tripoli until the early 1150s when it was probably granted by Raymond II of Tripoli to the Hospitallers. Certainly by the reign of King Amalric, the Castle was in the Hospitaller's control. It was the scene of a battle in 1163 between the armies of Nur Al-Din and those of King Amalric which resulted in defeat for Nur Al-Din.

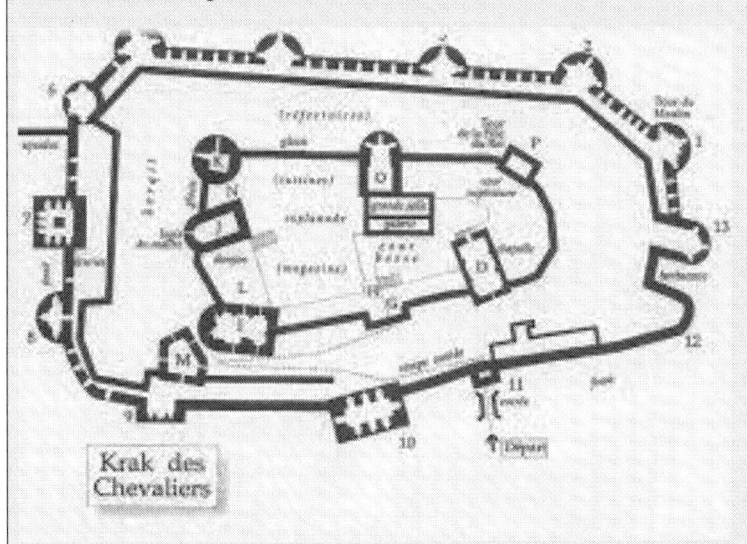

The castle survived many sieges and unlike many other castles in Outremer was not captured by Saladin after he had captured Jerusalem. Indeed, Krak Des Chevaliers was held as a strong point for the Order of St.John for many years, only being captured by Sultan Beibars in 1271.

Task: The Military Orders

Write a short exam style response to the following question;

Assess the extent to which the Military Orders overcame the military, political and financial shortfalls apparent in Outremer 1100-1187?

Write your response in no more than 500 words.

PART FIVE: Jerusalem changes hands and the Third Crusade

PART FIVE: Jerusalem changes hands and the Third Crusade

5.1 Damascus and the Assassins

5.2 The collapse of the Kingdom of Jerusalem

5.3 Nur Al-Din and Saladin

5.4 Preparing the Third Crusade

5.5 Fighting the Third Crusade

5.1 Damascus and the Assassins

In this topic we will;

- *Understand the importance of Damascus as a city that could unite the Muslim World or help to safeguard Outremer*
- *Explore the Sect of the Assassins*
- *Consider the view that Damascus and the Assassins demonstrate different kinds of relationship between the Franks and the Muslims*

Introduction

In this topic we will consider some Muslim groups that were sometimes in opposition to the authority of the Seljuk Turks and their representatives in Syria such as Zengi, Nur Al-Din and Saladin. In this topic we will explore the importance of the city of Damascus and why Christian and Muslim leaders alike desired to acquire this city and we will also explore the origins and function of the Isma'ili sect known as the 'Assassins'.

Damascus

Damascus is one of the world's oldest cities. It was important due to its position on the major routes of communication between Syria, Arabia and Egypt. The city of Damascus had been the capital of the Umayyad Caliphate that led the Islamic World until into the 10th century. After the collapse of the Umayyad Caliphate the focus of the Islamic world switched to a new centre of power; the city of Baghdad. Despite losing the prestige of being home to the Caliph, the city of Damascus remained an important city in the Islamic world.

Rulers of Damascus in the 11th century	
Ruler	Year
Duqaq	1095-1104
Tutush II	1104
Toghtekin	Atabeg of Damascus pre 1104 Ruler in own right 1104-1128
Buri	1128-1132
Buri's sons	1132-1139
Unur	1139-1149
Abaq	1149-1154
Nur Al-Din	1154-1174
Saladin	1174-1193

The rulers of Damascus in brief 1100-1149

Both Ridwan and Duqaq were the sons of the Seljuk Sultan Tutush I who ruled much of Syria at the end of the 11th century. Tutush I died in 1095 and when the First Crusade arrived in Syria and Palestine in 1097-1099, Damascus was ruled by Duqaq, who had seized control of Damascus and was a sometime rival to Ridwan of Aleppo; incidentally, his brother, and the two had fought a sporadic war before the arrival of the First Crusade.

The lack of unity between Ridwan and Duqaq in part enabled the First Crusade to capture Antioch and Jerusalem. In 1100 Duqaq attempted to ambush Baldwin when he travelled from Edessa to Jerusalem in order to become king. This opportunistic ambush failed and thereafter Duqaq did not attempt to attack the newly established kingdom of Jerusalem. Duqaq was succeeded by his son Tutush II, with Toghtekin as his *atabeg*. Tutush II however died within months of his father and Toghtekin became ruler in his own right.

Toghtekin was a military officer whose career began as a lieutenant serving Duqaq and Ridwan's father the Seljuk Sultan Tutush I.

Toghtekin served as *atabeg* (military governor under Tutush and maintained this position under Duqaq and Tutush II. Once Toghtekin became ruler of Damascus in his own right in 1104 he attempted to establish his own dynasty; the Burid dynasty. Toghtekin competed militarily with the Franks of Outremer on several occasions; in 1106 he forced the Franks to withdraw from their siege of Tripoli and in 1112 he prevented the capture of the port city of Tyre and combined with other Muslim leaders to attack the Galilee region of the kingdom of Jerusalem in 1113.

After 1113 however, Toghtekin seems to have pursued a more diplomatic relationship with Jerusalem, considering the kingdom now too well established to be overthrown by himself. Toghtekin did however attack the Franks of Northern Syria with mixed results. In 1124 Toghtekin failed to prevent the Kingdom of Jerusalem from capturing Tyre. In 1126 Toghtekin repelled an attack on Damascus by Baldwin II of Jerusalem, but towards the end of his reign found that his position in Damascus was increasingly under threat by the Franks of Jerusalem.

Toghtekin died in 1128 and was succeeded by his son Buri. Buri too faced pressure from the Franks. He was besieged in Damascus by the Franks in 1129 but succeeded in repelling the Franks. Buri was not to last long however, he was severely wounded by assassins in 1131 and never fully recovered, dying of his wounds in 1132. Thereafter Damascus experienced a period of upheaval as the sons of Buri, successive rulers were assassinated or died early. As a result Damascus was little able to interfere in the affairs of Outremer. With the death of Buri's three sons who all had died by 1139, the Burid dynasty ended.

Unur succeeded the sons of Buri, an *atabeg* who first came to prominence when in 1135 he commanded the army of Damascus when the city was attacked by Zengi. But for much of the next decade, Unur was often in other places than Damascus. From 1135-1137 Unur commanded the city of Homs in its resistance to Zengi. In 1138 Unur arranged a short lived peace treaty was arranged with Zengi, marked by Unur marrying one of Zengi's daughters. Unur also controlled Banyas for a time. Unur made a truce with Fulk in 1139 and for a few years relations between Jerusalem and Damascus were calm.

Unur returned to govern Damascus in 1139. The deaths of Zengi and Fulk should have relieved Unur of most of his major threats, however in 1148 Damascus became the target of the Second Crusade. The move took Unur by surprise. He had previously had tolerable relations with Jerusalem and the reason for the Second Crusade had been the loss of Edessa, a city several hundred miles further north. The Second Crusade assault on Damascus ended in failure for the Crusaders but Unur was forced as a consequence of this threat to make an alliance with his rival Nur Al-Din.

Unur died in 1149 soon after the end of the Second Crusade, probably of dysentery. He had children, but these were daughters, and one of them had been married to Nur Al-Din. Thereafter, Damascus was now increasingly seen as part of the territory of Syria, the northern parts of which had already been united; first by Zengi, then by Nur Al-Din and subsequently by Saladin.

Damascus as a linchpin

According to Tyerman (2006, p346) Damascus was a city that was inclined to alliance and diplomacy with Jerusalem, he writes "left to itself, Damascus tended towards alliance with Jerusalem". However, this statement may have been more an acknowledgement that, by itself, the city of Damascus was unable to effectively oppose the newly established kingdom of Jerusalem. Both Duqaq and Toghtekin opposed the establishment of Jerusalem. This may have been primarily due the new kingdom's aggressive acquisition of sea ports had a major detrimental effect on Damascus' trade links to the sea.

Damascus' trade may have been impacted by the establishment of the kingdom of Jerusalem, however Damascus did remain a vital point on the trade routes that ran along the edge of the desert between Northern Syria and Arabia and Egypt.

It's central position ensured that any ruler of Syria would hold the city as strategically important and the possession of this city as part of a wider empire would enable the ruler to acquire not only wealth through its position, but possession of Damascus was vital from which a successful invasion of the kingdom of Jerusalem could be launched, as did Saladin in 1187. Possession of Damascus also allowed a ruler to successfully unite the regions of Egypt and Syria. Again, it' central possession allowed a ruler to effectively govern both Northern Syria and Egypt.

> **Task: The city of Damascus**
>
> Write two statements – one in support of the following statement and one that challenges the following statement;
>
> *An independent city of Damascus was instrumental in helping maintain the safety of the states of Outremer.*
>
> These statements should be no more than 200 words each

The Assassins

The Assassins were a Shi'ite sect that, although accounting for only a small part of the Muslim population, demonstrates the political power that could be exerted through the combination of violence and religion. In this way the Assassins are a useful parallel to the Military Orders.

Origins and goals

The group was founded by an Iranian called Hasan As-Sabah around 1080. The Assassins were an Isma'ili sect, ultimately derived from Shia Islam and sponsored in part by the Egyptian Fatamid Caliphate in opposition to the Sunni Caliph at Baghdad and the Seljuk Turks.

There were however some key differences between the Assassins and the Fatamids. Shia Islam recognises the authority of twelve orthodox imans, the Assassins recognised only seven of these imans. The Assassins desired the restoration of radical Isma'ili rule over Islam. Their strict views on this orthodoxy put them in opposition to the Turks and the Caliph of Baghdad, who were Sunni Muslims.

Lacking the numbers and direct military strength to otherwise promote their own beliefs and agenda; the Assassins utilised assassination in order to remove opposition to them. Their name allegedly came from the use of hashish used by its killers before missions.

The Assassins originally based themselves at the town of Alamut in what is now Northern Iran. They spread gradually westwards into Iraq and from there into Syria, into the cities of Damascus and

Aleppo. From here they moved into the Nosairi Mountains along the Eastern border of the County of Tripoli, where they can be identified by 1132. In part it may have been the arrival of the Assassins that encouraged the Count of Tripoli to invite the Hospitallers Military Order to occupy Krak de Chevalliers in order to counterbalance their arrival.

In 1092 the Assassins murdered the powerful and influential vizier of Baghdad; Nizam Al-Mulk. This strike at the heart of the Caliphate caused much turmoil amongst the leadership at Baghdad and this turmoil rippled out into Syria just as the First Crusade arrived in Syria, encouraging internal rivalry and dissension.

The Assassins in Aleppo

After the murder of Nizam Al-Mulk, the assassins migrated gradually westwards, finding a home at Aleppo under the protection of Ridwan. Here the Assassins supported Ridwan and were used to remove political rivals such as Janah Ad-Daulah, the emir of Homs in 1103 and Khalaf Ibn Mula'ib, the emir of Apamea in 1106. Both of these assassinations resulted in some confusion in these towns and also enabled the Franks the opportunity to assert their own authority in these regions. The Assassins also inadvertently aided the Franks when they assassinated the powerful Atabeg of Mosul Mawdud in Damascus in 1113.

Ridwan's protection of the assassins however was somewhat resented by the people of Aleppo. After trying to seize control of Aleppo by seizing the citadel of the city when he died in 1113, they were rejected. Many Assassins were killed and the survivors driven out of Aleppo.

The Assassins in Damascus

The Assassins re-established themselves in Damascus after 1113 and continued to act against threats; real or perceived. In 1121 the Assassins murdered Al-Adfal, the Vizier of Fatamid Egypt. Al Adfal had opposed the establishment of the kingdom of Jerusalem and had for decades been the leading politician of Egypt. His death allowed the Fatamid Caliph to reassert his authority for a time.

Prominent Sunni leaders of Syria continued to be targeted. In 1126 Il-Bursuqi, Atabeg of Mosul was killed and it seems that their power was growing. In the same year the Atabeg of Damascus, Toghtekin gave the Assassins the border town-fortress of Banyas, partly in order to get them to leave Damascus. In 112, the people of Damascus followed the precedent set by Aleppo and, killing many assassins, drove the group out of the city.

The Assassins and the Franks

Preferring instead to establish themselves in the Nosairi Mountains, the Assassins sought an alliance with Baldwin II of Jerusalem and surrendered to him Banyas, which was uncomfortably close to Damascus. In 1148 Raymond of Antioch arranged an alliance with the Assassins against Nur Al-Din. Together they fought against Nur Al-Din and a group of Assassins were killed along with Raymond at the battle of Inab in 1149.

The Assassins were not always friendly to the Franks however, in 1152, for reasons which were never fully established, the Assassins killed Raymond II of Tripoli and in 1157 the Assassins were attacked by King Baldwin III when they tried to occupy the town of Shaizar.

Thereafter, relations gradually improved between the Franks of Outremer and the Assassins. In 1172, the Assassins of the Nosairi Mountains tried to seek an alliance with King Amalric. In return for their assistance, the Assassins requested that their villages near the Templar castle of Tortosa be exempt from paying taxes to the Templars. These taxes were negligible, but the Templars attacked and killed the Assassin ambassadors to Amalric.

From 1169-1193 the Assassins in Syria were ruled by Sheikh Rashid Al-Din Sinan; 'The Old Man of the Mountains' to whom even Saladin paid deference and respect. Saladin had good reason to be diplomatic to the Old Man of the Mountains; they tried to kill him at least twice and nearly succeeded on both of these occasions. In

1174 An Assassin tried to kill Saladin in his tent when he besieged Aleppo and the Assassins also tried again in 1176, also whilst Saladin was in a tent outside the town of Azaz. Saladin led a campaign against the Assassins, but broke it off when he awoke one morning to find that an Assassin had placed a knife and a hot cake on his bed next to him whilst he slept. This close call brought Saladin to make peace and thereafter he left the Assassins alone.

Task: The Assassins

Write two statements – one in support of the following statement and one that challenges the following statement;

The Assassins were instrumental in helping the Franks to establish the states of Outremer.

These statements should be no more than 200 words each

5.2 The collapse of the Kingdom of Jerusalem

In this topic we will;

- *Explore the major events and personalities in Jerusalem in the 1180s*
- *Consider the view that it was a failure of leadership that resulted in the loss of Jerusalem*

Introduction

In this topic we will explore the events of the final few years before Jerusalem was captured by Saladin in 1187. In particular we will focus on the power struggle between two factions in the kingdom of Jerusalem that almost came to the point of civil war. Unity did come, but this unity was ruined by the disastrous battle of the Horns of Hattin in July 1187.

King Baldwin's Will

King Baldwin IV died in March 1185. He was aged only 24 when he died killed by the leprosy that he had suffered with for most of his life. His heir was his nephew, another Baldwin and another child; Baldwin V was about seven years old when he was crowned king.

As a child, Baldwin V was obviously too young to rule a kingdom. He needed a circle of protectors and a regent to rule the kingdom in Baldwin's name. Under the terms of Baldwin IV's Will, he had issued instructions that Count Raymond III of Tripoli be appointed regent, until the child king should come of age. Also in the Will was a *caveat;* should Baldwin V die before he came of age, then Raymond should remain as regent until a joint decision had been made of the Pope, the Emperor of Germany and the Kings of England and France on two candidates; Baldwin IV's a Sibylla and Isabella. Also explicitly mentioned in Baldwin IV's Will was the command that Sibylla's husband; Guy of Lusignan be banned from holding any role in the regency.

Guy and Baldwin IV

It is fair to state that Baldwin IV intensely disliked his sister's second husband Guy of Lusignan. A relative newcomer to Outremer, Guy had few prospects in his native France and sought land and opportunity in the kingdom of Jerusalem. He had however managed to marry Sibylla and this marriage ensured that he would gain substantial property and claim through this marriage.

In 1183 during a period of illness for the king, Guy had been entrusted with command of the army of Jerusalem when Saladin sent an expedition across the border. Guy failed to bring the Muslim army to battle and was widely ridiculed for this perceived lack of action. Some rumoured that he was a coward; a grave insult to a knight. Perhaps this is too harsh a judgement. Guy had moved carefully and placed his army in such a way that Saladin's army could not attack him without disadvantage.

Guy, as ruler of Ascalon, had repeatedly stole from and murdered Bedouin caravans passing near to his fief. He continued this behaviour despite several truces with Saladin after 1183 and Baldwin IV's official representatives were banned by Guy from entering his fiefdom.

Raymond's regency

Raymond III was ruler of the semi-autonomous County of Tripoli and through his marriage also held large amount of lands in the kingdom of Jerusalem as Prince of Galilee; one of the major fiefdoms of the kingdom. One of Raymond's first acts was to arrange a four year truce with Saladin. Saladin agreed and the truce was made. Both had good reasons for wanting peace;

Raymond not only was the king under age, but the kingdom of Jerusalem was afflicted by a drought and crop failures. Despite repeated calls to Europe for additional military help in 1183-4, few knights and soldiers had come to Outremer and manpower was evidently a concern.

Saladin too had good reasons for desiring a peace with Jerusalem. He faced some minor rebellions in his lands of Egypt and also in Mosul. Saladin himself had been gravely ill for much of 1185 and finally, his lands would benefit from the trade of corn and food supplies to Jerusalem. It was not until April 1186 that Saladin managed to fully reassert his authority in Egypt and Mosul before returning to Damascus; which, given its centralised position, he made his principal power base.

Deception

In August 1186, King Baldwin V died. He had always been a child who suffered many illnesses, but his death brought further difficulties to the kingdom of Jerusalem. Baldwin V had spent much time in the care of Joscelin of Courtney, a friend of Guy of Lusignan, who had also worked with Raymond of Tripoli.

Under the terms of Baldwin IV's Will, the kingdom of Jerusalem would need to await the decision of the rulers of Europe to determine who would rule; the Princess Sibylla and her husband Guy, or Isabella and her husband, Humphrey of Toron. Joscelin convinced Raymond that he should call for a Council of the lords of the kingdom to meet at Tiberias. Joscelin himself would take the body of the young king to Jerusalem for burial. However, Joscelin had fooled Raymond. Whilst Raymond was at Tiberias waiting for the lords to arrive, Joscelin hurried to Acre and proclaimed Sibylla as Queen (and therefore Guy as king). Together, Joscelin and Guy garrisoned the strategic ports of Acre, Tyre and Beirut with loyal soldiers. After securing these important places, they entered Jerusalem; other influential supporters met them there including Reynald of Chatillon, Guy's brother Amalric, The Grandmaster of the Templars Gerard of Ridefort and also the Patriarch of Jerusalem Heraclius.

The Coronation dispute

Raymond tried to react to the proclamation of Queen Sibylla. He gathered support from other likeminded nobles of the kingdom; including Princess Isabella and her husband Humphrey of Toron, Balian of Ibelin, the Hospitallers and the lords of Sidon and Caesarea. Together they issued a statement that Sibylla should not be Queen.

However, this proclamation had no real effect and Sibylla was crowned. Sibylla had a strong claim to the crown. Not only had her mother been Queen, She was full sister to King Baldwin IV and the mother of King Baldwin V. More practically, her supporters had control of the city of Jerusalem itself, major castles such as Kerak and control of the seaports of Acre, Tyre, Ascalon, Jaffa and Beirut.

With some of his supporters electing to leave Outremer altogether, Raymond had one card left to play. He could inaugurate civil war. Whilst he was considering this move however, Humphrey of Toron (who since he was married to Princess Isabella was Raymond's candidate for the kingship) decided to act himself. He travelled to Jerusalem and pledged fealty to Guy and Sibylla. This act left Raymond with no other recourse but to submit. Civil war was averted and Guy and Sibylla would proceed as rulers of the Kingdom of Jerusalem.

Towards War

The truce with Saladin was maintained but in December 1186, Reynald of Chatillion decided on his own account to attack a Muslim merchant caravan travelling out of Egypt. Saladin protested this act to Guy and King Guy ordered Reynald to make amends. Reynald however refused to do so and Guy was unable or unwilling to force Reynald to submit.

War with Saladin became increasingly inevitable and the truce was effectively cancelled as both Guy and Saladin began to gather their forces. Whilst Guy gathered his forces, other lords of Outremer were more willing to ensure that they would not be involved. Prince Bohemund III of Antioch and Count Raymond of Tripoli both renewed their truces with Saladin. Raymond's truce in particular angered King Guy as it was to cover not only the County of Tripoli, but his fiefdom of Galilee (which was part of the Kingdom of Jerusalem). In practice this was an act of treason, as Raymond owed fealty to Guy for his possession of the lands of Galilee. King Guy intended to attack Raymond, but a peace was brokered by Balian of Ibelin to the effect that Raymond's truce would only apply to Tripoli. If he wished to keep control of his lands in Galilee, he would need to join Guy and fight Saladin.

War: The Springs of Cresson

On the 30th April 1187 Saladin notified Raymond that his son Al-Afdal would cross Galilee with a force of 7000 cavalry. Raymond agreed that this could occur and sent messages to warn his own men and other Christian forces in the area to stay away from Al-Afdal's men.

Two men however nearby decided to confront Al-Afdal. On the 1st May 1187 The Grand Master of the Templars Gerard of Ridefort and the Hospitallers' Grand Master Roger of Les Moulins, gathered around ninety knights and a few hundred sergeants and launched an attack on Al-Afdal. Heavily outnumbered, the result was fairly predictable; all but 3 knights were killed or captured. Roger of Les Moulins was killed; Gerard however managed to escape with two other Templar knights.

War was now inevitable. Al-Afdal's men had been attacked whilst travelling under terms of agreement with Raymond. Raymond of Tripoli now had no choice, he would have to submit to Guy and serve him in the war to come.

War: The Horns of Hattin

Both Saladin and Guy spent the remainder of May gathering their forces. By July the armies were in motion. On the 1st July 1187 Saladin crossed the river Jordan and the next day captured the town of Tiberias with an army estimated between 15-20,000 men. The castle of Tiberias remained uncaptured, within was the wife of Raymond of Tripoli commanding the defence.

At a council it was decided that the army of Jerusalem should march to help relieve Tiberias. Guy commanded an army of around 1200 knights; just over half of which were members of the Military Orders, and around 10000 infantry.

On the 2nd of July 1187 the army of Jerusalem was camped at Sephoria; a good campsite and a source of water which would have been an excellent place to fight a defensive battle. However, the decision was made to try and relieve the castle of Tiberias.

Guy's army set out the next day (3rd July) and journeyed towards the next available source of water; at Hattin. However the day was very hot and Saladin sent men to slow and delay the march. The Christian army was forced to halt for the night still short of Hattin and had to camp on a series of hills known as the 'Horns of Hattin'. Here they had no water (a well was nearby; but was dry) and suffered immensely.

During the night Saladin set fire to the scrublands at the base of the hills; causing further distress to the Christian army. In the morning the Christian army was faced with Saladin's full army confronting them, also in view was Hattin with its water source. The infantry of Guy's army launched an immediate attack and tried to break through to the water. They were defeated with heavy losses. The knights, more disciplined managed to repel repeated cavalry charges by Saladin's men, but defeat was certain. Raymond of Tripoli attacked with his forces and was 'allowed' to escape once he had broken through, likewise Balian of Ibelin also managed to fight his way clear. The rest of the army of Jerusalem was surrounded and destroyed.

Many were killed in the battle including the Bishop of Acre, along with whom was captured a relic of the True Cross. Some prisoners were taken including some 200 knights of the Military Orders, Guy of Lusignan, his brother Amalric, Gerard Grand Master of the Templars, Humphrey of Toron and Reynald of Chatillion.

Saladin handed over the knights of the Military Orders who were executed by some of Saladin's men; only Gerard of Ridefort was spared. Likewise; Reynald of Chatillion was personally executed by Saladin. The rest were taken into custody to be used as hostages later.

The Conquests of Saladin

The disaster at Hattin exposed the problems of manpower and distance from help for the Christian rulers of the kingdom of Jerusalem. The imprisonment of Guy was less of an issue; Kings had been captured before, but the destruction of the bulk of the effective fighting forces of the kingdom could not be easily replaced.

Now that he had destroyed one of the largest armies that the kingdom of Jerusalem could put into the field, the way was now clear for Saladin to begin to reconquer the Christian held lands whilst it was stripped of men.

Progress was rapid, Tiberias surrendered on the 5th July 1187, followed by the majority of the coastal ports. At first it may seem surprising that Jerusalem was not attacked until late in September 1187; some several months after the battle at Hattin. However, strategically speaking Jerusalem was low in the list of priorities. One of the reasons why the Franks had been able to secure their kingdom was through possession of sea ports. Saladin now moved to take control of as many sea ports as he could. Castles in the interior were also besieged and taken.

Below is a table listing some of the more notable Saladin's conquests after Hattin;

Saladin's conquests after Hattin	
Date	Event
5th July 1187	Tiberias Castle surrenders
10th July 1187	Acre surrenders
July 1187	Nablus and Toron surrender
	Jaffa taken by storm
	Tyre attacked but remains uncaptured
29th July 1187	Sidon surrenders
6th August 1187	Beirut surrenders
8th August 1187	Jubail surrenders
4th September 1187	Ascalon surrenders after a siege
September 1187	Gaza surrenders after Gerard orders the Templars there to do so.
	He is released as a result.
20th September 1187	Siege of Jerusalem begins
2nd October 1187	Jerusalem surrenders
22nd July 1188	Lattakiah surrenders
29th July 1188	Sahyun surrenders
December 1188	Kerak and Safed surrender after long sieges
January 1189	Belvoir surrenders after long siege

The siege of Jerusalem

After securing many sea ports Saladin brought his army to capture what many saw as the crowning achievement of his life; the city of Jerusalem. The Franks, commanded by Patriarch Heraclius and Balian of Ibelin elected to try and defend the city. They had the will, but the means were lacking. Only two knights remained in the city after Hattin. So Balian knighted squires and some 30 Bourgeois soldiers still within the walls and the bulk of the defence would be undertaken by merchants, clerics and other Frankish inhabitants of the city.

Saladin arrived before the city on the 20th September 1187 and laid siege. He first attacks began on the 26th September. By the 29th Saladin's siege engines had breached the city walls but despite fierce fighting Saladin's men were unable to enter the city. Once the walls were breached, the city of Jerusalem would inevitably be captured. No help could reach the city and Balian of Ibelin entered into negotiations to surrender the city. On the 2nd of October 1187, Jerusalem surrendered.

Saladin's terms were relatively lenient. There was no sack of the city, no massacre of the inhabitants which stood in strong contrast to the capture of the city by the First Crusade in 1099. Although some were condemned to slavery, the bulk of the Frankish population were able to ransom themselves and to leave the city under escort to the coast. The non-Frankish population were permitted to remain and Christian Holy sites were to be respected and remained accessible for pilgrims.

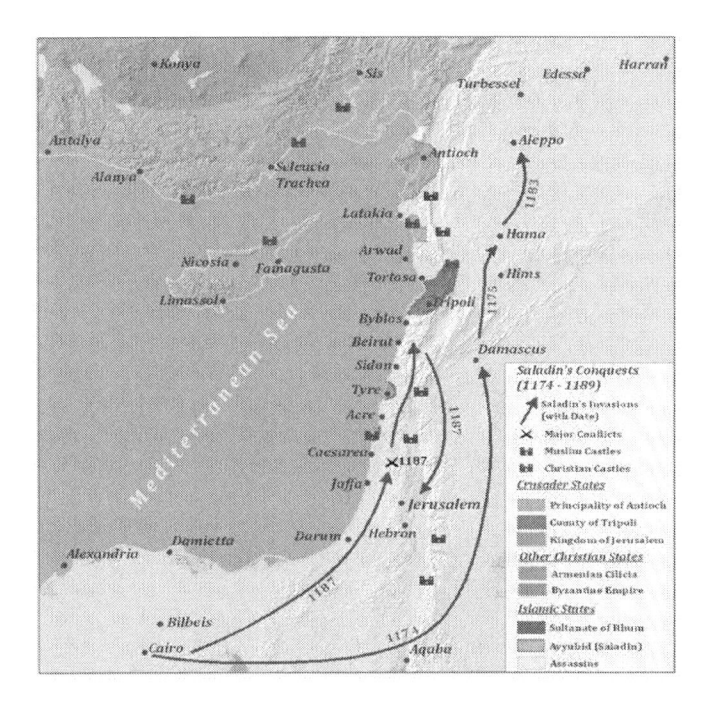

Saladin's mistake

Throughout his near triumphal procession in 1187-1188, Saladin made a crucial mistake. This mistake would allow the Franks to maintain a toehold in Outremer and give the expeditions of the Third Crusade an opportunity to counter attack. The mistake was not to ensure that he captured the port city of Tyre.

Saladin's forces were besieging the city in mid-July when a single ship managed to make its way into the harbour of Tyre. The ship carried Conrad of Montferrat, a crusader who had been distracted by the allure of Constantinople and remained there until, under suspicion for committing a murder in the city, Conrad had joined a ship sailing to Outremer carrying some 20 knights.

On the 14th July 1187, Conrad's ship arrived at Tyre and invigorated the defenders who were considering surrender. Conrad and his knights put fresh heart into the defence of the city and refused to surrender even when Saladin threatened to kill Conrad's father; a prisoner taken at Hattin. Conrad refused and his father was not executed. Shortly afterwards, Saladin moved on to attack other targets but tried to take the city again in November 1187. Again however, he was deterred by the strong fortifications and the numbers of Franks now beginning to use Tyre as their base in Outremer. A fleet of Saladin's ships were defeated outside Tyre in December and he ended his siege on 1st January 1188 to attack other, easier targets.

Task: The victory of Saladin

Write an exam style response to the following question;

To what extent do you agree with the view that Saladin's capture of Jerusalem was down to the mistakes of Guy of Lusignan?

Write your response in no more than 750-1000 words.

5.3 Nur Al- Din and Saladin

In this topic we will;

- *Understand the principle events of the careers of Nur Al-Din and Saladin*
- *Explore the challenges faced by these rulers and what they did to try and meet these challenges*
- *Consider the implications of increased Muslim unity for the Crusader states*

Introduction

In this topic we will explore the lives and careers of two Muslim rulers, Nur Al-Din and Saladin.

Timeline of Nur Al-Din	
Year	Event
1146	Death of Zengi, Edessa rebels and is recaptured and devastated by Nur Al-Din
1148	The Second Crusade – Nur Al-Din allies with Unur of Damascus
1149	Victorious in Battle of Inab and captures Homs
1150	Remnants of County of Edessa overrun, Joscelin of Edessa captured
1154	Annexes Damascus
1159	Treaty with Byzantine Empire
1161	Treaty with Jerusalem, undertakes *hajj* – (pilgrimage to Mecca)
1163	Defeated at Krak de Chevalliers
1163-1169	Contests control of Egypt
1170	Annexes Mosul
1174	Dies 15th May

The career of Nur Al-Din

Nur Al-Din

Nur Al-Din was the son of Zengi. Born in 1117 Nur Al-Din was the second eldest son. Through his career Zengi acquired control of large areas of Northern Syria including Mosul, Aleppo. When Zengi was murdered in 1146 his possessions were divided amongst his sons. The eldest son, Sayf Al-Din, inherited Mosul. Nur Al-Din, now aged twenty nine acquired Aleppo.

In 1146 Nur Al-Din was faced with an immediate challenge to his authority. Attempting to take advantage of Zengi's murder, the titular Count of Edessa, Joscelin III, briefly recaptured Edessa and tried to re-establish his County. Nur Al-Din acted quickly and savagely. Joscelin was defeated in battle and the city of Edessa was recaptured, the local Christian population, spared by Zengi were now devastated by his son. The male Christian population was massacred; the women and children were sold off into slavery. In order to prevent a repeat, the walls of Edessa were destroyed.

Nur Al-Din and Northern Syria

Nur Al-Din also kept a close watch on the progress of the Second Crusade. He was content to remain on the defensive when King Louis VII arrived at Antioch and was no doubt overjoyed when the Crusaders decided to leave Antioch and proceed south. Nur Al-Din profited from the Second Crusade by receiving an alliance with Unur of Damascus and, using reinforcements sent to him from his brother at Mosul, Nur Al-Din could put his resources to use against Antioch. A series of border raids occurred between Aleppo and Antioch in 1148-9 which culminated in Nur Al-Din's victory at the battle of Inab in 1149. Prince Raymond of Antioch was killed and his embalmed head sent as a trophy to the Caliph in Baghdad. Also in 1149 Nur Al-Din demonstrated his willingness to work with his Christian neighbours when he helped Count Raymond of Tripoli against Bertrand of Toulouse who was attempting to seize control of the County. In 1150 the remnants of Christian held Edessa were overrun and Bertrand was joined in captivity by Joscelin, titular Count of Edessa and remained in prison until his death in 1159.

> **A View of Nur Al-Din**
>
> *"Nur ed-Din thus emerged as the principal enemy of the Christians. He was now aged twenty nine; but he was wise for his years. Even his opponents admired his sense of justice, his charity and his sincere piety"*
>
> Runciman, A History of the Crusades, Book II, p243

Negotiations and annexations

The truce with Unur of Damascus did not last. Damascus was under pressure from Jerusalem but also from Nur Al-Din. Using a combination of military and economic pressure against Damascus until in 1154 when the people of Damascus surrendered and invited Nur Al-Din to assume control of the city. With the acquisition of Damascus, Nur Al-Din's Western frontier now encompassed almost the entire eastern frontier of Outremer. This was a new situation for the Franks of Outremer who would now need to deal almost solely with Nur Al-Din politically, economically and militarily. To the North however, another power was beginning to reassert its authority.

Nur Al-Din almost died of an illness in 1157 which re-occurred again in 1159. He managed to maintain his authority despite some attempts to deprive him of power through this period. Towards the end of the 1150s the Byzantine Empire had been re-establishing its position in Cilicia and was now making inroads into the territory of Antioch. Nur Al-Din was reluctant to confront the Byzantine Empire, and in truth such a confrontation would be unnecessary. Ideally, Nur Al-Din would want control of Antioch, but to do so would be to oppose the Emperor Manuel who also desired control of the city.

When Manuel arrived in Antioch in 1159 he forced the new Prince of Antioch, Raynald de Chatillon to give homage and agreed to an alliance with Nur Al-Din. Together Nur Al-Din and Manuel would attack Mas'ud, the Seljuk Sultan of Rum and deprive him of territory with a concerted attack. In return for the release of some 6000 Christian prisoners (including Bertrand of Toulouse), a treaty was also made between Nur Al-Din and Antioch

This treaty did not prevent Nur Al-Din from capturing Reynald of Chatillon in 1161 when Reynald decided to go raiding. No one offered to ransom Reynald and he would spend the next sixteen years in captivity. The occasion of Reynald's capture also resulted in a truce being established between Baldwin III of Jerusalem and Nur Al-Din.

Nur Al-Din, Islam and reform

Nur Al-Din's policies aimed at establishing a stable and prosperous domain under his authority. Nur Al-Din provided his lords and soldiers with land grants and used a more efficient system of taxation and bonuses in order to encourage trade and settled economies. Many of his soldiers were Turks and Kurds, people who traditionally had been nomadic and reluctant to settle in any single place. Nur Al-Din encouraged his soldiers to integrate with the indigenous inhabitants of his lands by granting land to his followers which he could in turn could raise finance from through a system of taxation. The result was an increase in wealth and prosperity in his territories which better enabled Nur Al-Din to expand his authority elsewhere.

A devout Sunni Muslim, Nur Al-Din undertook the *hajj;* a pilgrimage to Mecca in 1161 and throughout his life Nur Al-Din encouraged Islamic scholars and propagandists to come to his court. Nur Al-Din is known to have established at least 40 madrasa (Islamic schools) which he used in part to instil enthusiasm and cultural energy for aspects of Islamic religion. The concept of *Jihad* (struggle or effort) was encouraged under Nur Al-Din to develop not only the concept of Holy war, but also the effort to develop and establish stability and prosperity in his domains. Increasingly, and partly in response to the rhetoric of Christian Holy war, the Christians of Outremer were portrayed by Nur Al-Din as spiritual as well as physical opposition by judges, poets and scholars in Nur Al-Din's court.

Nur Al-Din and Egypt

In the 1160s Nur Al-Din increasingly directed his attention to Fatamid Egypt. The Fatamid dynasty that ruled Egypt was on the verge of collapse. A succession of viziers sought to control the Caliphs as figureheads whilst they governed and held the real power. The position of Vizier itself became unstable as they succumbed to assassination and internal rivalries and in 1163 the Vizier Shawar requested assistance from Nur Al-Din in order to shore up his position. Nur Al-Din agreed and sent one of his Kurdish generals Shirkuh (increasingly Nur Al-Din was in turn under pressure to find projects and lands for his ambitious generals) with an army.

Nur Al-Din supported Shirkuh's expedition to Egypt with an attack on the County of Tripoli, but was defeated at Krak de Chevaliers in 1163. Likewise, opposed by Amalric, king of Jerusalem, Shirkuh's invasion of Egypt was at first a failure, but in 1167 Shirkuh was sent to Egypt again and managed to secure this large country essentially for himself and for his nephew, Saladin who accompanied the expedition.

A Frankish view of Nur Al-Din

In the 1180s tutor of King Baldwin IV, Archbishop William of Tyre explored his views on increasing Muslim unity since Zengi and the dangers it posed to the Christian states of Outremer in the following passage William of Tyre considers Nur Al-Din.

"In former times almost every city had its own ruler...who feared their own allies not less than the Christians [and] could not or would not readily unite to repulse the common danger or arm themselves for our destruction. But now...all the kingdoms adjacent to us have been bought under the power of one man. Within quite recent times, Zengi...first conquered many other kingdoms by force and then laid violent hands on Edessa.

Then his son, Nur Al-Din, drove the king of Damascus from his own land, more through treachery of the latter's subjects than by any real valour, seized that realm for himself, and added it to his paternal heritage. Still more recently, the same Nur Al-Din, with the assiduous aid of Shirkuh, seized the ancient and wealthy kingdom of Egypt as his own...all kingdoms round about us obey one ruler, they do the will of one man, and at his command alone, however reluctantly, they are ready, as a unit, to take up arms for our injury. Not one among them is free to indulge any inclination of his own or may with impunity disregard the commands of his overlord."

Nur Al-Din's last years

Shirkuh died in 1169 leaving Saladin in effective control of Egypt as Nur Al-Din's representative in that country. In 1170, Nur Al-Din also took advantage of his brother's death in order to secure effective control of Mosul.

In theory Nur Al-Din reigned supreme in Syria and Egypt. In practice, the occupation of Mosul distracted Nur Al-Din at a time when Saladin was positioning himself as ruler of Egypt in his own right and communication between Syria and Egypt was still hampered in part by the presence of the Christian kingdom of Jerusalem and most notably the fiefdom of Outrejourdain in the south.

The fiefdom of Outrejourdain was in the desert between Syria and Egypt and a series of strong castles there; Montreal and principally Kerak controlled water sources and oasis in the region. If Nur Al-Din wanted to connect Egypt and Syria, he would need to control Outrejourdain. In 1171 and 1173 Nur Al-Din summoned Saladin to help him besiege the castles of Kerak and Montreal. Saladin refused on both occasions. Nur Al-Din was angered by this insubordination and made plans to remove Saladin by force. In 1174 Nur Al-Din began to gather an army at Damascus in order to attack Egypt but before it could march on 15th May 1174 Nur Al-Din died; probably of a heart attack. His son and heir was the eleven year old Malik as-Salih Ismail. Like what had often happened to the Christians of Outremer; the ruler of Syria now required a regent.

Conclusions

Unlike other brothers such as Ridwan of Aleppo and Duqaq of Damascus, the sons of Zengi did not immediately fall to bickering amongst themselves. Had Sayf Ad-Din and Nur Ad-Din done so, the position of the Franks in Outremer may well have been immeasurably strengthened.

Nur Al-Din sent a clear message with his sack of Edessa in 1146, he could be ruthless when he needed to be and he would act with swiftness and violence, but in 1159 and in 1161 Nur Al-Din demonstrated his willingness to work with Christians, establishing a series of truces. This did not prevent him from attacking the Christian states of Outremer when he deemed it necessary.

For much of his career, and despite the increasing rhetoric of ideas such as *jihad* that can be encountered in Islamic sources at this time, it could be argued that Nur Al-Din was more concerned with asserting his authority over his fellow Muslims. He targeted Damascus in the 1140s and early 1150s, he helped the Byzantine Empire attack the Seljuk Sultan of Rum in 1159 in order to consolidate his authority in the North and finally intervened in Egypt in the 1160s.

At the time of his death in 1174 Nur Al-Din had united Muslim Syria under his control and succeeded in removing the Shi'ite Caliphate of Egypt and installing in its place a regime that originated from his own resources. In answer to Nur-Al Din's single successful reign, two Kings of Jerusalem, Baldwin III and Amalric had ruled. Both had been energetic and encountered both success and failure but both had died young and Amlaric's heir was both a child and a leper.

Saladin (1137-1193)

Al-Malik al-Nasir Salah al Dunya wa'l-Din Abu'l Muzaffar Yusuf Ibn Ayyub Ibn Shadi al-Kurdi; rather better known as Saladin, was born in 1137. Saladin was neither Arab or Turk, but rather a Kurd, a Muslim people who were Sunni in their belief and obeyed the rule and authority of the Abbasid Caliph of Baghdad. Saladin's family were in the service of Zengi and then after his death his son Nur Al-Din, and it was in part through his families' service to Nur Al-Din that Saladin grew to prominence.

Saladin progressed from a relatively minor military officer in Nur Al-Din's army to becoming Sultan of Egypt and Syria. In many ways Saladin's career pathway was not too dissimilar to that of the Frankish military adventurers that founded the states of Outremer. Like Bohemund and Baldwin I who established Antioch and Jerusalem respectively, Saladin came from relatively humble and obscure origins and through a combination of political and military skill and leadership as well, according to William of Tyre, sheer good luck; Saladin would become both Sultan (literally; Power) of both the regions of Syria and Egypt.

Saladin and Egypt (1163-1174)

In 1163, Nur Al-Din dispatched an army to Egypt in order to respond to the appeal of Shawar, a vizier of Fatamid Egypt that had been deposed from his position in government and wished to reassert his control of the crumbling Fatamid Caliphate. This army was under the command of Shirkuh and as part of his military entourage, Saladin accompanied his uncle. Shirkuh was successful in reinstating Shawar but his presence in Egypt was soon resented.

The next year Shawar appealed to the only person able to help him drive out Shirkuh and his army; the King of Jerusalem, Amalric. Amalric duly invaded Egypt and fought a rather inconclusive campaign against Shirkuh. The war ended when both Shirkuh and Amalric agreed to leave Egypt in October 1164, leaving Shawar back in control as vizier of Egypt.

This state of affairs did not last for long however as in January 1167, Saladin, once again accompanied his Uncle Shirkuh in a new invasion of Egypt; this time sanctioned by the Caliph of Baghdad himself. Shawar once again called in Amalric to help him and Saladin was briefly besieged in Alexandria. Both sides again withdrew from Egypt in August of the same year. This brief truce did not prevent Amalric attempting to seize control of Egypt himself in 1168 and Shawar now seeking help from Shirkuh and Saladin. Amalric was forced to withdraw from Egypt, but this time Shirkuh and his army did not leave. Shawar was overthrown and murdered in January 1169, and controlled Egypt, but not for long. Shirkuh died in March of the same year.

Saladin now found himself in command of an army in Egypt that owed its allegiance to Nur Al-Din. However, this command was not uncontested. Saladin faced potential threats from within his own army as well as the army of the Fatamid Caliphate who viewed Saladin as an interloper who had long outstayed his welcome.

Through a combination of cunning and brutality, Saladin managed to completely destroy the Fatamid army regiment known as 'The Sudan' when it opposed him in 1170, and had replaced untrusted soldiers and officers with those of proven loyalty to himself. Saladin instituted a new regiment of soldiers loyal only to himself in Egypt, known as 'The Salahiyya'.

In the same year, Saladin repelled a combined Frankish and Byzantine attack on the Egyptian port of Damietta. Crossing the border Saladin captured the Frankish strongholds of Aila and Gaza; two strategic locations that allowed better access to invade the kingdom of Jerusalem.

In 1171 the last Fatamid Caliph died, Saladin did not attempt to continue this Shi'ite institution, but instead had the name of the

Abbasid Caliph declared in mosques across Egypt. Egypt was now officially part of the Abbasid Caliphate again after a gap of some two hundred years.

Saladin faced another attack in 1174 when a Sicilian fleet attempted to raid Alexandria, but Saladin faced increasing resentment from his official superior; Nur Al-Din. Saladin had refused to aid Nur Al-Din in attacking Frankish castles and possessions in Outlrejourdain in the past few years and by 1174 Saladin was faced with the threat of invasion by Nur Al-Din. This invasion never occurred due to the death of Nur Al-Din in May.

Saladin and Syria 1174-1187

Saladin wasted little time in grief for the death of his former patron. Saladin advanced out of Egypt shortly after news of Nur Al-Din's death and by October 1174 Saladin had occupied the important city of Damascus. Damascus had taken decades to fall to Nur Al-Din; it was taken by Saladin in a matter of months.

For the next few years Saladin was content to largely ignore the Franks of Outremer, instead he was occupied from 1174-1176 in asserting his control over much of Syria. However in 1177 Saladin did invade the kingdom of Jerusalem, only to experience defeat and a near death experience at the battle of Montgisard at the hands of the leper king Baldwin IV. Another attack on Christian territory in 1182, this time in Galilee was likewise repulsed as was an attempt to capture Beirut. In 1183, Saladin also failed to bring the army of Jerusalem to battle when it was commanded by Guy of Lusignan. These setbacks did not really last for long however.

This apparent reluctance to attack Christian targets with any sense of vigour encouraged some Muslims to criticise Saladin. One Muslim scholar, Ibn al-Athir admonished Saladin, with some justification, he accused Saladin of being more eager to attack Muslims than Christians. There were apparent grounds for this criticism. Saladin was happy to accept truces with Jerusalem for much of the period between 1174 and 1187 and Saladin would profit from these truces through wealth generated by trade with the Franks as well as being undisturbed in his attempts to acquire the rest of the lands formerly held by Nur Al-Din.

Saladin besieged Aleppo in 1174 and 1176 but on these occasions he failed to acquire control of the city. But he did acquire control of strategically important towns such as Homs and Shaizar in Northern Syria. In 1183, Saladin secured control of Aleppo and Mosul was his by 1186, these acquisitions came through the threat of force as well as the use of diplomacy. It was diplomacy that allowed Saladin to gain control of both Aleppo and Mosul. This was important as it ensured that the revenues and manpower of these cities and regions could be but to use to make further gains rather than exhausting them through military conflict. The manpower of Aleppo and Mosul would be combined with those of Damascus and Egypt in order to occupy the bulk of the kingdom of Jerusalem in 1187-1188 and in order to oppose the armies sent East in the Third Crusade.

Saladin and the Assassins

A favoured target of aggression by Saladin where the assassins; Shi'ites like, the *'Sudan'* regiment in Egypt, Saladin spent much of his time in the years between 110-1187 fighting against what he viewed as heretical Muslims. However, these attacks may have been less concerned with heresy and more concerned with the acquisition of power. Saladin attempted to remove the assassins as a threat through invasions of their territory in Northern Syria; however these attacks did not achieve the success he desired.

After at least two assassination attempts that nearly succeeded in 1174 and 1176 (both times whilst besieging Aleppo), Saladin came to a peace agreement with 'The Old Man of the Mountains' as the leader of the assassins was known, and thereafter the assassination attempts ceased.

A Frankish view of Saladin

Of Saladin, William of Tyre writes that he is;

"...a man of humble antecedents and lowly station, now holds under his control all these kingdoms, for fortune has smiled too graciously upon him. From Egypt and the countries adjacent to it, he draws an inestimable supply of the purest gold...Other provinces furnish him numberless companies of horsemen and warriors, men thirsty for gold, since it is an easy matter for those possessing a plenteous supply of this commodity to draw men to them."

Other Christians later viewed Saladin's character positively. He was wrongly assumed to have been knighted by Humphrey II of Toron at some point during the Third Crusade and many western sources portray Saladin as brave, chivalrous and possessing a reputation for justice

Task: Developing Exam techniques: An essay style response

It could be argued that of the two men considered in this topic; that it was Nur Al-Din that contributed more to the unification of Egypt and Syria and the subsequent recapture of Jerusalem than did Saladin or the activities of the Franks.

In order to explore this premise, write four statements, each of no more than 200 words.

1) Exploring the view that Nur Al-Din contributed more to the unification of Egypt and Syria and the subsequent recapture of Jerusalem than did Saladin.

2) Exploring the view that Saladin contributed more to the unification of Egypt and Syria and the subsequent recapture of Jerusalem than did Nur Al-Din.

3) Exploring the view that the Franks contributed more to the unification of Egypt and Syria and the subsequent recapture of Jerusalem than either Saladin or Nur Al-Din.

4) A concluding statement that summarises your view on this matter.

5.4 Calling the Third Crusade

In this topic we will;

- Understand the extent of crusade recruitment in Western Europe

- Explore the range of rulers and lords and the forces recruited for the Third Crusade

- Explore the events of the Crusade of Frederick Barbarossa

- Consider the view that the motives and priorities of the leaders of the Third Crusades differed markedly from those of the more humble crusaders

- Understand the reasons that led to the forces of King Philip and King Richard being delayed from reaching Palestine for several years

- Explore the journey of King Richard to Palestine

Introduction

In this topic we will explore the response in Western Europe to the capture of Jerusalem in 1187 by Saladin and what steps were taken to raise and launch a new Crusade whose aim was the recovery of the Holy City. We will also explore the reasons why it took the Kings of France and England some four years to reach Outremer.

The response in Europe

Despite repeated calls for assistance being dispatched from Outremer in the 1170s-1180s; by and large the European response was muted. No major expeditions were sent to Outremer in the ten years leading up to defeat at Hattin in 1187 and of the help that was sent; much of it came from the Military Orders, and the fighting strength of the Military Orders in Outremer had been decimated in the defeat at Hattin.

Many Europeans that had come on pilgrimage; such as Duke Henry the Lion of Bavaria had come to pray at the Holy sites, not to fight. On their arrival, these pilgrims saw a western society that seemed well established and entrenched in the East. The rapid collapse of the kingdom of Jerusalem that followed the disaster at Hattin could not have been easily foreseen, and in any event, after Hattin, the collapse of the kingdom could not be prevented, since quite simply there were too few Franks of fighting age left to oppose Saladin in Outremer, and no immediate help could be sent in sufficient numbers from either Western Europe or from places like the

Byzantine Empire. All Saladin needed to do was to use his large armies to surround and force the surrender of the castles and ports of Outremer; in this he was largely successful.

The exception was the strongly fortified port city of Tyre. Tyre was an ancient place; it had been established hundreds of years before Alexander the Great captured the city in the 330s BC; and it had taken Alexander seven months to capture the place. Tyre was about to surrender to Saladin in 1187 when a single ship's company of knights arrived there commanded by Conrad, Count of Montferrat.

Conrad's arrival reinvigorated the defenders of Tyre and Saladin decided to concentrate his efforts in capturing other places. This was a great mistake. By securing Tyre, Conrad provided a focus for the surviving nobles and fighting men of the kingdom of Jerusalem. This gathering at Tyre determined to send an official embassy to Europe; led by Archbishop Josias of Tyre was dispatched to Europe in order to request help.

Summoning the Third Crusade

Archbishop Josias of Tyre left Outremer towards the end of August 1187. Josias left before Jerusalem had been besieged by Saladin, but news overtook him and rumours were already circulating in Europe that Jerusalem was lost.

The response of King William II of Sicily

Josias landed in Europe in Sicily. He visited King William II of Sicily and informed him of the event of the disaster at Hattin and the capture of King Guy. William's first response was to don a hair shirt and undertake several days of penance and prayer. His second response was to make peace with the Byzantine Empire and recall his fleet that was raiding the coastlines of the Empire. His third response was to send his fleet and some 200-300 knights to sail directly to Outremer. This fleet would travel to Tripoli and would co-operate in the war in Palestine through the years 1188-1190. However when William died in November 1189, this fleet was recalled to Sicily.

The Papal Response; *'Audita Tremendi'*

Josias travelled from Sicily to Rome. Here Josias found Pope Urban III gravely ill. He died on the 20th October 1187, soon after Josias arrived. The co-incidence of the arrival of Josias and the death of Pope Urban III has often been interpreted as the news of the loss of Jerusalem being fatal to the Pope. In probability, news had not yet reached Rome that Jerusalem had been captured.

News now reached Europe that Jerusalem was lost and Pope Urban III was succeeded by his successor; Pope Gregory VIII. Pope Gregory VIII issued a circular commanding the Christians of Europe to respond to the loss of Jerusalem.

The *'Audita Tremendi'* was the Papal Bull issued to summon the Christians of Europe to a new Crusade. It was based in part on the Papal Bulls issued in order to authorise the Second Crusade and its particulars included;

- The loss of Jerusalem was lamented and mourned

- The loss of Edessa, some forty years previously had been a punishment for immorality that had been ignored

- A new Crusade was called to recover Jerusalem

- Those you would become crusaders should repent their sins and gather funds

- Crusaders were offered plenary indulgences

- The possessions of Crusaders would remain under the protection of the Church whilst they were away

- All wars in Europe would end and there would be a seven year truce

Another key evolution in the preaching of the Third Crusade was the use of the term *'crucesignati'*, Crusader. The participants of the Third Crusade were to be Crusaders; pilgrims were no longer encouraged to take part in what was essentially a military expedition. The *'Audita Tremendi'* was also a call to repent. Robbers, rapists and murderers across England and France sought the opportunity to repent of their crimes and join the crusade. In doing so, these criminals were able to escape justice for their crimes.

Having issued *'Audita Tremendi'*, Pope Gregory VIII died on the 17th December 1187.

A new Pope was elected; Clement III. Clement III was somewhat healthier than his predecessors and agreed with the idea of the Third Crusade. Whilst Archbishop Josias was sent to continue his mission to recruit the Kings of France and England, Pope Gregory went north of the Alps to recruit the most powerful secular ruler of Western Europe; The Emperor-King Frederick Barbarossa.

The Crusade of Frederick Barbarossa

Who was Frederick Barbarossa?

Frederick Barbarossa was the Emperor-King of Germany. When the news of the loss of Jerusalem reached him he was in his late sixties and had ruled Germany as King and Emperor for over three decades. In his youth Frederick had been to Jerusalem and was a veteran of the Second Crusade. He had served his Uncle, Conrad the King of Germany as his chief lieutenant during the Second Crusade. Frederick had spent much of his reign as ruler of Germany fighting in Italy against forces allied to the Papacy. Relations with Pope Urban III had been unsettled; since in 1187 the two had been in a state of war. However the new Pope Gregory VIII and his successor Clement III both patched up a peace treaty and relations improved.

Taking the Cross

Frederick Barbarossa took the cross on 27th March 1188, several months after the Kings of England and France. Frederick made his preparations carefully, but rapidly. He announced that his eldest son Conrad would remain in Germany to govern. His second son, Frederick of Swabia would accompany the Crusade expedition. Frederick's main political rival in Germany; Duke Henry the Lion of Saxony was given a choice, surrender his lands, accompany the crusade or go into exile for a period of no less than three years. Duke Henry chose exile and went to England.

It is almost certain that Frederick order preparations for his crusade to begin months before he took the cross in March 1189 as his expedition set off May 1189; only 2 months after Frederick officially took the cross.

Organisation

The German Emperor Frederick Barbarossa also seems to have overlooked the use of the Saladin Tithe. Instead he insisted that his army would march together, but each contingent would have to pay its own way. In this respect, as well as in its direction of march, the army of Frederick Barbarossa was attempting to recreate the expeditions of the Frist and Second Crusade. This allowed Frederick to gather his large army quickly and to set out much sooner than the English and French contingents.

Frederick's army was large. Numbers in the sources estimate between 80-100,000 soldiers, including 20,000 knights. Whilst these numbers are probably exaggerated, the army was certainly large. Several sources record that Frederick's army took three days to pass at two different locations. If this was the case the army may well have numbered between 60-70,000. The size of the expedition was reason enough for it to march by land and not sail. No single fleet would have been able to accommodate such a large number and the cost would have been immense. Through force of personality and the possession of a large number of fiefs and vassals; Frederick was able to amass a huge army for the Third Crusade.

This method however was problematic. Frederick Barbarossa united and commanded his army through the sheer force of his own personal charisma and personality. When Frederick died however, his army rapidly disintegrated into groups, many deserted and returned to Germany, some remained in Antioch, others continued under Frederick's son, Frederick of Swabia, but he was unable to lead only a small proportion of the German Crusade to the siege of Acre, and when he died there soon after; even this remnant dispersed.

Barbarossa's Crusade

Emperor Frederick left Ratisbon in May 1189 and largely followed the same route of both the First and Second Crusade. Before he set out Frederick sent letters to the rulers of Hungary, the Byzantine Empire and the Seljuk Sultan of Rum requesting that his army could pass peacefully through these realms and also requesting that food and supplies be made available to his men. Frederick also sent a letter to Saladin requesting that he meet him in battle in November 1189.

The Byzantine Empire

The German army passed peacefully enough through Hungary; inspired in part by the availability of food and supplies as well as the harsh discipline imposed on any individual that broke the rules established by Frederick. It was when the Crusaders reached the Byzantine Empire that it faced greater difficulties.

In July 1189 the Byzantine Empire was a very different place to that visited by Frederick during the Second Crusade. In 1189 the Byzantine Empire was in a state of fragmentation and indeed of collapse. Manuel's son Alexius II had been usurped and killed by Andronicus Comnenus who ruled with a tyrannical hand from 1183-1185 before being overthrown and murdered by an enraged mob in the Hippodrome of Constantinople. He had been succeeded by Isaac Angelus a minor nobleman who had come to power by instigating the revolt that overthrew Andronicus.

All was not well with the Empire during the reign of Isaac Angelus;

- The armed forces of the Empire had not recovered from their defeat at Myriocephalum in 1176

- The Empire had been at war with Sicily from 1184-1187

- Cyprus was in revolt, ruled by Isaac Comnenus

- Cilicia had been lost to the Armenians

- Bulgaria was overrun with bandits and rebels

- Serbia was in the process of becoming its own independent state

- Isaac Angelus had also formed an alliance with Saladin against the Seljuk Turks

As a result, the Empire was not well prepared to receive such an immense army as Fredericks. The German crusaders were attacked by Serbians and Bulgarians. The local Byzantine army detachments refused to assist the Crusaders and were accused of complicity in these attacks.

The situation was not improved by Isaac's own ambassadors to Frederick defecting and advising the Germans to attack Constantinople and overthrow Isaac. In a desperate move to encourage the Germans to cross into Asia via Gallipoli rather than at Constantinople; Isaac imprisoned Frederick's representatives to hold as hostages. Frederick in turn occupied a city and spent the winter of 1189-90 there. He also sent messages back to his son Conrad in Germany requesting that he raise a fleet that could be used to attack the Empire. The situation had the potential to degenerate into farce.

However, wintering in Northern Greece was a sensible precaution for Frederick. His army could therefore travel across Asia in the summer months and not repeat the errors of the Second Crusade by marching through Anatolia in the winter months. Peace was restored between the two Emperors and it was agreed that the Germans would cross into Asia via Gallipoli. This crossing was completed in March 1190.

The death of Barbarossa

Travelling in April and May across Anatolia was sensible for such a large force. Temperatures were not too hot and food supplies more plentiful. However, the Seljuk Sultan did not agree to the safe passage requested. His men harassed the Crusaders but the size of the army deterred the Seljuks from opposing them in a straight battle.

In reprisal for these attacks Frederick marched on the Seljuk capital of Iconium (Konya) and after a sharp battle, forced the Sultan to retreat. The city was seized and plundered on 17th May 1190. By early June 1190, Frederick's army had reached Cilicia and was approaching the territory of Antioch when disaster struck.

On the 10th June 1190 the Emperor Frederick died. What happened is uncertain. Perhaps he died of a heart attack after swimming in a particularly cold river, perhaps he was thrown from his horse into the river, or perhaps it was a stroke. Whatever happened, Frederick died on the 10th June 1190.

A disaster for the Third Crusade?

Frederick had almost managed to bring a large, intact army to Outremer. Had he survived his large army might have been able to achieve what Richard I could not; capture Jerusalem. Frederick's death however fragmented his army. His son Frederick, the Duke of Swabia, been able to keep the Crusade together then he may also have achieved the aim of recapturing Jerusalem. However, the Duke of Swabia did not have the personal charisma required to keep the large German army together. Some sections immediately left the army there in Cilicia, and more left once the army reached Antioch. Frederick Barbarossa was buried in the Cathedral of Antioch and his son, eager to see the Crusade through, continued into Palestine leading an ever smaller force. In August 1190, Frederick Swabia reached Tyre and proceeded on from there to the siege of Acre. At Acre Frederick of Swabia would die like thousands of others; of disease during the long drawn out siege.

The kings of France and England

It was just as well that the Pope declared a European wide truce in the *'Audita Tremendi'*. The Kings of France and England had been fighting a rather inconclusive border war for several years in 1187 and this in itself had provided sufficient distraction for the knights and nobles of western Europe, who did not have far to travel to partake in war, pillage and destruction. England was ruled by King Henry II, the Plantagenet king who had ruled England, much of Wales and France for decades. His adversary was King Philip II of France; also known as Philip Augustus. Henry's son and heir was Richard of Poitiers; better known as 'Richard the Lionheart'. Richard was not a loyal son, often in revolt or conspiracy against his father, but when he heard news of the Crusade in November 1187, Richard swore to take the cross and join the crusade. Such a hasty move further alienated Henry from his son as Henry was somewhat more reluctant to partake in the crusade.

In January 1188 Archbishop Josias met both Kings at the town of Gisors on the border of the duchy of Normandy. At Gisors the two kings agreed to a truce and both determined to pledge themselves to the Third Crusade. Joining the kings at Gisors was also Philip, the Count of Flanders. It was decided that all the forces of England, France and Flanders would travel together to Jerusalem. The followers of the English King would wear White Crosses, the French would wear Red Crosses and the followers of the Count of Flanders would wear Green crosses.

Other rulers were not reached by Josias; and the appeal of the Crusade was somewhat less attractive to the rulers of other countries; King Canute VI of Denmark, King Sverre of Norway and King William the Lion of Scotland all refused to take the cross and recruitment from these kingdoms was much less than that of England, France and Germany.

The motives of Philip and Richard

Was the news of the loss of Jerusalem and the urge to restore it to Christian control sufficient enough reason to go on Crusade?

King Philip

According to Steven Runciman, King Philip motives for going on Crusade went beyond that of considered Christian duty;

> "...he was no idealist, and he went crusading merely from political necessity."

Runciman 1954, p34

In 1187, King Philip of France was in his mid-twenties, but had already been King of France for some ten years. His views of Crusading may well have been influenced by the views of his Father on the matter, Louis VII who had led the Second Crusade to the fiasco outside Damascus. Despite the piety of Louis VII, that one experience was enough Crusading for him.

However, King Philip needed to go on Crusade because he was struggling as king. He had been in a series of wars with his rival Henry Plantagenet, who in addition to being King of England was also overlord of more territory of France than King Philip himself. King Philip was badly in need of the goodwill of the Church and needed a way to ensure tighter control of the power Counts and Dukes of France. King Philip also faced a dilemma, if the English king was to go on Crusade and Philip did not, then those French lords that were going on Crusade would likely fall under the influence of the English King. Likewise, if King Philip went on Crusade and the English King did not. Then he risked being unable to defend his lands from any attempt to dispossess him.

The solution therefore required both rulers to go on Crusade.

King Henry II

King Henry was also somewhat reluctant to go Crusading. He had previously resented attempts to recruit men and money to be as he saw, wasted in Outremer and this reluctance was not helped by Henry's age and state of health. Henry was already ill when he agreed to go on Crusade at Gisors in January 1188. His health was not helped by his son's rebellion and Henry was only able to make a peace with Richard and Philip a few days before his death. Henry had however prepared some of the ground for his successor; permitting the raising of the Saladin Tithe, and preparing the fleet in England, which sailed under the Archbishop of Canterbury.

King Richard

King Richard was in his early thirties at the time of the loss of Jerusalem. The eldest surviving son of Henry, Richard was a powerful lord in his own right as the Duke of Poitiers. Richard was eager to prove his mettle as a knight and spent much of his life fighting in one conflict or another; including against his father. For Richard, the pull of Outremer may have been in part down to vanity. If he could restore Jerusalem to Christian control; he would possess a fame and reputation greater than any of his contemporaries. Richard had already announced his intention to go on Crusade in November 1187; several months before his father and the French king.

The Saladin Tithe

It was also decided at Gisors to arrange and regulate taxes that would finance the Crusade expeditions. The Saladin Tithe was a 10% flat rate tax on income and moveable property of all subjects of the kings. Only those that were to go on the Crusade expedition were to be exempt and therefore the application of this tax was a great encouragement to many to join the crusade; particularly the wealthy and those who could afford to best fight as knights. Many peasants had little disposal income and less moveable property that could be taxed. Lords and knights on the other hand had more coin, more luxurious goods and livestock, and so faced a large tax bill. The Saladin Tithe could be avoided if an individual went and joined the Crusade.

The lands of the English king were better organised and regulated and the Saladin Tithe was rigidly enforced most effectively by King

Henry and subsequently by his son and heir Richard. However, King William of Scotland was subject to King Henry and the Saladin Tithe, however he was unable to compel his lords to participate in raising the Saladin Tithe. Henry also had to face some abuse of this extraordinary tax. A Templar knight, called Gilbert of Hoxton tried to steal the Saladin Tithe that he was entrusted with. Philip of France had less direct control over his lands and taxation and was therefore less able to implement the Saladin Tithe. This would ensure that Philip had less money to raise his expeditionary force and less able to maintain it once he arrived in Outremer.

Raising Revenue and recruitment

Each Crusade leader needed to raise revenue in order to finance themselves and the expeditions they wished to lead to Outremer. The Saladin Tithe could raise impressive amounts of cash, but whilst the King of England proceeded with the rigorous application of the Tithe; King Philip II of France was not able to enforce the Saladin Tithe effectively. As a result, although almost all of the French Counts joined the Crusade, they raised their own forces and commanded themselves. The French King could only afford to finance his immediate household and a small additional contingent.

Richard I on the other hand not only stringently applied the Saladin Tithe across his lands; he also sold crown lands and appointed officials to posts that they paid for. The result was wholesale corruption. Richard's brother and the future king John, was able to acquire large amounts of land in SW England and more unwisely was able to live on these lands. The result was that the longer Richard I was away from his kingdom, the more John was able to assert his authority.

Arab historians also mention on several occasions some of the techniques that the Christians used to encourage recruitment. Conrad of Montferrat is said to have produced a picture of Jerusalem being captured, whilst the contemporary Iraqi historian Ibn al-Athir (1160-1233) mentions the production of posters depicting Jesus being struck in the face by an Arab. Such pictures combined with recruiting drives by priests and secular leaders were just some of the techniques used to encourage recruitment.

Some detailed documentation also survives in England illustrating the preparation and effort involved; numbers of arrows, horseshoes created and loaded onto ships, numbers of pig carcasses salted and likewise prepared for transportation.

Dissent and delay

The meeting at Gisors promised a Crusade response from the rulers of England and France, however this Crusade response faced delays and procrastinations as it became clear that the Papal truce was less important than the immediate squabbles of the lords of the land.

Richard of Poitiers faced a revolt in his lands in what is now Southern France in June 1188 and in addition he could not halt a border war with his neighbour and rival the Count of Toulouse. Despite his families' record in Crusading history, the current Count of Toulouse had little interest in heading to Jerusalem and was happy to ignore the Papal Truce. The border war escalated and King Philip of France decided to intervene and invaded Richard's lands. King Henry in turn began to attack King Philip's land in Northern France. By January 1189 this war took on a new twist when Richard of Poitiers rebelled against his father and joined the French king in attacks on Henry's lands in Normandy, Maine and Anjou. Peace was not restored until the 3rd of July 1189 and only three days later, King Henry of England himself died, leaving Richard King of England.

Persecution in England

The death of Henry brought peace to Western Europe. Richard was crowned in England on 3rd September 1189 and preparations for the Third Crusade could continue now, undistracted by war.

However, some communities were disproportionately affected by the preparations for the Third Crusade. In England many people were resentful of the Saladin Tithe and, combined with the news of the loss of Jerusalem, some people looked closer to home for a target on which to vent. King Richard I's coronation was celebrated by some with attacks on the Jewish communities. In places such as London Jews were targeted and massacred, and in York the local Jewish community was forced to take shelter in Clifford's Tower were they were besieged and some were forced to commit suicide before the remainder were burned alive. The rioters then proceeded to York Minster, where they burned the tax records that had assessed how much they owed for the Saladin Tithe.

THE CRUSADES 1095-1204

The size of the armies of the Third Crusade

The Crusade armies that came from Europe between 1186-1190 are fairly well documented. We know that the following lords and kings commanded their own forces;

- Emperor Frederick Barbarossa
- King Richard of England
- King Philip of France
- Count Henry of Champagne
- Duke Henry of Burgundy

There were other smaller forces led by individuals such as the Count of Nevers and James of Avesnes.

Numbers

- Emperor Frederick Barbarossa is recorded as leading an army of 20,000 knights and 80,000 infantry. In probability this force was smaller – perhaps 40-60,000 in total.
- King Richard of England led an army that sailed to Outremer on a total of 219 ships – 100 of which were paid for and carried his own personally raised army. 100 ships could carry perhaps 6000 knights and soldiers. Gerald of Wales mentions 3000 Welsh mercenaries (spearmen and archers) in Richard's army so the total for Richard was probably around 17,000 sailors, knights and infantry.
- King Philip of France directly commanded an army of some 650 knights and 1300 squires carrying perhaps 50 ships.

Smaller but notable contingents sailed to Outremer including those commanded by the following lords;

- Count Henry of Champagne
- Count Louis of Thuringia
- Duke Leopold of Austria
- Duke Henry of Burgundy
- Individuals also sailed out to Outremer – including a Spanish knight known only as *'The Green Knight'* who was present at Acre by the end of the year 1189.

It could be estimated that approximately 80-100,000 knights, infantry, sailors and non-combatants set out from Western Europe to participate in the Third Crusade. Some women joined the Crusade as servants, cooks, washerwomen, prostitutes and indeed as fighters. Some women are recorded as fighting in the battles around Acre in 1189-1191.

The Kings set out

The Kings of France and England set out from Vezelay together with their personal armies on the 4th July 1190. There had been delays including the death of King Philip's wife and the delay caused by the wars between the leaders. Together the Kings travelled in close company to Lyons before separating to reach their ports of departure. Both kings agreed to sail to Outremer and some time would have been spent in ensuring that sufficient ships were available to transport their armies to the Holy land.

Both kings agreed that the expedition should be subject to strict rules;

- Food and supplies were to be made available and subject to strict price controls

- Gambling was forbidden for the soldiers

- Debts incurred on the expedition were to be repaid in full

- Future conquests were to be shared equally between Richard and Philip

Richard travelled to Marseilles and Philip travelled to Genoa. Both Kings agreed to rendezvous on the island of Sicily where they would winter and avoid the storms that might devastate the fleets if they sailed during the winter. However, Richard had other ideas. Disliking the idea of the sea journey to Sicily, Richard instead travelled by land through Italy. Richard travelled swiftly and reached the Sicilian port of Messina on the 3rd of September 1190. Philip sailed and arrived at Messina on the 14th September 1190. Here both kings planned to wait, winter and ensure that other forces could join them. Richard in particular, also had other good reasons to visit Sicily.

Sicilian adventures

The island of Sicily was part of a vibrant and energetic Norman kingdom. However, King William II of Sicily had died in November 1189. He had been married to Richard's sister Joanna, but their marriage had been childless and the new king of Sicily was Tancred; William's cousin. King William had left in his will a sizeable inheritance as well as the promise of warships. Tancred was reluctant to hand over this treasure to Richard and not only refused to do so, he also decided to imprison Queen Joanna.

On his arrival in Messina, Richard demanded the return of his sister as well as the money. King Philip tried to broker peaceful negotiations between the English and Sicilian Kings but Richard had a large army at hand and was determined to have his way. Messina was forcibly occupied by the English troops in October, other Sicilian towns captured and a monastery full of Orthodox monks were made homeless. Richard also seized control of a part of the Sicilian fleet and set fire to it.

King Philip was shocked and angered by Richard's actions. He was resident in Messina when the English troops sacked the city and Richard had shown a disregard for Philip's diplomacy. Relations deteriorated further when Richard, who was unmarried, rejected a marriage between Philip's sister Alice and Richard. Alice, according to Richard had a dubious reputation which made her unsuitable. This undiplomatic response was made into a worse insult when Richard announced his intention to marry Berengaria of Navarre, who now joined Richard in Sicily with the intention of accompanying the Crusade.

Peace was restored between Tancred and Richard when Tancred agreed to release Queen Joanna, who would also join the expedition to Outremer, and Tancred also paid Richard 20,000 ounces of gold to Richard in lieu of the inheritance, and an equal amount to Queen Joanna. Richard now had substantially more money to spend on his Crusade.

The Kings wintered in Sicily and Philip set sail for Outremer on the 30th March 1191. Philip's fleet sailed without incident directly to Outremer and arrived at Tyre in mid-April 1191. From there the French fleet sailed down to the siege of Acre, which they reached on 20th April 1191.

For Richard however, his journey was less smooth. Departing from Sicily on the 4th April 1191, his adventures in the Mediterranean would continue.

Richard and Cyprus

Richard's fleet sailed from Sicily to the island of Crete and then onto the island of Rhodes which he reached on the 22nd of April 1191. He remained here until the 1st May 1191 when he sailed to Cyprus in order to deal with a problem.

The problem was one of those problems that arose out of accidental circumstance. A storm had scattered part of Richard's fleet on the approach to Rhodes. One ship was lost in the storm and another three were swept by strong winds to the island of Cyprus. Here two of the ships were wrecked. The third ship made safe harbour was carrying Richard's sister Joanna and his bride to be Berengaria of Navarre.

The island of Cyprus was in 1191 effectively an independent state. It had revolted from the Byzantine Empire in 1185 when the Emperor Andronicus was killed and replaced by Isaac Angelus. The military governor of the island was Isaac Comnenus, a relation of Andronicus and he objected to the usurpation of the Imperial throne. Isaac Comnenus however decided that rather than welcoming and offering hospitality to the shipwreck survivors of Richard's fleet, he decided instead to imprison them whilst holding Joanna and Berengaria as hostages.

Richard arrived with part of his fleet off the coast of Cyprus on the 8th May 1191. Isaac Comnenus tried to encourage Richard to leave and refused to hand over his prisoners. He did however release Joanna and Berengaria. Richard married Berengaria on the 12th May 1191 in the company of several important visitors from Outremer including Guy of Lusignan and Bohemund III of Antioch who had sailed over to greet Richard.

Richard decided that Isaac Comnenus should be dealt with. In a three week campaign Richard defeated Isaac in battle and captured several of his castles. By the end of May 1191 Isaac was captured and imprisoned in silver chains. He had agreed to surrender so long as he was not 'bound in irons', so Richard honoured this and used silver manacles instead.

Capturing Cyprus secured for Richard large quantities of plunder and control of the island. Richard had no need for Cyprus so sold the island to the Templars for 100,000 Bezants – of which he received 40,000. Later, the island would be transferred to Guy of Lusignan who paid Richard the remaining 60,000 Bezants. The occupation of the island of Cyprus was also a foreshadowing of what was to come. Cyprus was a Byzantine province and its seizure by Western Europeans would be followed within a fifteen years by other large parts of the Byzantine Empire, including the capital city of Constantinople.

From Cyprus Richard and his fleet sailed to Tyre, reaching that place on the 6th June 1191. Richard was refused admittance by soldiers loyal to Conrad of Montferrat and King Philip, so Richard took his army and travelled down to the siege of Acre, which he reached on the 8th June 1191.

Task: Research Task

Consider the Third Crusade, alongside the 1st and 2nd Crusades as well as the other less known Crusading events.

- Explore the similarities and differences in the preparations and journeys of these expeditions to Outremer.

- Explore also the motivations and reasons for these Crusades – consider how prominent religious piety was in the motivations for leaders and followers to go on Crusade?

- To what extent does the evidence suggest that the organisation of Crusades improved?

- To what extent does the evidence suggest evidence that the leadership of the Crusading expeditions improved?

For each bullet point write a response of no more than 500 words.

5.5 The Third Crusade

In this topic we will;

- *Understand the scale and extent of the military assistance sent to Palestine from Europe*
- *Understand the major events of the Third Crusade*
- *Consider the strategies utilised by Saladin during the wars of Palestine*
- *Consider the strategies utilised by the Frankish leaders during the wars of Palestine*

Introduction

In this topic we will discuss the major events of the war in Palestine that was fought from 1188-1192. In particular we will explore the sources of help that reached Palestine in these years and the arrival of the Royal armies commanded by Kings Philip and Richard the Lionheart. We will also consider the diplomatic steps undertaken by both sides throughout this period.

Help for Outremer 1188-1189

Conrad of Montferrat was not the only source of help to reach Outremer in 1188-89. A succession of fleets travelled to Outremer and their presence helped to keep the vital ports of Tyre and Tripoli in Frankish hands.

The Green Knight

Saladin returned to attack Tyre in the summer of 1188. Here additional forces had arrived to bolster those commanded by Conrad of Montferrat. In particular a single knight attracted much attention. Renowned for his skill in battle, a knight from Spain, identified only as 'The Green Knight' so impressed Saladin that he arranged to meet with him. Saladin's purpose was to try to arrange a truce with Tyre and also to try and recruit the Green knight into his own service. However, the Green knight refused both the offer of employment and the truce. The Franks would not accept any truce that did not involve the restoration of the lands taken in the past few years.

The Sicilian fleet

William of Tripoli sent a large fleet soon after he heard the news of the disaster of Hattin and this fleet, commanded by the Sicilian Admiral Margaritus, reached Tripoli by the end of April 1188. This fleet deterred Saladin's Egyptian naval squadrons and helped to keep both Tyre and Tripoli in the hands of the Franks. The Sicilian fleet also influenced Saladin's decision not to continue with the siege of Krak des Chevaliers.

Saladin was eager to understand the motives of the Sicilian fleet. He met Admiral Margaritus in Northern Syria at Lattakieh and the Sicilian fleet also gave assistance to Bohemund III, Prince of Antioch. Saladin had conquered several castles and towns in Northern Syria but desisted from further assaults when he arranged a truce with Bohemund III in September 1188. However, the assistance given by this Sicilian fleet was only to last for two years. By the end of 1189 these ships had been recalled to Sicily on the news of the death of King William II of Sicily.

Saladin releases his prisoners

Saladin appears to have been attempting diplomatic solutions alongside his goal of reconquering the lands held by the Franks during 1187-1188. Saladin had captured many notable prisoners at the battle of Hattin and pursued a policy of releasing these prisoners in return for the surrender of castles and towns. In September 1187 the Grandmaster of the Templars, Gerard of Ridefort was released after he ordered his Templar knights to surrender the fortress of Gaza. Humphrey of Toron was released in May 1189 after his possessions had been captured. King Guy was released in July 1188. He had tried to order Ascalon to surrender; but the garrison had ignored the commands of the king. Saladin released him anyway after received from Guy and oath to leave Palestine and never to fight against Muslims again. Guy ignored this oath after his release, but Saladin probably expected this response, but released him anyway.

Why release these prisoners? For Saladin each siege took time, manpower and money, and there were a great many fortified castles, towns and ports in Outremer. The release of a noble prisoner in return for surrender was probably a good deal for Saladin. These nobles had been defeated once, they could be defeated again. Some, particularly King Guy, were seen as a divisive figure who may help to foster division and difficulties amongst the Franks by splitting their unity. This policy attracted criticism from among Saladin's supporters; the contemporary historian Ibn al-Athir saw this policy of clemency as a weakness and one that allowed the Franks to regroup.

Saladin also disbanded much of his army at the end of 1188. Keeping an army together was a costly and difficult enterprise, and quite simply, in 1188 there was little for them to fight. Saladin could or would not attack Tyre with any enthusiasm and Tripoli was covered partially under the truce arranged with Bohemund III of Antioch. Saladin's large army was drain on his finances, but also he realised that help would be coming from Western Europe; by allowing his army to go home for the winter, he could let them relax, spend their earnings and return to him in 1189-1190 more enthusiastic than they would be if he made them keep in army camps all winter.

Saladin's whereabouts January- August 1189

Saladin himself spent the months of January to March 1189 in Jerusalem and Acre, rebuilding fortifications, reorganising these places before spending March and April 1189 in his capital city of Damascus. From April to August 1189, Saladin was present at the siege of Beaufort, a strong castle in Palestine still holding out.

Guy vs Conrad

In 1188 the Franks did indeed split into two divided factions. Tyre was commanded by Conrad of Montferrat and he attracted the support of many Frankish barons including Balian of Ibelin. Guy was also well connected in Europe. He was related to both Frederick Barbarossa and King Philip of France. He could expect assistance from lords arriving from Western Europe from the lands of these rulers.

Guy on the other hand based himself with Queen Sibylla at Tripoli. In Europe he had owed allegiance to King Richard and so hoped to attract the support of Crusaders coming from the lands of the English king. He also had the continued support of the Templars.

After his release, In late 1188, Guy marched to Tyre and demanded entrance to the city. Conrad refused, declaring Guy was no longer king, it was up to the kings of England, France and the German Emperor to decide who would rule the kingdom of Jerusalem.

Towards the siege of Acre

On the 6th April 1189 a new fleet arrived from Western Europe. This fleet was from the Italian city of Pisa and numbered 52 ships. The Pisans were commanded by their Archbishop and arrived at Tyre.

Another arrival at Tyre in April was King Guy. He led another small army south from Tripoli and again demanded entrance to Tyre. Again Conrad refused. However, Guy did manage to obtain the support of the Pisans, they had squabbled with Conrad over trading rights. Other forces had been arriving in Palestine in the past few months and numbers were growing. These forces would need to be used.

Saladin was still focussed on the siege of Beaufort and several strategies began to be considered;

- An attack on Saladin at Beaufort
- An attempt on ports north of Tripoli
- An attempt on ports south of Tyre

Beaufort was a strong castle, but to attack Saladin directly would be to attack his strongest force. An attempt was made to capture the port city of Sidon in July 1189, but this was repulsed. The third option was to attack southwards, towards Acre.

Acre was the largest and most important port in the Kingdom of Jerusalem. The city was heavily fortified, but had a large harbour and had been the wealthiest city of the Kingdom, more wealthy even than Jerusalem.

Guy decided to attack Acre. With a small army of several thousand men, a few hundred knights and soldiers recruited from the fleets of the Pisans, the Sicilians and other arrivals, Guy marched on Acre in August 1189.It was a brave move. Acre was a strongly fortress in its own right, but its garrison was large, Saladin having posted 5-6,000 men in the city to protect it. However the move may have wrong-footed Saladin. He expected the Franks to try to attack him at Beaufort, or failing that use the march on acre as a feint, to encourage him to abandon his siege.

Guy however knew that reinforcements were on the way. By also being seen to act, he would provide an attractive alternative to Conrad, who refused to join him and remained in Tyre. Guy reached

Acre on the 28th August 1189. He attempted to capture the place by storm on the 1st September 1189 but was repulsed. The fleets of the Pisans and the Sicilians blockaded the city by sea. The siege of Acre had begun.

The Siege of Acre

The siege of Acre was a brutal and bloody affair that lasted almost two years. The siege saw many attacks by both Christians and Muslims and casualties were immense. As we shall see many leaders died during the siege, many more suffered illness and of the common soldiery on both sides of the battle lines the losses were huge. Some liken the siege to the battles of attrition fought in the First World War. What is clear from the sources however is that both sides required constant large scale reinforcements in order to hold out in their respective positions.

The siege was won by the crusaders in time, because they were able to continue to bring large numbers of forces to the siege for longer than Saladin was able to do.

September 1189: The arrival of James of Avesnes and Saladin

Soon after the siege of Acre began, in September 1189 a fleet of Danish and Flemish ships; estimated to number 500, though probably were much fewer, arrived at Tyre to bolster the forces of Conrad of Montferrat. Very probably these were citizens of coastal communities and did not include any great lords. Likewise another small fleet from Flanders, commanded by a Flanders knight called James of Avesnes arrived either in late September or in October 1189. James of Avesnes would take a leading role in the siege of Acre and die at the battle of Arsuf in 1191. Another leading lord from Europe was Count Louis of Thuringia who arrived soon after James of Avesnes.

These fleets were not commanded by the leading men of the Crusades. What they did bring however was a steady stream of reinforcements and supplies to Outremer and enable the Franks to maintain control of the vital ports of Tripoli and Tyre, but also enable the Franks to continue the siege of Acre; control of which was necessary for the Crusade to continue towards its ultimate goal.

Saladin arrived at the siege of Acre on the 15th September. He had captured Beaufort and now came to deal with Guy. Saladin launched an immediate attack on Guy's camp. This attack was repulsed and so

Saladin set up his own fortified camp a few miles from that of the Crusaders, who also fortified their own camp.

At the end of September Conrad joined Guy and the others at Acre, bringing with him the men from the fleet of Danish and Flemish ships that had recently arrived.

October –December 1189: Battles and attrition

On the 4th October Guy led the Crusading army out to attack Saladin's army. Guy now had about 30,000 soldiers and Saladin probably had about 20,000 men. The battle was fierce, Guy had to lead a rescue attempt to save Conrad and Gerard of Ridefort was captured in the battle. He was executed by Saladin and can be counted amongst the perhaps 4000 Crusader deaths in this battle. Saladin lost a similar amount of men.

On the 31st October, a fleet from Egypt managed to break through to the harbour of Acre and bring in supplies and men for the garrison of the city. Another convoy would manage the same feat on the 26th December 1189.

In November 1189 another fleet arrived from Europe; the fleet, of about 35 ships, English and Flemish, left England in August 1189 and would winter in Portugal where they helped to capture the fortress of Silves for the Portuguese King before continuing to Palestine, arrived. Saladin too called on additional forces, summoning soldiers from Mosul and Egypt; men who had been disbanded in the previous year.

Winter 1189-1190

The siege continued through winter; with the Crusaders besieging Acre, but in turn being blockaded by Saladin's army that prevented the Crusaders from easily raiding the area for food supplies. There were no major battles but many skirmishes as well as some fraternisation between Saladin's men and the Crusaders. Saladin faced growing criticism from his own men, unhappy that they had not defeated the Crusaders and that they were forced to remain in the field over winter. In the Christian camp Guy and Conrad had reached reconciliation; with Conrad recognising Guy as king, in return Conrad was guaranteed possession of Tyre and further conquests. In March 1190 Conrad returned to Tyre to arrange for food supplies and reinforcements to be shipped to the army. Conrad returned at the end of March and his fleet defeated a fleet of Saladin's outside Tyre. One ship crew was captured and these men were horrifically tortured and killed by a group of Crusading women.

The siege continues May-July 1190

On the 5th May 1190 the Crusaders again attempted to capture Acre but failed. Saladin retaliated on the 19th May and began an 8 day battle in which no decisive result was obtained other than heavy casualties. Another battle was fought on the 25th July which resulted in some 5000 Crusader casualties.

These heavy losses decimated the Crusaders, but these dead soldiers were replaced. On the 28th July Count Henry of Champagne arrived with a large French fleet of some 50-60 ships. Henry had with him many Counts of France who had not waited for the Royal expeditions to set out. Henry was instantly regarded as the commander of the Crusaders around Acre. He was well connected, nephew of both King Philip and King Richard and was therefore seen as a unity leader. In Early October 1190, an English fleet commanded by Baldwin, Archbishop of Canterbury arrived. He had set out with king Richard from Marseilles in August 1190, but unlike the king had sailed directly to Palestine. Another large army arrived from the North on the 7th August 1190. Frederick the Duke of Swabia led the remnant of the German Crusade down to Acre and took a leading role in the siege.

With the arrival of Duke Frederick to lead the Germans present at Acre, Count Louis decided to leave. He had been ill for a long time and took ship for home but died on the return journey. What this demonstrates is that the continuing arrival of ships from Europe also saw departures. The siege had been long drawn out and still had no sign of ending. Many Crusader doubtless deserted during the siege of Acre, some are known to have joined the defenders of Acre and served in the garrison of the town.

Duke Frederick announced his arrival at the siege with an assault on the city, this like the others failed and once demonstrating again that the fortifications were strong, seemed now content to join the others in their camp.

The arrival of the additional forces seems however caused some concern for Saladin. He now relocated his camp further away from Acre and the Crusaders; an additional 5 miles needed to be travelled to bring the two opposing forces into confrontation. This suggests that Saladin was already expecting Acre to fall sooner or later and did not want to risk his field army until it had been reinforced.

Autumn and Winter; marriages and fatalities 1190-1191

In autumn Guy suffered the personal loss of the death of Queen Sibylla, but also their infant daughters; all in the space of a few days. In addition to the obvious grief, Guy's claim to kingship had been based on his marriage to Sibylla. The rightful heir to the throne of Jerusalem was now Princess Isabella, wife of Humphrey of Toron.

Humphrey however would be an unsatisfactory king; he was widely regarded as possessing too timid a personality. Balian of Ibelin therefore suggested that Isabella divorce Humphrey and marry Conrad of Montferrat. Isabella was not too keen on the idea; Humphrey was young and attractive, whereas Conrad was middle aged and battle scarred. He also had two other wives, one in Constantinople and one in Italy. However the marriage was arranged in spite of the Archbishop of Canterbury threatening to excommunicate all involved. Archbishop Baldwin died on the 19th November 1190 and the marriage went ahead a few days later. Conrad and Isabella withdrew from Acre and returned to Tyre, where they had a daughter in 1191. Guy of Lusignan refused to abdicate and insisted being called the king of Jerusalem.

The siege continued, an attack on Acre was repulsed on the 31st December 1190 and military operations wound down in January and February as winter set in. henry of Champagne became critically ill in January, Duke Frederick of Swabia died of a disease on the 20th January 1191. Frederick was buried in a cemetery near Acre and the site would in 1198 become the founding location of the Germanic Military Order; the Teutonic Knights.

The Crusaders suffered from severe food shortages in the winter of 1190/1 and many died. Saladin used the winter to force a way through to Acre and was able to resupply and reinforce the city in February for a few days. In March the Crusaders were heartened by the return of ships bring food supplies and the arrival of Duke Leopold of Austria with a small army. He would command the Germans in Palestine at the siege for a time until insulted by King Richard.

The arrival of Kings Philip and Richard

In April 1191, the siege had now reached its twentieth month. Both sides were exhausted by the fighting, the diseases and the food shortages. Saladin had few additional men that he could call up to serve in his army. The crusaders still had large numbers, but tens of thousands had died outside Acre already. The siege may not have continued, but for the arrival of the long awaited kings of France and England. The kings of France and England, brought large, fresh and well equipped armies intact to Acre at a time when all other participants were exhausted by the struggle.

King Philip; the Bad Neighbour and the Cat

King Philip arrived at the siege of Acre on 20th April 1191. Philip's army included 650 knights and 1300 squires and he also brought horses, food supplies but most importantly he brought skilled engineers and materials for the construction of siege engines. With Philip also arrived Hugh, Duke of Burgundy and Count Philip of Flanders with their men.

Philip took command of the Crusade forces outside Acre and ensured that the siege was more efficiently prosecuted, but he also decided to wait for King Richard and his larger army to arrive before he would launch any large scale attacks.

Philip constructed many siege engines including a catapult called 'Bad Neighbour' and a siege ladder called 'The Cat' (which was destroyed by fire). The Duke of Burgundy also built a catapult, Count Philip of Flanders constructed two, The Templars and the Hospitallers also each paid for and crewed one each. Another catapult called 'God's own sling' was paid for by a collective of minor lords. This large number of siege engines enabled the walls of Acre to be heavily bombarded, several towers collapsed and breaches occurred. Count Philip of Flanders died of a disease on the 1st June, only a few days after his arrival. His death would cause problems for King Philip, his siege engines would be bought by King Richard on his arrival.

King Richard arrives

King Richard arrived at Tyre on the 6th June 1191. He was refused admittance by Conrad's men so Richard led his army down to Acre, arriving on the 8th June 1191. He arrived and almost immediately succumbed to a sickness that was ravaging the camp. Both Richard and Philip fell ill in June to a sickness called 'arnaldia', perhaps scurvy, that caused Richard's hair and nails to fall out. For a time it was thought that King Richard would die. Despite the sicknesses and continued losses, the Crusaders probably numbered over 25,000 combatants at any given time.

Richard continued to lead his men in the siege of Acre through his illness, even constructing a hut from which he could take shots with a crossbow at the defenders of Acre. In addition to the siege operations being conducted by land, the combined English and French fleets ensured that the naval blockade was tight. Both Kings continued to recruit men to their armies from among those in the area whose lords had died or left Palestine. King Philip paid his new recruits 3 gold pieces a month, when he arrived however, the much wealthier King Richard paid his recruits 4 gold pieces per month.

The surrender of Acre

Saladin too received reinforcements. His soldiers came from Sinjar, Homs, Shaizar, Mosul and Egypt. Despite the arrival of these fresh soldiers, Saladin could not get his men to attack the Crusaders in full force and could only launch distracting attacks when the Crusaders made serious assaults on Acre , as they did on the 3rd of July and again on the 11th July. Saladin planned a major attack for the 5th July, but could not get his men to undertake the assault on the Crusader's camp.

Low on supplies and suffering heavy casualties, the defenders of Acre opened negotiations to surrender the city on the 4th July. On the 12th July, after surviving the heavy attacks of the day before, the garrison surrendered. The terms of the surrender were that;

- Acre would surrender
- All its contents were surrendered
- The garrison of 2700 men and their families would be ransomed for 200,000 dinars by Saladin
- The True Cross, held by Saladin, was to be returned to Christian control
- 1500 Christian prisoners, held by Saladin, would be released

Saladin was not part of these negotiations but agreed to honour these conditions. Whilst preparations were made the Acre garrison was retained and the kings would share control of the city.

Divisions

During the siege of Acre the Crusaders, whilst united in their goal of capturing the city, had been less united on other fronts. The question of the kingship of Jerusalem was raised again, with Richard and the Pisans supporting the claims of Guy, whilst Philip and the Genoese supporting the claims of Conrad of Montferrat.

Another dispute arose over the inheritance of Flanders. Count Philip of Flanders died outside Acre on 1st June 1191. He had no heir and his fiefdom was one of the most important and wealthiest in France. King Philip needed to arrange for the inheritance of these lands and was not able to arrange this whilst he was in Palestine. When Philip demanded of Richard half of the island of Cyprus (at Vezelay it had been agreed that all conquests should be shared equally) Richard refused unless he was given half of Flanders. This was unacceptable to Philip and tensions remained between the two kings. Philip was jealous of Richard's wealth and the way he seemed to becoming the leader of the crusade.

A third dispute arose shortly after the capture of Acre. Acre was occupied by the Crusaders and the banners of the French and English were raised. Duke Leopold of Austria however placed his own banner alongside them, stating his claim as leader of the German contingents of the Crusade. Richard however ordered that

Leopold's banner by thrown into a ditch. This so angered Duke Leopold that he abandoned the Crusade a few days later, swearing revenge. He would get this revenge later.

King Philip goes home

After the capture of Acre, King Philip decided to return to France. An agreement and reunion was patched up between the two kings. Richard did not want Philip splitting the leadership in the crusade, but he did not want Philip to be his enemy in Europe whilst he remained in Palestine.

Philip needed and wanted to go home. He was ill and had been ill almost constantly since he had arrived and he needed to return to France to deal with the issue of Flanders. He also suspected that Richard was plotting to kill him. Philip resented the way Richard spent his money in camp to pay for support, and Philip could not match Richard's wealth.

It was agreed that Philip would leave his army in Palestine under the command of the Duke of Burgundy. Philip also agreed not to try to attack Richard's lands in Europe whilst Richard was absent. In return Philip would support Guy's position as king, Conrad would be his heir and they would share the revenues of the kingdom of Jerusalem.

King Philip travelled to Tyre, arriving on the 31st July 1191 and set sail for Europe on the 2nd August. He had organised the siege of Acre decisively and skilfully and his siege engines had really helped to dishearten the garrison. However, it appeared that two kings were an impediment to the success of the Crusade, whilst both were present it would be inevitable that there would be factions in the crusade leadership. A single king of Europe could achieve more unity of leadership.

Negotiations between Saladin and Richard

Richard had been in communication with Saladin soon after his arrival in Palestine. It must be borne in mind that throughout the Third Crusade, the opposing leaders were in communication through a series of ambassadors. This communication did not prevent serious outbreaks of violence and atrocities however.

On the 11th August 1191 Saladin sent a portion of the ransom and released some of his prisoners as agreed. However, the prisoners released did not include the noble captives that were the ones specified. In return, Richard refused to release any members of the captured Acre garrison. Negotiations reached a stalemate until the 20th August 1191 when Richard, impatient at the delay, decided to send Saladin a most horrific message.

The 2700 survivors of the Acre garrison and their families were paraded before Saladin on the 20th August 1191 and then Richard ordered his men to massacre them all. Saladin's men watched in horror and anger as they saw the Acre garrison murdered. Some tried to rescue them but were repulsed. The massacre was not Richard's finest moment. He was criticised by many, including the Jerusalemite barons. Richard may have had practical reasons for this action, he would need to leave men to guard the Acre garrison and he would need to pay to feed them. He also sent a message to Saladin that he meant business.

The battle of Arsuf

On the 22nd August 1191 King Richard led the Crusade army south from Acre along the coast road in the direction of Jaffa and Ascalon. Accompanying the expedition was the English and Pisan fleets. Conrad of Montferrat did not accompany the Crusade and remained at Tyre. Saladin shadowed Richard's army attacking when he could but focusing on blocking any change of direction towards Jerusalem and seeking out a suitable battlefield. By the beginning of September 1191, Saladin had chosen his battlefield; Arsuf, just inland from Jaffa, and blocking the approach to Jerusalem.

On the 7th September 1191 the battle of Arsuf was fought. Richard was cautious. He kept his men under close control in several divisions. Whilst Count Henry of Champagne was left in charge of the baggage with a strong guard, Richard deployed the remainder for battle.

Saladin opened the battle with an infantry attack, which was repulsed, whilst the rest of Richard's army was showered with arrows, Saladin followed the attack up with a cavalry attack on the Hospitallers, who were positioned on Richard's left flank. The attack was severe and nearly broke through. The Hospitallers pleaded for Richard to launch a charge by the knights, but the plea was refused, however the Hospitallers took matters into their own hands and attacked anyway. This forced Richard to support them and he ordered all the knights in the army to charge. The result was that Saladin's army was routed and forced to retreat. Despite being defeated, Saladin did not suffer many casualties. The Crusaders also did not suffer too many losses; they lost around 100 knights, including James of Avesnes.

Indecision

Saladin retreated to Ramleh, near Jerusalem. Richard did not pursue but remained on the coast and instead rebuilt the fortification of Jaffa which gave the Christians another port fortress on the coast of Palestine. The Crusader army remained at Jaffa from September to Mid-November 1191. Both Richard and Saladin continued in diplomatic exchanges, but nothing was agreed. Richard never met Saladin, but had much contact with Saladin's brother Al-Adil and at one point discussions reached a point where it was suggested that Al-Adil marry Richard's Sister Joanna and govern Palestine jointly. Joanna refused and likewise Al-Adil refused to entertain suggestions that he become a Christian. The strategic city of Ascalon and the Holy City of Jerusalem were demanded by Richard, but Saladin refused both. Jerusalem was his great victory over the Christians and of religious significance to Islam. Ascalon meanwhile was strategically important as it was positioned astride the coastal routes from Egypt to Jerusalem.

In Mid-November 1191 Richard marched from Jaffa to Ramleh and camped at this town for six weeks. Saladin retreated to Jerusalem and summoned fresh armies from Egypt to meet him near Jerusalem. Eventually, Richard decided to continue the journey towards Jerusalem; however his already slow march was further delayed by atrocious weather. At Beit-Nuba, a village some 12 miles from Jerusalem, Richard halted his march and considered his next step.

Saladin had two significant armies; one in Jerusalem, which was well protected with walls and food provisions and another army was positioned within a few miles of the city. Richard had a large army, but If Richard attacked Jerusalem, he would be attacked by the other army. Likewise, if Richard tried to attack the army outside Jerusalem, he risked being attacked in turn by the army at Jerusalem. His army was not large enough to divide and do both tasks. Richard was at an impasse. He decided to retreat on the 8th January 1192 back to the coast.

Back and forth

The retreat in January 1192 caused great resentment in the army. The French began to abandon Richard's army and in April 1191, Hugh Duke of Burgundy ordered all French forces to return to Acre. Hugh had his own problems, he was leader of the French forces loyal to King Philip, still a significant force, but he had ran out of money.

King Richard decided to operate along the coast. At the end of January Richard moved to and occupied Ascalon and spent 3 months rebuilding the fortifications of the city, only interrupting this stay with a swift journey to Acre to stop the Pisans and Genoese from fighting each other and also in continuing his negotiations with Al-Adil. On the 20th March 1192 a deal in principal was agreed; the Christians were to keep what they had conquered and also would be able to visit the Holy sites in Jerusalem as pilgrims. Latin priests could also stay in Jerusalem to oversee the Christian holy sites. The city of Beirut too could be restored to Christian control so long as it was unfortified. This agreement was agreed in principal; however it would take some time before it was implemented.

The murder of Conrad Montferrat

King Richard needed to go home. He had discovered that he could not capture Jerusalem, and if he could, how would the Franks of Outremer keep control of it? Richard had heard reports that his brother John was taking control of England, ignoring Richard's chosen representatives. Also King Philip was rumoured to be plotting attacks on Richard's lands in Northern France.

Richard decided to call a council. He appealed to the Frankish barons of Outremer to support Guy of Lusignan as their king. He was received in silence. No-one wanted Guy as King. Richard now realised this and so agreed that it should be Conrad of Montferrat who was the new king. Richard's nephew, Henry, the Count of

Champagne was sent to Tyre to tell Conrad that he was to be anointed king. Guy was sent to rule Cyprus which he now bought off Richard.

Henry of Champagne reached Tyre on the 20th April 1192 and informed Conrad that he would be king. Eight days later, on 28th April 1192, Conrad was murdered in the streets by two assassins. One was killed in turn and the other captured and interrogated. The assassin stated the murder had been ordered by the 'Old Man of the Mountains' as a reprisal for stealing goods belonging to the assassins, however Richard was rumoured to have been involved as well.

Conrad's widow Isabella had already been married twice. She would remarry some seven days after the murder of Conrad. Her husband was Count Henry of Champagne who would in turn become King. Henry and Isabella would live in Acre, which now became the capital of the new Kingdom of Jerusalem.

Back and forth again

Although a treaty had been in agreed in principal between Richard and Saladin, it was not yet ratified. Richard took the opportunity of the delay to capture Saladin's final port on the coast, Daron which he captured on the 23rd May 1192. The garrison of Daron was systematically massacred by Richard's men; perhaps through excessive enthusiasm on the side of the Crusaders, or as part of a deliberate policy by Richard to send Saladin another message to agree to the treaty.

Whilst Richard was engaged at Daron, the French Crusaders at Acre decided to press for another march on Jerusalem. The reunited Crusade gathered at Ascalon and, in spite of Richard's reluctance plans were made for a new attempt on Jerusalem.

On the 7th June 1192 the Crusade army set out and reached Beit-Nuba on the 11th June. Here the army remained for a month. Saladin had at Jerusalem a large and well equipped army and was prepared to defend the Holy city. He had however restored the True Cross to the Church of the Holy Sepulchre. Saladin was confident that he could defend Jerusalem through the summer months ahead.

The Crusaders remained at Beit-Nuba, a Muslim caravan on route to Jerusalem was captured giving the Crusaders additional supplies, but Richard, supported by the local nobles advised a retreat rather than an attack. If an attack on Jerusalem went ahead the army would suffer from lack of water, it would be most likely a long siege reminiscent of Acre and success was far from assured. The question of long term success was also uncertain. Even if Jerusalem was captured, could the Franks keep hold of it when the 3rd Crusade returned home? None of the major lords of the Crusade with the exception of Henry of Champagne) were eager to remain in Outremer. On the 4th July 1192, Richard ordered a retreat to the coast.

Jaffa

Richard had returned to the coast with the Crusade army. The French contingent now made preparations to return home. At the end of July 1192, Richard was at Acre when news reached him that Saladin had launched an attack.

Saladin decided to attack the newly fortified city of Jaffa. Moving from Jerusalem in mid-July, Saladin besieged Jaffa from the 28th-31st July. After the walls had been breached, the garrison of Jaffa agreed to surrender. On the 31st July the less than 50 knights of the garrison were being escorted through the city in preparation for surrender when King Richard arrived by sea. He had some 50 ships carrying 80 knights, 400 archers and some 2000 Italian sailors. At the news of Richard's arrival the 49 knights of the Jaffa garrison renewed the attack and urged Richard to join them in the street fighting now taking place. Richard was at first reluctant, but hearing news of the battle just beginning decided to join in. Richard waded ashore with his soldiers and drove Saladin's men out of the city in some bitter hand to hand fighting. Subsequent fighting occurred when Saladin attempted to oust Richard and his men from Jaffa before the main Crusade army arrived from Acre by land. On the 5th August Richard's small army defeated some 7000 men of Saladin's army in a well fought battle.

Peace

On the 2nd of September 1192 the treaty of peace, long agreed in principal in March was finalised. The treaty allowed the following;

- A 5 year peace treaty was in place.

- The Christians were to keep what they had conquered.

- The Christians were allowed to visit the Holy sites in Jerusalem as pilgrims.

- Latin priests could also stay in Jerusalem to oversee the Christian holy sites.

- The city of Beirut was restored to Christian control so long as it was unfortified.

- The city of Ascalon was to remain in Christian control so long as it was unfortified.

The crusade had not succeeded in recapturing Jerusalem, but access to the Holy sites had been safeguarded. King Richard allowed his men to visit Jerusalem as pilgrims but refused to do so himself. Richard had secured his reputation as a warrior and a knight. He had commanded his men skilfully in battle and had consistently attempted to achieve a diplomatic solution with Saladin. Quite early on both Saladin and Richard had realised that neither had the strength to achieve an outright victory. Richard could not recapture Jerusalem, but Saladin had not been able to totally eliminate the Franks in Palestine.

The Kingdom of Jerusalem had been re-founded from the two cities of Tyre and Tripoli. It now possessed control of a coastal strip of land some 10-15 miles wide and ninety miles long; much smaller than it had been previously. But the Second Kingdom of Jerusalem was now viable; it included the cities of Beirut, Jaffa, Ascalon and most importantly, Acre. These ports would ensure communication with Europe and provide wealth through trade and the pilgrim traffic, which could also continue. Several important castles were still in Frankish hands including Krak de Chevaliers and Tortosa.

Costs

The cost for both sides however had been immense. Below is a list of some of the Christian nobility dead as a result of the Third Crusade;

- The German Emperor Frederick Barbarossa
- Queen Sibylla and her two daughters
- Gerard of Ridefort, Grand Master of the Templars
- Philip Count of Flanders
- Count Louis of Thuringia
- Duke Conrad of Swabia
- Count Conrad of Montferrat and Tyre
- James of Avesnes
- Archbishop Baldwin of Canterbury

It has been estimated that of all those who participated on the Christian side, a figure that could approach or even exceed 100,000 individuals in the Third Crusade over 50% died. Some 20% of those dead were casualties killed in battle, with another 30% dead through disease and starvation. Saladin too lost huge numbers of brave men and women as well as many of his 1187-8 conquests. He had however ensured that he kept control of Jerusalem.

Richard would leave Acre on the 9th October 1192, he was shipwrecked near Corfu and decided to travel the rest of the way across Europe. In Austria Richard attempted to travel in disguise but was discovered and imprisoned by Duke Leopold of Austria who now had his revenge for the humiliation at Acre. Leopold kept Richard as a prisoner until February 1193 when he became prisoner of the new German ruler, Henry VI. Henry VI ransomed Richard for a vast sum in March 1194, by which time King Philip of France had invaded Richard's lands in France. Recovering these lands cost Richard his life. In March 1199 Richard was killed by an arrow at a siege of a small and unimportant castle.

Saladin's achievements

Saladin had succeeded in preventing the Crusaders in their goal of recapturing Jerusalem. However he had suffered much damage to his prestige amongst his own men. Some still saw Saladin as an adventurer who had acquired his position through ambition and trickery. Saladin had managed to keep his field armies intact in spite of constant warfare and little prospect of capturing wealth and booty from 1186-1192, a period of six years. Saladin had managed to fight a defensive war and preserve control of his primary prize; Jerusalem.

A Modern assessment of Saladin

Some more modern Western writers have been critical of Saladin as a military man during the Third Crusade;

"As a military man, Saladin showed his mettle on numerous occasions, especially against his Muslim foes early on. His famous victory at Hattin, so often named in this connection cannot be considered his finest hour, as the result of the battle had as much to do with Frankish bungling as with any strategic genius on Saladin's part. It was his sense of geopolitics – of who to attack and when – that, with a few notable exceptions, such as Tyre, revealed his gifts. Yet for all that, after Hattin, his military record was miserable – a chain of defeats and prolonged periods in the field that alienated his commanders and, in the worst cases, turned his troops against him".

P.Cobb 2014, p203

Unlike the Crusaders of 1099 and the treatment of Muslim prisoners by Richard, Saladin had treated most (not all) of his prisoners generously. Saladin could not prevent the loss of Acre and perhaps could have acted more decisively to defeat Guy during the early stages of the siege. However, the Crusaders were never able to win a decisive victory over Saladin, despite them often having larger numbers of men. Saladin however ensured that he survived the Third Crusade in possession of the most valuable prize; Jerusalem and had ensured that the Second Kingdom of Jerusalem was only a small fraction of its former self. Saladin had managed to keep control of important regions such as Oultrejourdain, which allowed him safe communication between his provinces of Egypt and Syria.

Task: Examination style responses

Write a response to each of the following statements giving your view on the representation contained with the statement;

- *Bickering and dissension ensured that the Third Crusade could not succeed*
- *The Third Crusade would have succeeded in recapturing Jerusalem if Frederick Barbarossa had lived*
- *The city of Jerusalem was nothing to Richard and everything to Saladin*

Write each response in no more than 200 words

Essay Question

Write a response to each of the following examination style question'

To what extent do you agree with the view that the Third Crusade was a failure?

Write your response in no more than 700 words

PART SIX: The Fourth Crusade

PART SIX: The Fourth Crusade and A Level examination preparation

6.1 Preparing the Fourth Crusade

6.2 The Fourth Crusade

6.3 Modern Historical views of the Fourth Crusade

6.4 AS Level Exam Questions and Techniques

6.5 A Level Exam Questions and Techniques

6.1 The Fourth Crusade: Summoning and recruitment

In this topic we will;

- *Understand the circumstances as to why the Fourth Crusade was called*
- *Explore the motives of those involved with the Fourth Crusade*
- *Understand the nature and challenges posed by the Fourth Crusade*

Introduction

In this topic we will explore the reasons for the Fourth Crusade, why it was called for in the first place, who wanted to go on the crusade and the problems faced by Fourth Crusade that led to its diversion and dispersal.

The context: the German Crusade of 1197

Frederick Barbarossa had died on the North Syrian border in 1190. His second son Conrad of Swabia, who was his second in command, died outside the walls of Acre in 1191. The Germans had then been led at Acre by Duke Leopold of Austria until he was insulted by King Richard I. He had left Palestine in July 1191. German participation in the Third Crusade then had been hampered by unfortunate deaths, a loose leadership structure and the machinations of the kings of England and France.

For the new ruler of Germany, the eldest son of Frederick Barbarossa, King Henry VI had unfinished business with Palestine. Everywhere, King Henry VI was on the march, King Richard had been his prisoner in 1194, only being released on the payment of a huge ransom and an oath of submission to Henry's authority. He had also occupied the kingdom of Sicily, overthrowing King Tancred and he had promised crowns to rulers as far away as Armenia and Cyprus. The Pope, Celestine III was afraid of Henry VI, he neither condemned nor approved of Henry's ambition, afraid to support him, but unable to oppose his power and authority.

King Henry VI was in Sicily in 1196 and had plans to lead a massive force to Palestine in due course. More immediately, he sent to Palestine an advance navy and army under the command of the Count of Holstein and the Archbishop of Mainz. This expedition landed at Acre in August 1197. Henry of Champagne, king of Jerusalem did not welcome them, he had the treaty of Jaffa with the

Muslims, and Palestine had largely been at peace since the end of the Third Crusade.

The Germans immediately decided to attack. Without consulting Henry of Champagne or the other leading Franks of Palestine, the German army marched inland towards Jerusalem. Hearing of their approach, the ruler of Jerusalem, Al-Adil decided to confront them. The Germans had hoped to make up for the failures of the Third Crusade, however on hearing of Al-Adil's approach, the German leaders fled, leaving their men to stand alone. The brave German infantry prepared to fight and their resolution deterred Al-Adil, they could retreat unmolested.

Henry of Champagne gathered his soldiers, the Germans had not been wanted or requested, but he would join them whilst they were here. In a strange incident, Henry died whilst reviewing his soldiers in Acre in September 1197. He fell out of a window, taking with him his court little person Scarlet. Queen Isabella, married three times and widowed twice, was now required to marry again to provide the kingdom with a ruler. It was decided to appoint Amalric, elder brother of Guy of Lusignan and, now that Guy had died (in 1194), King of Cyprus. He would arrive in Acre in 1198.

In the meantime, the Germans joined with the Franks of Palestine in a new expedition. In October 1197, the armies captured Sidon and Beirut. On this success, the Germans decided to try to capture Jerusalem. In November 1197, the Germans entered Galilee and laid siege to the castle of Toron. It was here that armies from Egypt, led by Saladin's son Al-Aziz confronted them in February 1198. The German leaders, already hearing news that King Henry VI had died in Sicily, routed away again when confronted with serious opposition. This time the German infantry joined them in their rout and all of them fled to the coast and returned to Europe. With the exception of the recovery of Beirut and Sidon, the German Crusade of 1197 ended in failure.

A new pope, a new Crusade.

In early 1198, Pope Celestine III died. He was succeeded by Pope Innocent III. Pope Innocent saw an opportunity to reassert the authority of the Papacy. The German Empire was divided, Henry's son and heir, Frederick was an infant and was in Italy. Henry's brother, Philip of Swabia aspired to rule Germany, whilst in France, King Richard I and King Philip II were at war. Innocent saw that, despite the failure of the Third Crusade and the German Crusade of 1197, there was still enthusiasm for Holy War.

In August 1198 Innocent III requested a New Crusade. Preachers were despatched across Europe to recruit whilst other priests were sent to the ports of Italy and Southern France to enquire about transportation by sea. There were to be no armies travelling by land and no groups of pilgrims. Like the Third Crusade the expedition was to be a military one aimed at recapturing the Holy city of Jerusalem.

Papal Organisation

Pope Innocent explicitly created guidelines for the crusade. Crusaders would serve for a minimum of two years in Palestine. They would have their possessions protected by the Church and plenary indulgences were explicitly clarified. Any confessed sins of crusaders, for any crime they may have committed would be forgiven, so long as they were confessed to a priest.

Innocent's aim was to capture and hold Jerusalem and to restore the Frankish lands in Outremer. To do this he arranged for stringent guidelines and clear rules for the Crusaders. What he failed to do however was to get a king to lead the expedition.

Pope Innocent hoped to acquire the support and assistance of the Byzantine Empire in his crusade. Between the years 1198-1202 It is known that the Pope and the Emperor Alexius III exchanged at least 8 embassies and 12 letters. The Pope wanted the Emperor to submit to Papal authority in religious matters and also to help the new crusade. Alexius III rejected the authority of the Pope, but would help the Crusade if the island of Cyprus was returned to Byzantine control. The result was a stalling in negotiations, but did not lead to outright hostility on behalf of the Pope towards Constantinople. As late as 1203, the Pope is known to have explicitly forbade any attack on Constantinople.

The reluctance of Kings

The Pope sent a legate named Peter Capuano to the kings of England and France. He attempted to bring about reconciliation and a peace that would last for 5 years. He also attempted to encourage one of the two to lead Innocent's new Crusade. Richard and Philip however were engaged in a bitter border war. Philip II had been a reluctant crusader during the Third Crusade and had no intention of undertaking another one.

Whilst Richard was in Palestine and then in prison, his lands had been attacked or subverted by his brother John and the King of France and since his return Richard had been constantly engaged in reasserting his authority. Richard was furious that Philip had attacked his lands whilst he was absent on Crusade and had no enthusiasm for Papal requests that he head back out to Palestine. Peter Capuano irritated Richard so much so that at one point he threatened to have the Papal legate castrated. Richard therefore had no intention of joining the crusade, and his death in April 1199 brought about a succession crisis between his nephew Arthur his brother and John. This succession crisis ensured that little or no help would come from Angevin lands.

Despite the failure to attract a king to lead the new Crusade, the preparations continued. In December 1199 Pope Innocent ordered a tax of 2.5% to be raised on clerical property and profits. This would create a common fund for use by the crusaders to cover expenses such as transportation and supplies.

Fulk of Neuilly

The principal preacher of the crusade was Fulk of Neuilly. This established monk and preacher was very much in the same mould as St. Bernard of Clairvaux and toured much of France in 1199-1201. In particular he focused his preaching in Northern France, in Flanders, Normandy, Brittany and in the Ille de France. Fulk claimed that he had personally signed up some 200,000 Crusaders for the cause. This however was a gross over-exaggeration. He also received donations as he toured and announced that these donations would fund the crusade. Again, this was an exaggeration. Fulk was accused of amassing a fortune in donations; which he kept for himself. These accusations shattered Fulk's reputation. He retired from public life and further involvement in the Crusade and died soon after. His reputation in tatters.

Leadership?

So far the Fourth Crusade had failed to recruit a king, and its principal preacher had been accused of embezzlement of Crusade funds. It was not a great start. However in the winter of 1199-1200 some prominent lords were planning to join the crusade.

In Northern France, a group of young nobles met, and through the course of a hunt and a preaching sermon by Fulk of Neuilly, it was announced that these young nobles would join Innocent's new Crusade.

The young nobles included;

- Theobald, Count of Champagne
- Louis, Count of Blois
- The Count of Flanders, Baldwin IX of Hainault

Here was a nucleus of young nobles around which Pope Innocent could build his crusade. All three men were young; all three men were wealthy, so wealthy in fact that they rivalled the King of France in riches. All three came from families with a pedigree in Crusading.

Theobald of Champagne was the brother of Henry of Champagne who had joined the Third Crusade, married Queen Isabella and become king of Acre, and who had recently died by falling from a window in 1197. He was also the nephew of both King Richard of England and King Philip of France.

Louis, the Count of Blois could point to Stephen of Blois, a participant in the First Crusade and who was killed in Palestine in 1102.

Baldwin of Flanders also could point to his families' crusading record. He too had a relative who fought in the First Crusade and he had become Count of Flanders through the death of his relative Philip outside Acre in 1191.

All three also had another reason to desire a journey elsewhere. They were in theory vassals of King Philip of France, however, in the war between Richard and Philip they had sided with Richard. Now that Richard was dead they could expect a degree of censure and punishment from King Philip.

These young lords determined to present themselves as the leaders of the Fourth Crusade. Together with other lords they decided that they would act together through a committee. They would travel out on Crusade together and it was decided by them to seek assistance in their travel plans. Of the three, only one possessed the means to raise and operate a fleet. Baldwin of Flanders had a fleet which he summoned and dispatched direct to Palestine. He himself would join the others.

At a series of meetings in 1201 at Soissons and Compiegne, the French leadership consolidated their plans. Given that the Franks in Acre had a peace treaty with their Muslim neighbours and that the crusade had not been requested from that quarter, it was agreed to honour this treaty and use the crusade forces to initially attack Egypt, not Palestine. In this strategy the French Counts had listened to what King Richard had considered to be the best strategy for a new campaign. An attack on Egypt was the best way to recapture Jerusalem, as the resources and positioning of Egypt would always make it difficult, if not impossible to hold onto the city of Jerusalem. This decision was made in secret by the leadership and kept from the majority of the Crusaders. The crusade propaganda still stressed that the goal of the expedition was to recapture Jerusalem and that the Crusade would arrive in Palestine.

This plan was kept so secret that even Baldwin of Flanders's own fleet was not sent instructions to sail to Egypt. Instead it sailed on its own to Palestine.

An embassy was sent to the Italian trading cities in order to commission a fleet to transport the main part of the crusade. This embassy was a group of knights including Geoffrey of Villehardouin, a veteran of the Third Crusade who had spent four years as a prisoner after being captured outside Acre in 1190. Only Venice was in a position to help. The embassies that were sent to Genoa were refused outright. The Pisans also refused on the grounds that they were unable to transport a large crusade force.

The embassy to Venice

The embassy of French crusaders, of whom Geoffrey of Villehardouin was part reached Venice in February 1201 and negotiations continued until April 1201. Venice was one of several Italian city states that depended on trade with the East for its continued success. Venice had extensive trade with the Byzantine Empire, the Latin sates of Outremer and also Egypt. Each year fleets of trading ships went to the Eastern Mediterranean and the Black Sea and returned bringing trade goods such as spices, silks and slaves. In more recent years, however Venetian trade had fallen behind their rivals the Genoese, particularly in relation to Constantinople and the Black Sea, where the Genoese had privileged trade rights.

The Venetians had helped to construct the kingdom of Jerusalem with fleets that dated back to the beginning of the 12th century. It was their fleet that had helped Baldwin II conquer the city of Tyre in 1124. As a result the Venetians had also had trade links with Palestine and Syria, but these trade links were perhaps less well established than the Genoese.

The current ruler of Venice, Doge Enrico Dandolo had reigned from 1192 and was in his late eighties or early nineties when the embassy of the Fourth Crusade reached Venice. He had also just reached an agreement with the Egyptians to increase trade links with the city of Alexandria. Perhaps 10% of Venetian trade was with Egypt. Despite this agreement Dandolo agreed to supply the Fourth crusade with all the transportation and supplies it would need.

The Treaty of Venice 1201

The agreement of April 1201 between Venice and the Fourth Crusade stipulated that Venice would supply transportation for some 4500 knights and their horses, 9000 squires without horses and an additional 20000 infantry. In addition, the Venetians agreed to feed and supply all these men for a period of a year. They would also supply 50 warships of their own to escort the transports and the destination would be Egypt.

In return the Crusaders would pay 85000 Venetian marks and any conquests made would be shared equally between the Crusaders and the Venetians. All would be made ready by June 1202 at which date the expedition would sail. Crusaders would reach Venice by this date. The payment of the 85000 marks would be made at regular intervals;

- 15000 Marks by 1st August 1201

- 10000 Marks by 1st November 1201

- 10000 Marks by 2nd February 1202

- 50000 Marks by 2nd April 1202

Geoffrey of Villehardouin and the embassy agreed these terms on behalf of the Crusade leaders and left a sum of 5000 Marks as a down payment towards the first instalment.

Problems

The embassy and the Venetians planned for a Crusade army of some 33500 men plus 4500 horses. This was then to be a mammoth undertaking that would require Venice to obtain or construct between 200-300 ships in addition to their war fleet of 50 ships. This would certainly be one of the largest crusades; twice the size of Richard I's expedition in the Third Crusade and perhaps equalling the combined fleets of the Third Crusade. The Venetians themselves acknowledged this and stated that they would need to cease all trading activity in order to have ships and crews sufficient in number. The price was high – but calculated at the going rate previous expeditions. Given that the Fourth Crusade was to be the Venetian's sole source of income for several years, the cost was justifiable.

However, the onus then was on the Crusade leaders to find the manpower and the funding that could fulfil their part in the bargain that they struck with Venice. The three French Counts, no matter how wealthy, lacked the means themselves to fulfil this agreement. They needed additional lords and their retinues to join them. Additional lords were willing to join the crusade, but they had not been part of the agreement with Venice and were under no obligation to participate in it. Other lords raised their own forces, their own transportation and sailed directly to Palestine. Here then was a fatal flaw in the planning. The Counts had no legal or moral authority over lords.

This problem was compounded on the 24th May 1201 when Count Theobald of Champagne died suddenly. He had been the driving force behind the Counts of Northern France's decision to go on Crusade. He left some 50000 French Livres to fund part of the expedition, which was approximately worth around 20000 Venetian marks; half of which was spent on financing the soldiers and the other half was available to pay for the Venetian fleet.

Boniface of Montferrat

In August 1201, another lord announced suddenly that he would join the crusade. Boniface of Montferrat was an Italian noble and supporter of both Duke Philip of Swabia; a candidate for the crown of the German Empire and also the King of France Philip II. His decision to join the crusade may well have been due to these prominent connections. Philip of France had been opposed recently by both Louis of Blois and Baldwin of Flanders and by sending a friend and supporter like Boniface of Montferrat, King Philip may have been hoping to exert some measure of control over these wayward vassals whilst they were on Crusade.

Boniface was also a man with connections to the Franks of Outremer. His father had joined the Second Crusade whilst it had been his brother Conrad, who had been the hero of Tyre in 1187, arriving to save the city from Saladin with a single ship and a small company of knights. Conrad had gone on to be declared king of the Kingdom of Jerusalem but had been murdered by assassins in the streets of Tyre in 1192. Another brother, the eldest named William, had been married to Queen Sibylla of Jerusalem in 1176 and had been the father of King Baldwin V of Jerusalem.

Byzantine connections and intrigues

Finally, Boniface of Montferrat had several connections to previous Byzantine Emperors. Not only had Boniface's brother Conrad been married to the sister of the Emperor Isaac II, still another brother, called Renier had married to a daughter of the Emperor Manuel Comnenus. These marriages had not ended well. Conrad had to flee Constantinople in 1187 after being involved in a murder, whilst Renier had been executed after the failure of a palace coup in 1182. These past relations would be crucial as they revealed a wider web of connections leading to the heart of the Byzantine Empire and these connections would in 1204, lead ultimately to the Crusader attacks on Constantinople and the sack and capture of the Imperial capital itself.

Boniface, as mentioned above, also was friends with Duke Philip of Swabia. Philip was the brother of the recently deceased German Emperor Henry VI and was involved in a succession struggle with others for control of Germany. After declaring that he would join the crusade, Boniface travelled north to visit Duke Philip.

The Germans had not really been the primary target of recruiters for the Fourth Crusade, now with Boniface taking the cross, German involvement in the Crusade would increase as Duke Philip was eager to fulfil his brother's plans and ambitions, including his plans for recapturing Jerusalem and in particular, his hostility to the Byzantine Empire.

In 1195, The Byzantine Emperor Isaac Angelus lost his throne in a coup led by his brother Alexius Angelus. Isaac was deposed, blinded and imprisoned. His son, also called Alexius, was also imprisoned. In 1201 Prince Alexius managed to escape from his prison and fled to Germany to seek refuge at the court of his brother in law, Philip of Swabia. Prince Alexius wished to depose his uncle and see his father (and himself) restored to ruling the Byzantine Empire. Prince Alexius was with Duke Philip when Count Boniface of Montferrat visited Philip towards the end of 1202.

Duke Philip was married to Irene Angelina, the daughter of the deposed Byzantine Emperor Isaac Angelus. He was therefore hostile to the current Byzantine Emperor Alexius III, who had deposed, blinded and imprisoned Isaac, who was also his brother.

Task: Connections and intrigues

Considering the information above, how would you classify the motivations and or relationships those who join the Fourth Crusade? Ensure that you explore the following;

Consider;

- Political reasons
- Familial connections
- Religious motivations

Spend no more than 30 minutes on this task

Debts and solutions

The agreement also stated that the Crusade army was to be some 33,500 men strong. When the Crusaders began to arrive at Venice it soon became apparent that this number was not going to be reached. When the deadline for the expedition to sail was reached in June 1202 there were not enough crusaders and a large portion of the money required by Venice was still outstanding. The Crusaders that had arrived were kept in isolation on an island away from the city and forced to purchase supplies from Venice at high prices.

By September 1202 and despite all the efforts of the Counts of Blois and Flanders and the Count of Montferrat, only some 20000 Crusaders had arrived and 34000 Venetian Marks, 40% of the amount, was still outstanding to Venice. Venice in turn needed the additional funds to pay off their own considerable expenses. They had a fleet and the crusaders were still substantial in number. A solution emerged if the Crusaders could work for the Venetians in some way, they could pay off their debt and their journey could get under way.

Task: Identifying the strengths and weaknesses of organisation of the Fourth Crusade

Assess what you have learned in the material above.

Make two lists; One identifying the positives and the other the weaknesses of organisation in the Fourth Crusade.

Consider the role of the Pope, the legacy of the German Crusade of 1197, the situation in Palestine, the French Counts, Venice, and Boniface of Montferrat.

Do you think that the positives outweigh the negatives? Do you think that the expedition could have ever achieved its' goals or do you think that the aims of the Pope were realistic?

Spend no more than 45 minutes on this task

6.2 The Fourth Crusade: Summoning and recruitment

In this topic we will;

- *Explore the major events of the Fourth Crusade*
- *Understand the why the cities of Zara and Constantinople became military targets*
- *Consider the motivations of the leaders that led to the outcome of the Fourth Crusade*

Introduction

In this topic we will explore the events of the Fourth Crusade, we will consider why the Crusaders and the Venetians attacked the city of Zara and then went on to capture and ransack the capital of the Byzantine Empire; Constantinople.

Delays and indecision

By June 1202 the Crusaders had mustered at Venice, with the most prominent lord present being Baldwin of Flanders. According to two eyewitnesses; Geoffrey of Villehardouin and Robert of Clari both stated, that of the 33500 expected Crusaders, only between 10000-13000 had actually arrived. In July 1202, the Papal legate, Peter Capuano, arrived, and not content with narrowly avoiding castration at the hands of Richard I, Peter declared on his own authority that the sick, poor and the non-combatants among the Crusaders were allowed to go home; their vows need not be fulfilled. Peter Capuano remained with the Crusaders for some weeks and then decided to sail directly to Palestine. Even the Papal Legate had chosen not to sail as part of the main Crusade expedition.

Boniface of Montferrat arrived at Venice in August 1202, he had been liaising with Peter of Swabia, Prince Alexius and also the Pope. He arrived to find the Crusaders few in number, the Venetians demanding their money and a harbour full of ships that should have sailed according to the agreement made several months ago.

In September 1202, Doge Dandolo suggested to the Crusaders a solution to the impasse that they had reached. If the Crusaders would help Venice capture the nearby port city of Zara on the Dalmatian coast, the booty captured would be used to pay off the remaining 34000 Venetian marks that were still owed.

An attack on Zara would give the Crusaders something to do. Some had been at Venice for nearly six months and it would remove the

Crusaders from Venice and its marshy surroundings and unhealthy climate and allow them to spend the winter at the more comfortable location of Zara. They would need to spend the winter somewhere, as it would be too dangerous to risk a winter sailing to Palestine.

Zara however was a controversial decision.

Zara

The city of Zara was a city some three days sailing distance from Venice. Zara was an old city, its inhabitants engaged in trade and traditionally had been a part of the Byzantine Empire. More recently the city had been subject to Venice and currently was part of the kingdom of Hungary. The population of Zara were Christians and Christians who followed the primacy of the Pope of Rome. Their overlord Emich, the King of Hungary, had also recently decided that he would become a Crusader and had announced this decision to Pope Innocent III. In theory King Emich was pledged to Innocent's Crusade. More likely however King Emich had taken the cross in order to deter any aggression from Venice.

According to Robert of Clari the plan to attack Zara was agreed by both Dandolo and the Crusade leadership; however the bulk of the crusader force was kept in ignorance until they arrived at the city. Boniface of Montferrat did not immediately sail with the expedition; he travelled to see Philip of Swabia again. The crusaders were commanded by a committee of Counts led by Baldwin of Flanders and Louis of Blois.

Peter Capuano too knew of the attack – and approved. He declared that it was better to attack Zara, a Christian city, whose overlord was a crusader, rather than to allow the Crusade to disperse through lack of an alternative plan. Pope Innocent III reacted somewhat differently. Hearing that the crusaders and Venetians were attacking Zara, he excommunicated the whole expedition.

The Crusaders and Venetians set sail from Venice on the 8th November 1202 and arrived at the city on the 11th November 1202. The people of Zara were awed by the force facing them and began to negotiate surrender; however these negotiations were thwarted when a group of Crusaders informed the people of Zara that the Crusaders would never attack their co-religionists. Heartened by this news, the city chose to resist. The siege began and the crusaders did indeed join in.

On the 15th November 1202 Zara surrendered and the city was sacked. Some of the population was massacred and others sold into slavery. Tension remained between the Venetians and the Crusaders, some troops fought each other in a dispute over the division of the treasure and booty taken from Zara. Some Crusaders, including Simon of Montfort returned to Italy and from there arranged their own expedition to Palestine in 1203. However, the majority of the Crusaders were forced to remain at Zara over the winter. They could not afford to make alternative travel plans and to travel across the Balkans was too dangerous. The Venetians took the booty from Zara, but declared that there was still an amount owed by the Crusade.

Prince Alexius and the decision to attack Constantinople

Boniface of Montferrat returned to the crusade in December 1202. He had conspired with Duke Philip of Swabia (also an excommunicate) and others and made certain arrangements. In early 1203 Pope Innocent III sent a letter to the crusaders at Zara. He lifted the ban of excommunication on the Crusaders (the Venetians were still excommunicated) and instructed the Crusades not to attack any more Christian lands – unless they impeded the crusade or for *'another just or necessary cause'*.

By April 1203 the Crusade and the Venetians were still at Zara. The delay is difficult to understand as it was now possible to set sail. What was required however was a destination. The announced aim was Jerusalem but originally the Crusade leadership had decided on an attack on Egypt. Venice had a trade agreement with the ruler of Egypt and so may have been reluctant to attack here.

Then the papal letter arrived with a declaration – do not attack Christians, unless for *'another just or necessary cause'*. Shortly after this letter arrived, a *'another just or necessary cause'* arrived. In April 1203, Prince Alexius of the Byzantine Empire joined the expedition with an offer too tempting to refuse.

Prince Alexius was the son of the deposed Emperor Isaac II and been imprisoned by the new emperor (his Uncle) called Alexius III. Prince Alexius had escaped in 1201 and made his way to the court of his brother in law, Philip Duke of Swabia. Prince Alexius reached Duke

Swabia towards the end of 1201. In February 1202 Prince Alexius had travelled to Rome but his appeal for help had been rejected by Pope Innocent III. From March to November 1202 Prince Alexius had been at Philip of Swabia's court and had met Boniface of Montferrat in both 1201 and 1202. It was not until after events at Zara that Prince Alexius decided to approach the Crusaders and Venetians directly.

One possibility is that after being rejected by the Pope in February 1202, Boniface of Montferrat had acted on behalf of Philip of Swabia and Prince Alexius both, representing their policies diplomatically. Prince Alexius must have been either confident of the outcome or desperate with no other option when he approached the Crusaders and Venetians outside Zara in early 1203.

Prince Alexius announced a great offer to the assembled Crusaders and Venetians. In return for them helping him to return to Constantinople and overthrow his Uncle. Alexius would pay the Crusaders and Venetians a huge sum of 200,000 silver marks, he would agree to submit the Byzantine Church to the authority of the Pope and he would also join the Crusade expedition with 10000 men from the Byzantine army. Once the Crusade had recaptured Jerusalem 500 Greek knights would be used to help protect the Holy city and be paid for by the Byzantine Empire.

The Byzantine Empire had been long protected by paid mercenary soldiers. The Crusaders and Venetians would now become in effect paid swords that would attack another Christian people in order to finance their original mission of Holy War.

Constantinople

The City of Constantinople was the capital city of the Byzantine Empire, the successor state to the Roman Empire that had ruled almost all of Europe. In the 4th century the Emperor Constantine had created for himself a capital city; a 'New Rome' and it was named after himself. The people of Constantinople referred to themselves still as Romans and although they now spoke Greek rather than Latin, they considered themselves as the direct descendants and inheritors of the Roman Empire.

The city of Constantinople was in 1203 the greatest city in Europe. It had a population of at least 300000-500000, seven times the estimated population of Paris or Venice and over ten times the population of Rome or London. Constantinople had the largest building in the World until the twentieth century in the shape of the Church of Agia Sofia and was filled with monuments from antiquity and relics of the Christian faith. Thousands of Muslims, Italians and Jews lived here alongside the Greek population and traders came from as far as Russia and India to sell their goods. Its wealth and splendour had astounded pilgrims and visitors from Europe. Quite simply, there was no other city even close to rivalling it in wealth and splendour in Europe.

The state of the Empire

The Empire had undergone many trials and tribulations in the distant past. More recently however the Empire was in a period of instability and weakness. Since the death of the Emperor Manuel in 1180, the Empire had lurched from crisis to crisis.

Manuel's son Alexius II had become Emperor as a child in 1180. By 1183 he had been usurped and murdered by Manuel's cousin Andronicus Comnenus. Andronicus Comnenus was a brutal murderer and authoritarian but had been unable to achieve victory in a war with the Sicilians and seen the second city of the Empire; Thessalonica captured. Andronicus had been killed by an angry mob in 1185 and replaced by a new Emperor and a new dynasty.

Isaac II Angelus had come to the throne of the Empire by accident. An inoffensive nobleman, he had been suspected by Andronicus of conspiring against him. Rather than face arrest and execution, Isaac had killed the officer sent to arrest him and inspired the people of Constantinople to rise up against Andronicus. Isaac however was a weak emperor, corrupt and vacillating. He had done little to restore the Empire and instead spent money which should have been spent on the army and navy on himself and his cronies. In 1195 Isaac too fell to a palace conspiracy led by his brother Alexius, who now replaced him as Emperor Alexius III. Isaac was blinded (a traditional way of symbolising that a ruler was now unfit to rule) and imprisoned.

Prince Alexius therefor aspired to overthrow his uncle and restore his father the legitimate Emperor Isaac and would rule as co-Emperor with him.

In 1203 the Byzantine military forces were still large by any standards, but they were in decline. The Emperor Manuel had led the cream of the Byzantine army to death and defeat in 1176 at the battle of Myriocephalum. Since 1176 the Byzantine army had never recovered. It was primarily composed of mercenary regiments; drawn from France, Germany and Italy; from Turkish peoples like the Cumans and the Pechenegs and men from Serbia, Croatia and Bulgarians from the Balkans. The Imperial regiments were few and far between and most of them were far from Constantinople, stung out in border fortresses in the Balkans or in Anatolia. The Emperor did however have an elite palace regiment called the 'Varangian Guard' originally made up of Russians and Vikings, it was now mostly made up of Danish and English career soldiers and they had a fearsome reputation.

The Byzantine navy under Manuel had been large and able to attack Egypt. Now it had been starved of funds and experienced sailors for over twenty years and for the past decade the Byzantines had relied on Italian city states to do most of the naval protection. In 1203 the Crusade and Venetian forces would only be opposed at sea by *'20 rotted skiffs'*.

The view of Gunther of Paris

A fabulously wealthy city, a weak Emperor, a disposed but legitimate heir to the throne protected by minimal naval defences and an army that although large was mercenary and suspect as well as inefficient. Add to this the promise of large rewards and huge military assistance in their future endeavour, the Crusaders and the Venetians found the allure of Constantinople too great to resist.

Shortly after the events of the Fourth Crusade, a writer and historical source named Gunther of Paris stated five reasons to explain why the Crusaders and Venetians were persuaded to attack Constantinople;

- Religious – the promise of Church unity.

- Political – the influence of Philip of Swabia and his aspirations to become the leading man of Europe.

- Legal – Prince Alexius had a strong claim to the throne of the Byzantine Empire.

- Pragmatic – the Crusaders and Venetians had the manpower and needed the money promised.

- Opportunist – The Venetians could increase their own trade opportunities, wealth and power through helping Prince Alexius take Constantinople and damage their Genoese and Pisan rivals at the same time.

THE CRUSADES 1095-1204

Task: 5 Reasons

Consider the five reasons stated by Gunther of Paris stated above.

For each faction involved in the expedition to Constantinople in 1203 explore and briefly explain which of these reasons might be most important reason why they would support the action.

Consider the following groups;

- Prince Alexius
- Crusaders
- Venice
- The Pope

Consider also if any of these factors might have had little or no appeal or even encouraged opposition to the expedition.

Spend no more than 30 minutes on this task.

The attack on Constantinople

Having decided to place Prince Alexius back in control at Constantinople, the expedition departed Zara at the end of April 1203. On the island of Corfu in May 1203 the Crusaders almost fragmented as they found Prince Alexius uninspiring and also because the bulk of the Crusaders still desired to sail to Palestine. It was with difficulty that the Crusade leaders managed to persuade their men to keep on track.

On June 24th 1203 the expedition reached the area of Constantinople. They had been unopposed in their journey by the Byzantine fleet (such as it was). Whilst some men took to looting the towns near the city, the Venetians sailed Prince Alexius past the city walls to parade hi and to drum up support in the city. The response was disappointing. Nobody knew who Prince Alexius was by sight or by reputation. Alexius returned to camp and the expedition prepared to attack. Byzantine forces were in the area, and in greater number, but they did little or nothing to oppose the Crusaders and Venetians.

On the 5th July 1203 the attacks on the city began. On the 17th July the attacks on the city, using siege engines provided by the Venetians managed to cause a fire within the city. The fire destroyed a large part of a city district and the attacks were contained, however Emperor Alexius III lost heart by the attacks and fled the city.

Isaac and Alexius

The Crusaders and Venetians had not captured the city in July 1203. But with the cowardly retreat of Alexius III, the people of Constantinople decided to restore Isaac Angelus as Emperor and admitted Prince Alexius who was crowned alongside his father as Alexius IV on the 1st of August 1203.

The campaign had been a success. However, now Alexius V had to make good on his promises. He raided the treasury and churches to raise some 100000 silver marks. This large sum was divided, 50000 went to the Venetians directly for their services, 34000 was given to the Crusaders, who them immediately gave this sum over to Venice as final payment for the money owed. Another 16000 silver marks were given to the Crusaders to pay for their expenses- expenses mostly owed to the Venetians. Venice therefore received almost all of this money.

Alexius IV also discovered a major problem. He had little or no support amongst either the people or the nobles of Constantinople. Nobody knew who he was and since he had been imprisoned whilst young, he had no faction to support him and his father was ill, blind and discredited from his past career as Emperor. Alexius would not be likely to be able to keep his throne on his own.

Alexius IV therefore approached the Crusaders and the Venetians with a new proposition. If they would remain in the city until March 1204, they could protect him and wait in safety whilst he gathered together his own powerbase and also brought together the Byzantine army units he promised to join the crusade. The leaders agreed.

The bulk of the crusaders were unhappy with this decision. But by this time most of the leaders were paying for the loyalty of their own retinues with money and supplies. The pious genuine crusader that was not serving Baldwin of Flanders, Louis of Blois or Boniface Montferrat had once again limited alternatives, if they could not afford to arrange sea passage themselves they could not leave.

In the meantime the Crusaders and Venetians offended the people of Constantinople with their behaviour and attitude, treating the city like a conquered place. A mosque was burned down and street fighting occurred between the city folk and the Crusaders. Elements in Constantinople decided to force the foreigners to leave; the Venetian fleet was attacked as people tried to set fire to it on the 1st January 1204.

The sack of Constantinople

At the end of January 1204 a Greek conspiracy deposed Isaac and Alexius IV. Isaac was incarcerated and died soon after, whilst Alexius IV was murdered in his cell on the 8th February.

The new Emperor was another Alexius, surnamed Murzuphlus. Alexius V Murzuphlus was crowned the new Emperor in early February 1204. Murzuphlus determined to confront and expel the Venetians and Crusaders. The Venetians and Crusaders took up positions outside the city and determined to attack on land and by sea.

Murzuphlus resisted with the larger but unreliable Byzantine forces in and around the city. Battles continued throughout March 1204 and on the 6th April the Crusaders and Venetians were repulsed from the city walls with heavy losses. The expedition was faced with a quandary, if they left they would be forced to retreat back to their homes and face the wrath of the Pope for attacking a Christian people. Their reputation would be in tatters and Venice would be finished as a trading power. They had no option but to continue their attacks.

On the 12th April 1204 the crusaders and Venetians managed to breach a sea wall and enter the city. Street fighting commenced and the decision was in balance when the Emperor Murzuphlus gave up the struggle and fled the city. With his retreat most opposition ended, the Varangian guard saw no reason to continue in the defence if the Emperor they had sworn to serve had fled. The city surrendered.

The sack of Constantinople lasted for several days, thousands were massacred, the church of Agia Sofia was desecrated and used as a horse stable whilst a prostitute was placed in the seat of the Patriarch to sing rude songs. The Greek nobles and senior clergy fled the city and began to seek refuge in other parts of the Empire.

Over 300000 silver marks of booty was seized and officially counted, more treasure would have been taken unofficially. 10000 horses were also seized as well as countless other valuables. During the past year much destruction had been mete out on the city – over 500 acres of the city had been burned down, sculptures from antiquity had been destroyed in the past year, including a 5th

century BC statue of a giant Athena that had stood in the city for centuries.

The Pope heard of the sack of Constantinople some months later. He wrote an angry letter expressing his fury at the attack but by then of course, it was too late. In early 1205 the Papal Legate Peter Capuano arrived at Constantinople having spent the past year in Palestine. In opposition to the Pope's desires, when he arrived he ordered that the Crusade be dissolved.

Aftermath

There was little or no desire amongst the participants of the sack of Constantinople to proceed to the Crusade.

Doge Dandolo died of natural causes in 1205, the Venetians had done very well out of the project. They had large amounts of wealth to ship back to Venice, they also seized control of many islands in the Aegean and strategic ports on the Greek coast such as Methone and Monemvasia.

The Crusade leadership decided to carve up the Empire amongst themselves. Baldwin of Flanders was elected to become Emperor. He would rule Constantinople, but not for long. He would be captured in battle by a Greek and Bulgarian army in 1205 near the city of Adrianople. He would never be released. Louis of Blois was killed in battle the same year whilst Boniface of Montferrat would declare himself king of Thessalonica, angry that he had failed to be elected Emperor. Boniface would not long outlive Louis. He was killed in battle in 1207 fighting against Greeks who still opposed Latin rule.

The Latin Empire of Constantinople would last from 1204-1261, when the Greeks would retake Constantinople. It achieved little other than providing an alternative destination for European knights and adventurers seeking new lands that previously had travelled out to Outremer.

Contrasting views on the Fourth Crusade

Sir Steven Runciman is damning of the actions and outcome of the Fourth Crusade;

"There was never a greater crime against humanity than the Fourth Crusade,"

Runciman (1954, p130)

For Runciman the Fourth Crusade was the inevitable culmination of gathered hostility towards the Byzantine Empire, hostility that can be first identified in the First Crusade, when the Crusaders accused the Byzantines of attempting to thwart the expedition to liberate Jerusalem. For Runicman the capture of Constantinople in 1204 saw the end of Hellenistic civilisation in Europe and made the subsequent capture of the city to the Muslim Ottoman Turks in 1453 inevitable.

For Tyerman (2006) the Fourth Crusade's main failure and consequence was that the Crusaders were totally unable or unwilling to encourage Church unity between the Latin and the Greek Orthodox. All future relations between Greeks and Latins was hampered by suspicion of each other's actions. Thereafter the question of Church unity would be a feature in most if not all diplomacy between Constantinople and the Latin states of Europe.

The Latin Empire also failed to be establish itself in any meaningful or long-lasting way, but it did encourage the Greek empire to be divided amongst rival claimants. When the Greek empire was re-established at Constantinople in 1261, it was established with a focus on the Greek Christian faith rather than on the basis of a state or differing regions. The result was widespread political fragmentation in the lands previously seen as part of the Byzantine Empire which continued until into the 15th century when the Greek Byzantine Empire had disappeared.

THE CRUSADES 1095-1204

Task: Examination style response

Write a response to the following question;

"To what extent does the evidence support the view that the Fourth Crusade was always going to attack and capture the city of Constantinople"

In your response ensure that you explore the organisation and declaration of the Crusade in 1199-1200, as well as the motives and participation of the various factions as well as its progression from Venice, to Zara to Constantinople.

Write your response in no more than 750 words

6.3 Reference topic 1: Glossary and ruler lists

Glossary

Abbasid – The dynasty of Caliphs that ruled in Baghdad from 762 after overthrowing the Umayyad Caliphate in 750.

Acre - A port city of the kingdom of Jerusalem

Antioch – A major city in Northern Syria

Ascalon - A port city of the kingdom of Jerusalem

Atabeg - A title of nobility among Turkish groups, a military governor.

Ayyubid - The dynasty of Sultans founded by Saladin in Egypt in 1174.

Baron - A title of minor nobility among Latin Europeans, a lord of a castle or manor.

Beirut – A port city of the kingdom of Jerusalem

Caliph – Muslim civil and religious ruler, regarded as a successor to Muhammad.

Caliphate – The regions and provinces that recognise the authority of a Caliph

Count - A title of nobility among Latin Europeans, denoting a ruler of a region or province.

Danishmends - A Turkish dynasty based in Northern Syria and Anatolia sometimes rivals to the Seljuks.

Duke - A title of high nobility among Latin Europeans, denoting a ruler of a region or province often granted to a relation to the ruler of the Kingdom or Empire.

Edessa – A city in Northern Syria.

Emir - A title of nobility among Arab groups, a military governor or ruler of a town, castle or city.

Fatamid - Shia Islamic Caliphate based primarily in Egypt and descended from the daughter of Mohammad, Fatima. Founded in 909 and lasting until 1171.

Galilee – A region in Palestine, North of Jerusalem and part of the kingdom of Jerusalem

Knight – A mounted warrior and title of minor nobility.

Mamluk – An Arabic slave soldier.

Oultrejourdain - A region in Palestine, South of Jerusalem and part of the kingdom of Jerusalem.

Outremer – The 'lands beyond the seas' the lands conquered by the Latin Christians during the Crusades.

Ortoqids – A Turkish dynasty based in Northern Syria and Palestine and sometimes rivals to the Seljuks and to the Fatamids.

Patriarch – The highest ranking Christian Church Bishops.

Pilgrim – An individual undertaking a journey of religious significance to a Holy site.

Seljuks – A Turkish dynasty led by Sultans and in the theoretical service of the Abbasid Caliphate. Based principally in Northern Syria and Anatolia.

Serjeant – A professional infantry or cavalry soldier of non-noble rank in a Latin Christian army.

Sidon - A port city of the kingdom of Jerusalem.

Sultan – A position of authority representing secular authority in a Caliphate, in theory subordinate to a Caliph, in practice often in possession of ultimate authority.

Tripoli - A port city on the coast.

Tyre - A port city of the kingdom of Jerusalem.

Umayyads - The dynasty of Caliphs that ruled in Damascus until overthrown in 750.

Select list of Rulers

Rulers of France

Philip I – 1060-1108

Louis VI – 1108-1137

Louis VII – 1137-1180

Philip II – 1180-1223

Rulers of England

William II – 1087-1100

Henry I – 1100-1135

Stephen – 1135-1154

Henry II – 1154-1189

Richard I – 1189-1199

John – 1199-1216

Rulers of Sicily

Roger I 1062-1101

Simon 1101-1105

Roger II 1105-1154

William I 1154-1166

William II 1166-1189

Tancred 1189-1194

William III 1194

Henry I (VI of Germany) 1194-7

Frederick I (II of Germany 1197-1250

Rulers of Germany

Henry IV – 1056-1106

Henry V – 1106-1125

Lothar III – 1125-1137

Conrad III – 1138-1152

Frederick I – 1152-1190

Henry VI – 1190-1197

Philip of Swabia 1198-1208

Byzantine Emperors

Alexius I - 1081-1118

John II - 1118-1143

Manuel I – 1143-1180

Alexius II – 1180-1183

Andronicus – 1183-1185

Isaac II – 1185-1195 & 1203-4

Alexius III 1195-1203

Alexius IV 1203-1204

Nicholas 1204

Alexius V Murzuphlus 1204

Rulers of Jerusalem

Baldwin I - 1100-1118

Baldwin II - 1118-1131

Fulk - 1131-1143

Baldwin III - 1143-1163

Amalric – 1163-1174

Baldwin IV – 1174-1185

Baldwin V – 1185-1186

Guy of Lusignan – 1186-1192

Isabella I 1192-1205 (with husbands)

Rulers of Edessa

Baldwin 1198-1100

Baldwin II 1100-1118

Joscelin I 1119-1131

Joscelin II 1131-1150

Popes of Rome (select list)

Gregory VII- 1073-1085

Urban II – 1088-1097

Paschal II – 1099-1118

Calixtus II - 1119-1124

Innocent II - 1130-1143

Celestine II 1143-1144

Eugenius III – 1145-1153

Alexander III - 1159-1181

Innocent III – 1198-1216

Rulers of Edessa

Raymond IV of Toulouse - 1102-1105

William Jordan - 1105-1109

Bertrand - 1109-1112

Pons – 1112-1137

Raymond II – 1137-1152

Raymond III – 1152-1187

Bohemund IV of Antioch 1187-1233

Rulers of Antioch

Bohemund I -1098-1105

Tancred –regent 1101-1103 & 1105-1108

Tancred ruler – 1108-1112

Roger of Salerno -1113-1119

Baldwin II of Jerusalem (regent) - 1119-1126

Bohemund II - 1126-1130

Baldwin II of Jerusalem (regent) - 1130-1131

Fulk of Jerusalem (regent) - 1130-1136

Raymond of Poitiers -1136-1149

Constance - 1149-1153 & 1161-1163

Reynald of Chatillon -1153-1161

Bohemund III - 1163-1201

6.4 Reference topic 2: Resources and further Reading

Further Reading

Author	Title
Asbridge, T.	The Crusades: The War for the Holy Land
Cobb, P	The Race for Paradise; An Islamic History of the Crusades
Comnena, A	The Alexiad
	Chronicles of Joinville and Villhardouin
	The First Crusade: Chronicle of Fulcher of Chartres
Edbury, P,W.	The Conquest of Jerusalem and the Third Crusade: Sources in Translation, (Continuations of William of Tyre, including the Chronicles of Ernoul)
Edward, P. Chartres	The First Crusade: The Chronicle of Fulcher of and Other Source Materials
Frankopan, P.	The First Crusade: The Call from the East
Gillingham, J.	Richard I,
Holmes, G.	The Oxford History of Medieval Europe
Madden, T.	The New Concise History of the Crusades
Nicholson, H.	Chronicle of the Third Crusade: A Translation of the Itinerarium Peregrinorum et Gesta Regis Ricardi, (Anonymous)
Richards, D.S.	The Rare and Excellent History of Saladin, Baha al Din Shaddad
Runciman, S.	A History of the Crusades
Smith, R.	The Crusades: A Short History
Tyerman, C.	God's War
Tyerman, C.	How to Plan a Crusade,

Online Resources

http://digicoll.library.wisc.edu/cgi-bin/History/History-idx?type=browse&scope=HISTORY.HISTCRUSADES

Kenneth Setton, ed. *A History of the Crusades, vol. I*. University of Pennsylvania Press, 1958

http://sourcebooks.fordham.edu/halsall/sbook.asp

A useful compendium of sources and links

http://www.thearma.org/essays/Crusades.htm#.WGPNLlyij1Y

article by Professor Madden

https://worldhistoryproject.org/topics/the-crusades

Timeline of the Crusades created by the World History Project

https://europeanhistory.boisestate.edu./crusades/timeline/1095-1099.shtml

Timeline of the Crusades created by Boise State University

Printed in Great Britain
by Amazon